MOVING ON

A Guide to Good Health and Recovery for People with a Diagnosis of Schizophrenia

Roz D'Ombraine Hewitt

KARNAC

First published in 2007 by
Karnac Books Ltd.
118 Finchley Road, London NW3 5HT

British Library Cataloguing in Publication Data

A C.I.P. for this book is available from the British Library

ISBN-10: 1 85575 442 8
ISBN-13: 978 1 85575 442 3

Edited, designed and produced by The Studio Publishing Services Ltd.
www.publishingservicesuk.co.uk
e-mail: studio@publishingservices.co.uk

Printed in Great Britain

10 9 8 7 6 5 4 3 2 1

www.karnacbooks.com

D

MOVING ON

CONTENTS

To the contributors

ACKNOWLEDGEMENTS

My thanks go to the many people who helped with the writing of this book, but I especially want to thank the contributors: Alistair Macdonald, Anne, Cathleen, Carol, Carole, Caroline, Charles Plover, Chris, Clive, Darren, David, Elaine, Eve, Gillian, Gita, Gladstone Henry, Graham Cockshutt, Jacob, James, Jan, Janet, Jeanette Simpson, Jo, John, John Exell, Jon Williams, Linda Hart, Lisa, Liz Pitt, Liz Skelton, Marie, Mark, Martin Reynolds, Michael, Molly, Narinder, Nicholas, Norman Wood, Philip, Richard Jameson, Rachel Studley, Rita, Robert, Sharon, Sheila Edwards, Simon Graham, Shuresh Patel, Spike, Stephen Miles, Susan Salsman, Tally, Timothy, Tony, and William.

ABOUT THE AUTHOR

Roz D'Ombraine Hewitt is a journalist and broadcaster. She has wide experience of writing on health issues and especially mental health and well-being.

INTRODUCTION

This book is about good health and recovery for people with a diagnosis of schizophrenia. When someone is diagnosed as having schizophrenia it is on the basis of symptoms caused by severe disturbances in their thoughts, perceptions, emotions, and behaviour. Chapter One describes the symptoms associated with a diagnosis of schizophrenia, the myths and misconceptions that surround the condition, and how a diagnosis is arrived at.

Despite extensive research, there is no consensus on the cause of schizophrenia—or agreement that it is a specific illness, but in Chapter Two the main theories are described.

Personal accounts and research evidence indicate that for some people antipsychotic medication lessens the symptoms associated with schizophrenia. Chapter Three describes these drugs, their side-effects, the reduction of, and withdrawal from, medication. The chapter also has information on antidepressants and other prescribed treatments.

For many individuals, ongoing support is a key factor in their being able to recover and stay well. Chapter Four describes the role of mental health professionals and other people and organizations who can provide this support.

Research consistently shows that, compared to the general population, people with a diagnosis of schizophrenia are much less healthy. Developing a more active and healthier way of life is the subject of Chapter Five, which includes sections on improving psychological health and well-being, stress management, diet, exercise, relaxation, and ways of combating stigma.

Chapter Six covers routes into paid employment, the effects of the Disability Discrimination Act, and has guidelines on how to remain well at work. There are also first-hand accounts from people who have returned to work.

Surveys often report that people with schizophrenia would like to be offered complementary therapies and counselling as well as, or instead of, medication. Chapter Seven examines the evidence for the most popular and accessible complementary therapies. The relevant merits or otherwise of different forms of counselling and psychotherapy are discussed in Chapter Eight.

Appendix I is a guide to state benefits and entitlements and Appendix II is a guide to the English and Scottish Mental Health Acts.

Most of the first-person accounts in this book are from interviews. Other accounts have been taken from material that originally appeared in The Schizophrenia Association of Great Britain Newsletter and Voices magazine, and are reprinted with their permission. In each case I tried to get in touch with the individual contributor. Unfortunately, I was unable to contact Jeanette, John, Norman, and Spike, but have included them in my thanks on the acknowledgements page.

I wish to emphasize that the views of the contributors are individual to them. They are not intended to be seen as representative of others with a diagnosis of schizophrenia. Nor is it suggested that what the contributors found helpful will necessarily benefit someone with similar symptoms. However, it is hoped that their experiences will be useful to others in their recovery.

Schizophrenia is a word which some people with the diagnosis feel stigmatized by, do not agree with, or see as a meaningless "label". Several contributors to this book have said that they prefer to describe themselves as mad, or having psychosis. Some researchers and clinicians reject the use of the word schizophrenia on the grounds that it is unhelpful or unscientific. However, as yet, there is no agreement on an alternative, so for the want of a "better" word, schizophrenia and diagnosis of schizophrenia are used interchangeably in the book and I hope that this will not cause offence.

Roz D'Ombraine Hewitt
London, 2006

CHAPTER ONE

What is schizophrenia?

S chizophrenia is a psychiatric term, used when a person has symptoms that arise from extensive and severe disturbance in their thoughts, perceptions, emotions, and behaviour. Schizophrenia was originally formulated and classified as a disease by two nineteenth century psychiatrists, Emil Kraepelin (1856–1926) and Eugen Bleuler (1857–1939), and the diagnosis has been used by the medical profession for almost a hundred years. However, there are several misconceptions about what psychiatrists mean when they use the term, and about the people who are diagnosed with schizophrenia.

What schizophrenia is not

Schizophrenia does not mean that someone has a split, or double personality, as in Robert Louis Stevenson's novel about the man who alternated between being good Dr Jekyll and evil Mr Hyde. There is a psychological condition known as multiple personality disorder, but research suggests that it is rare (Davison & Neale, 1990).

This particular misconception may stem from the word schizophrenia itself, which was coined by Bleuler in 1911, from the Greek word *schizen* meaning split and *phren* meaning mind. Bleuler believed the symptoms indicated that a person's mind was psychologically split, or fragmented, from various parts of itself and from reality. Nor is schizophrenia about someone being ambivalent or undecided on an issue, though people talk of being "schizophrenic" about things.

There is sometimes confusion between the terms psychotic and psychopath. In sensational film and TV drama the word "psycho" is often used to describe a vicious serial killer, but psychosis is a state of consciousness in which a person's thinking and behaviour are so severely disordered that they are out of touch with reality, whereas psychopathy is not a mental health problem. A psychopath's thinking and behaviour is in touch with reality. He or she thinks, perceives, and speaks in a rational manner. But people diagnosed as psychopaths lack what is generally called a conscience, or a sense of morality. They seem able to commit acts of great cruelty and violence without feeling shame, remorse, or pity for their victims. In recent years the medical profession has used the term less frequently, replacing it with "antisocial personality disorder".

The word schizoid is sometimes used pejoratively to imply that a person is mentally unstable or even deranged. However, people who have been diagnosed with schizoid personality are neither of these. Although they may appear cold and aloof and lacking in empathy for others, generally they just seem to prefer their own company, pursuing solitary interests.

People who have been diagnosed as having a schizotypal personality may also be self-absorbed and uncommunicative, to the point where their behaviour is thought of as eccentric. But an individual with this so-called personality disorder tends to have strange or unclear speech and hold bizarre and unrealistic beliefs. For this reason the disorder has been described as a mild form of schizophrenia.

How is schizophrenia diagnosed?

Unlike many illnesses—diabetes or cancer, for instance—schizophrenia cannot be detected in a blood sample, body fluids, bacteria, or abnormal cells, and the symptoms associated with the illness can also be experienced by people with other mental health problems, such as depression or post traumatic stress. However, psychiatrists do use a set of criteria in making a diagnosis of schizophrenia. The first one was compiled by Kraepelin in 1919.

Kraepelin's classification

Kraepelin's classification system was based on his observation of the inmates of nineteenth century asylums. According to how they fared, he classified them into two groups. Those patients who experienced symptoms such as hallucinations, delusions and an inability to think clearly or to concentrate, but who eventually recovered, he described as having manic depression.

Patients with similar symptoms, but which, typically, had begun in their early (praecox) life and whom he believed would therefore inevitably experience intellectual and psychological decline (dementia), Kraepelin classified as having dementia praecox, the early term for schizophrenia.

Some researchers argue that the cluster of symptoms associated with schizophrenia is not sufficient evidence for a single diagnosis (Bentall, Jackson, & Pilgrim, 1988) and, moreover, that Kraepelin's classification system is fundamentally flawed, since there are no clear distinctions between the different mental health conditions and their supposedly defining symptoms often overlap. Also, contrary to Kraepelin's earliest predictions, many of his "dementia praecox" patients recovered. Kraepelin did later change his original definition, and subsequently reported recovery rates of around 2.6%. After further studies, he increased this figure to up to 5.5% (Tsuang & Faraone, 1997).

However, it is now estimated that about one in six people will recover from a first and only episode of illness, about ten per cent of people will be virtually disabled by their symptoms, while most people will experience bouts of illness, interspersed by—often long—periods of comparative good health, when their symptoms are less severe or in remission (Jablensky et al., 1992).

None the less, Kraepelin's system forms the basis of two of the most widely used sets of diagnostic criteria: the *ICD-10* (*The International Statistical Classification of Diseases and Related Health*

Problems, 10th edition), published by the World Health Organiz-
ation (WHO) and the *DSM* (*The Diagnostic and Statistical Manual of
Mental Disorders*), which is published by the American Psychiatric
Association.

DSM-IV, the fourth edition, is widely used in the UK. It sets out
the number of symptoms that must be present, to what degree, and
for what length of time, for psychiatrists to justify a diagnosis of
schizophrenia.

DSM-IV criteria for a diagnosis of schizophrenia

There are several systems for diagnosing schizophrenia, but in the
UK psychiatrists tend to use the criteria set out in the American
Psychiatric Association's *Diagnostic and Statistical Manual*, currently
the fourth edition (*DSM-IV*), and diagnose schizophrenia when
specific symptoms indicate that:

- there is a severe disturbance in a person's mental state to the
  extent that it may affect his or her thoughts, perception and attention, emotions, posture, movement and social and life skills.
- this disturbance is not in any way due to the effect of alcohol,
  prescribed or non-prescribed (recreational) drugs, a brain injury
  or a recognised brain disorder, such as a tumour, or a mental
  problem like mania or depression.
- to fulfil the diagnostic criteria, two or more of the following
  "Criterion A" symptoms will need to have been present for at
  least one month (or less if the symptoms have been treated)

     delusions or hallucinations,
     speech disturbance, such as incoherent or disorganised
     speech
     very disturbed movements and behaviour, for instance, cata-
     tonic immobility,
     negative symptoms, such as apathy and affective flattening.

NB if delusions are considered bizarre, or hallucinations comprise
two or more voices talking/arguing with each other or a voice
which keeps up a running commentary on the person's thoughts or
actions this one symptom is sufficient to meet Criterion A.

Also: "Criterion B" symptoms need to be evident. These cover a
person's social and occupational abilities. For a significant period of

time since the disturbance(s) began, someone's ability to function on a day-to-day level will have deteriorated markedly. Specifically, compared to before the symptoms began, in two or more areas of their life, for example, their work, personal interactions, or self-care, the levels will have reduced noticeably.

Duration: The person shows continuous signs of disturbance for at least six months. This must include at least one month of Criterion A symptoms (or a lesser period if the symptoms are successfully treated).

Reprinted with permission of The American Psychiatric Association

Again, unlike with most illnesses, there is no essential symptom that must be present for schizophrenia to be diagnosed. However, psychiatrists look for those that appear linked to disturbances in a person's thoughts, emotions, movements, and behaviour. These disturbances can result in a wide range of symptoms, though often someone diagnosed with schizophrenia will have only some of these.

Thought and speech disturbances

People's thoughts can be disturbed in both the form, the way in which they are organized and spoken, and the content, the actual thoughts that they express. For example, a person's speech may become incoherent. The phrases or ideas expressed are not connected, or only in a very fragmentary fashion, so that a listener is left bewildered, as if they have missed some important part of the conversation.

A person may also use neologisms, words they have made up which are meaningless to someone else. Their speech may ramble from one topic to another, as if they were continuously being distracted. Or it could comprise a series of seemingly unrelated statements. This is described as "loose association" or "tangentiality". Or, when ideas are expressed very quickly, in what can sound like an endless monologue, it is termed a "flight of ideas".

But someone may also suddenly stop speaking in mid flow, apparently having lost their train of thought. This tendency is called "blocking". "Perseveration" is the term for a persistent repetition of words and ideas—although a person may say very little.

This "poverty of speech" may be accompanied by "poverty of content" when, however much or little they talk, the person's speech contains scant information, although it is more usual for some-one to have disturbances in what they say, rather than how they say it, and these content disturbances are often expressed as "delusions".

Delusions

Delusions are beliefs that most individuals would view as at odds with, or misinterpretations of, reality. For example, someone might be convinced that his or her thoughts are no longer their own, but have been inserted into their brain by an external source—so-called "thought insertion"—or that their ideas are being broadcast so that other people can pick them up and know exactly what they are thinking.

The belief that they are receiving secret coded messages from well-known people they see on television, or being convinced that mysterious forces are spying or plotting against them—and that even their closest friends and family are part of the conspiracy—are other commonly-held delusions.

Naturally, people often feel tormented by such "persecutory delusions", as they're called, though rarely do they drive someone to become violent. Nor are delusions necessarily frightening or disturbing. Someone may happily believe themselves to be the president of America, or a popular Hollywood star, for instance. These are called "delusions of grandiosity".

Richard, a former actor, recalls finding his grandiose delusions very enjoyable.

> I inhabited a wonderful fantasy world and it was great fun. I once thought that I was both the star and director of an enormous film being made all over London. As an actor this was fabulous—the fulfilment of all my ambitions. After a morning on my imaginary film set, I headed for an ice-rink. Still believing myself to be a big star, I wasn't surprised to be greeted by popping flashbulbs. Only much later did I realize that the "flashbulbs" were really a photo booth in action.

Although Richard later realized that the flashing photo booth was independent of his fantasy, at the time he drew it into his delusion. This is known as a delusion of, or ideas of, reference. Unaware that their thinking is disturbed, individuals do not doubt the reality of their delusions, so that virtually any incident may be used as supporting "evidence". Someone in the grip of a delusion may, for instance, interpret the conversation of people on a bus, a wrong telephone number, or being offered a cup of tea, as proof that they are being spied on, plotted against, or poisoned.

Clinical evidence, however, suggests that delusions may help people cope with social or emotional problems. A psychiatrist, Anne Hassett (1998), recorded how an elderly and isolated woman was convinced that for three years it had been her responsibility to care for a plumber who lived in her roof. After being encouraged to take antipsychotic medication, the woman ceased to believe the plumber existed. But she soon felt so lonely that she took matters into her own hands and stopped using medication—and the plumber returned.

Hassett believes the case illustrates the need for clinicans to realize that delusions may serve a useful purpose and simply removing them may leave a painful void in a person's life. Research also suggests that delusions are not "meaningless" (Bentall & Kinderman 1998), but tend to reflect people's concerns about their life and position in society (Bentall, 1994) and are attempts to make sense of their experiences (Maher, 1988). In a study of first-person accounts of delusions (Stanton & David, 2000), many participants reported retaining some delusional thinking after their recovery. Most attributed their recovery to a combination of medication, psychotherapy, social support, and personal coping strategies.

Disturbances in perception and attention

Disturbances in perception will, of course, dramatically affect people's experience of the world. A person may have a sense that their surroundings are somehow different or unreal; that the environment is flat and colourless, or that objects, buildings, or people suddenly feel too close—or very far away. These perceptual changes can be so disorientating that people are afraid to leave their homes or even to move around freely indoors.

At the same time, someone can find it very hard to focus his or her attention or to "think straight". Mark recalls that during his final year at university he had difficulty with even the simplest mental task and found it impossible to concentrate on his course work.

> It started with me not being able to add up my change—it just seemed too difficult. At college I'd sit in the library reading and re-reading a book, but nothing would stick. It was like my brain wasn't there so that there was nowhere for the information to go. I'd put on the telly, but I couldn't follow it. Trying to watch the picture and listen to what was being said was too much for me to handle and I couldn't make sense of any of it.

As people's mental abilities lessen, their physical senses may go into overdrive and they become hypersensitive to every sight, sound, and smell. Light can seem blinding, noise deafening and odours overpowering and their skin feels so sensitive that it is painful for them to be touched. This was Lisa's experience.

> My skin looked perfectly normal, but it felt sore and painful, as if I had sunburn. Night times were the worst. I'd lie in bed and feel an awful burning all over my body and sometimes a crawling sensation, like there were insects living under my skin. I was always washing and putting on the cream my GP prescribed, but it did no good.

Lisa was also convinced that her body itself was changing. The psychiatric term for this disturbance is "dysmorphobia".

> One day my mother saw me counting the hairs in my comb. I explained that I was going bald and wanted to save them for when I didn't have any hair left. I also became obsessed with the size of my nose. It seemed to be growing bigger and also my jaw. That especially worried me because I thought that it might push my teeth out.

In addition to fears that parts of the body are changing, someone may believe that his or her whole body has changed in some fundamental way; that it has turned into a machine or some sort of alien creature, for example. The most vivid and disturbing distortions in perception are called "hallucinations".

Hallucinations

People under the influence of alcohol or drugs may hallucinate and hear voices. So may people with severe depression or mania. It is estimated that two to three per cent of the population hear voices. Of these, one in three is likely to develop a psychiatric illness (Romme, 2004).

Hearing voices is very common among people diagnosed with schizophrenia. Although the voices are only in the person's head, he or she may be convinced that it is another person or persons speaking. One theory of hallucinations is that they are a disorder of "inner speech", the sort we "hear" in our heads when, for example, we rehearse something we intend to say to someone.

Another theory of hallucinations is that they are caused by an abnormality in the part of the brain that interprets external speech. Brain imaging techniques have shown that when people use inner speech a region known as Broca's area is active. One study (McGuire et al., 1995) shows that this area is activated when people who do not have a diagnosis of schizoprehrenia repeat in their minds the sort of remarks typical of an unkind "voice", such as, "You idiot! Why are you so stupid?" However, if they imagine an alien voice saying the same sentence, their brains show activations in a different area, which monitors internal speech and differentiates between that and external speech.

Interestingly, the researchers found that when people with schizophrenia imagined an alien voice repeating a hallucination-type message, their brains were not activated in this monitoring area. Therefore, it seems, their brains mislead them into thinking that an internal message is coming from the outside.

Hallucinatory voices tend to be critical and unkind. People may hear several different voices at the same time, voices which argue and lose their temper with each other. Gladstone Henry's experience of hearing voices was published in *Celebrating Black Heritage: A medley of inspiration* (Sharing Voices, Bradford).

Rid These Voices

> No more can I take it
> Won't someone hear me
> Won't someone hear me
> Long time I've been going through this tribulation,

> No more can I take it.
> My mind's split in two
> My mind is split right through
> And there's nothing I can do
> Voices in my head,
> Can't sleep at night
> In my bed
> O Jah
> Where can I find a Red[1]
> To rid these voices in my head.

At times voices command individuals to harm themselves or to harm others. What is experienced as unrelenting persecution may lead some people to act in an angry or violent way (Taylor, 1985). But, despite sensational newspaper reports that create an impression that people with schizophrenia are inherently violent, the statistics tell a different story. In *Schizophrenia: A Very Short Introduction* (2003), the authors Christopher Frith and Eve Johnstone explain that only about three or four per cent of violent acts are committed by people who have been diagnosed with schizophrenia. This is fewer than such acts by people who have been diagnosed with depression or a personality disorder.

The authors also point out that there is about a one per cent risk that people with schizophrenia will commit a murder. Added together, therefore, about ninety-six per cent of violent crimes, including murder, are committed by people who do not have a diagnosis of schizophrenia. But whether or not someone has a mental health problem, there is a consistently strong link between violent behaviour and excessive drug or alcohol consumption (Monahan, 1996; Walsh, Buchanan, & Fahy, 2002). (The psychiatric term for someone who experiences hallucinations, numerous "systematized" delusions, and ideas of reference is "paranoid schizophrenic".)

Although many voices are abusive, some people, like Spike, have reported positive changes in the way their voices speak to them.

The voices used to scream out all day. They still talk all day, but it's supportive now. The voices are my only real allies. They keep me up rather than knock me down and now, after quite a long time, are on my side. I still have problems, but the voices are there, a constant reminder that I'm all right—whatever people may believe.

Although the content may change, as Spike found, voices tend to be very persistent. Research has shown that both hallucinations and delusions might relate to a person's life experiences. One theory is that voices may be "replays" of previous abusive incidents (Janssen et al., 2004). The drama therapist John Casson cites several such examples in his book, *Drama, Psychotherapy and Psychosis* (2004).

Many voice-hearers, including people with schizophrenia, report having benefited from attending self-help groups, such as those of The Hearing Voices Network, where they are able to share their experiences and learn techniques for managing voices. (See Chapter Eight.)

An experience of psychosis

Eve was thirty-seven and working in an accounts department when she first became ill. This is her description of how the symptoms began.

> Overnight things started to go haywire. I had difficulty concentrating on my work and getting to sleep. When I did drop off I had terrible nightmares about huge snakes eating my body. I dreaded going to the office. I was convinced that my colleagues were trying to poison me. I confided in a friend. She said it was probably stress and advised me to take a holiday. I took her advice, but on the flight out I heard voices. The other holidaymakers were talking about me: saying I was ugly and no good at my job. I spent virtually the whole fortnight in my hotel room. When I did venture out I thought everyone was talking about me, calling me names and laughing at me. Back home, I returned to work, but things quickly got even worse. It was getting harder and harder to cope. After everyone had gone home I'd spend hours at my desk trying to catch up, but nothing made sense. I was still terrified my colleagues were going to kill me. I was certain that they had a clever way of getting poison into my food. I lost a lot of weight because I scarcely ate anything.
>
> One weekend I just broke down and told the friend. She said I needed help and to see my doctor. But the voices told me not to

leave the flat or they'd kill me. That evening my friend came round and said she was ringing my GP. He made an appointment for me to see a psychiatrist. My friend said she'd come with me. I told her that I wouldn't keep the appointment. There was nothing wrong with me. It was other people who were ganging up on me and they should be stopped. That's what I told the psychiatrist when my friend eventually got me to see him. I really couldn't believe that I was ill. Eventually, I was persuaded to be admitted to hospital as a voluntary patient. But I still didn't think there was anything wrong with me.

Hallucinations can affect the other senses too. "Gustatory" hallucinations occur when someone's sense of taste is disturbed. With "olfactory" hallucinations it is the sense of smell that is affected. John's account of bodily—"somatic"—hallucinations appeared in *Voices*, the magazine of the Hearing Voices Network (Spring, 2003).

Imagine a person you cannot see attacking you. I thought it was spirits who would punch me and physically beat me up when I was trying to get to sleep. Also, between 5.45am and 7.30am, one would punch me very hard in order to wake me up. It is hard to wake someone up who is on major tranquillisers because all they want to do is sleep. After a while you can't take anymore so you have to get up. You can only take so much. When you are half or totally awake they leave you alone. [p. 7]

Disturbances in posture, movement and facial expression

One form of these disturbances is when people squat immobile, or maintain an unusual posture, sometimes for long periods of time, described as being in a state of catatonic immobility. This was said to be common when people spent long periods in the old mental hospitals (Davison & Neale, 1990)—and even commoner in the original prison-like asylums. Richard Warner, author of *Recovery from Schizophrenia: Psychiatry and Political Economy* (1994), suggests that catatonia may have been a response to the long and punitve regime routinely endured by the inmates of these late nineteenth century institutions, with poverty and unemployment their only prospect if they were eventually discharged.

In some instances, prolonged immobility is followed by extreme agitation. Someone can suddenly become highly energized, pacing up and down, talking continuously and incoherently, waving their arms about and gesturing repeatedly. Other forms of movement disturbance include strange facial expressions or grimaces (Davison & Neale, 1990).

Affective (emotional) symptoms

I loved cooking and reading and writing letters and especially listening to music. They'd been loads of things in my life and in the end I didn't want to do any of them. A tiny part of me wanted to want them back because they'd brought me so much pleasure and I knew I was missing out. But I wasn't able to care about anything really. [Caroline]

One of the affective symptoms Caroline experienced is described as "flat" or "blunted affect". A person looks and feels apathetic, as if completely drained of energy and emotion. His or her voice tends to be flat and toneless and the eyes have a blank, lifeless expression. People diagnosed with schizophrenia often say that blunted affect is one of the most difficult symptoms to cope with.

This extreme loss of interest may also be a side-effect of medication (Healy, 2005) or an indication that someone is depressed. Although depression is not regarded as an "identifying" symptom, like the rest of the population, many people with schizophrenia experience periods of mild to severe depression. In part, this may stem from the difficulties of coping with their symptoms and emotional, social, and financial problems. (Chapters Three, Five, and Eight have suggestions for managing depression.)

Rather than being withdrawn and apathetic, however, some people's behaviour becomes very outgoing, though completely out of context. This "inappropriate affect", as it is called, means they may laugh when they hear sad news or become furious at being asked to perform a simple social act, such as moving down a crowded bus. Sometimes a person may switch abruptly from one emotional state to another for no apparent reason.

Loss of social and life skills

It is often the case that people with schizophrenia feel unable to cope with the demands of everyday living or to interact with others. They don't look after themselves adequately and neglect their personal appearance and hygiene. They may lose weight through not eating regularly, or eat excessively. There's also a tendency for them to withdraw from social contact—including their friends and family—and they have difficulty making eye contact, or being physically close to others.

Wide variation of symptoms

The wide variation in the number and severity of the symptoms experienced by people first led Bleuler to suggest that schizophrenia was a group of illnesses, rather than just one and, therefore, should be called schizophrenias. More recently, it has been argued that as the symptoms are neither unique to the diagnosis, nor always present, the term schizophrenia is not scientifically or therapeutically useful and should be abandoned. This is the subject of Mary Boyle's book *Schizophrenia: A Scientific Delusion?* (1993). However, for the time being, schizophrenia remains the term used by the medical profession, who divide the symptoms into "positive" and "negative".

Positive symptoms

These are disturbances and distortions of ordinary behaviour such as delusions, hallucinations, and other forms of bizarre or previously uncharacteristic behaviour.

Negative symptoms

These refer to the lessening or loss of behaviours that enable someone to engage in ordinary daily life. They include emotional flatness, apathy, inattention to personal appearance and hygiene, social withdrawal, and lack of concentration.

Schizoaffective disorder

Should a psychiatrist believe that someone's symptoms are not sufficiently severe or clear-cut to warrant either a diagnosis of schizophrenia or bipolar disorder, also known as manic depression, he or she may make a diagnosis of schizoaffective disorder. Personal accounts suggest that it is not unusual for someone to be given a diagnosis of manic depression, schizophrenia, or schizoaffective disorder on different occasions.

This is understandable, since people with schizoaffective disorder experience the extreme mood swings associated with bipolar disorder: mania, alternating with depression. They also may have hallucinations, delusions, and feelings of disassociation, when they feel detached from their own body and reality.

Who is diagnosed with schizophrenia?

Throughout the world, in every community and from every background, around one person in 100 is diagnosed with schizophrenia at some time during his or her life. These include children and middle-aged and elderly people, but most often it is young adults, between the ages of eighteen and twenty-four. Statistically, men are more likely to develop schizophrenia in their late teens or early twenties, and women in their twenties or early thirties.

Research shows that there is a significantly higher incidence in men (Aleman, Kahn, & Selten, 2003; McGrath et al., 2004) of about four to one (McGrath, 2005). In the UK there is a disproportionately higher number of people from black and ethnic groups, who are more likely to be involuntarily hospitalized. This includes black Africans (Davies, Thornicroft, Leese, Higgingbotham, & Phelan, 1996) and people of South Asian origin (Bhugra et al., 1997; King, Coker, Leavey, Hoare, & Johnson-Sabine, 1994). From the African-Caribbean community the rate is estimated at between two and twelve times higher than in the general population (Harrison, Owens, Holton, Neilson, & Boot, 1988; Wessely, Castle, Der, & Murray, 1991; van Os, Castle, Takei, Der, & Murray, 1996).

In 1992, the mental health charity Mind, supported by the Department of Health, responded to the high number of black

people compulsorily detained in hospital, diagnosed with schizophrenia and given high doses of medication, by setting up the
Diverse Minds programme. Its continuing aim is to make mental
health services more responsive to the needs of people from black
and ethnic groups.

What are the early signs?

The ways in which people become mentally unwell varies. One
individual's symptoms may start very suddenly, sometimes following a period of stress or illness. Or there is a gradual change in
mood and behaviour, with the person possibly feeling tired and list-
less and withdrawing from social contact. Either way, psychiatrists
describe this as the "prodromal" (preliminary) phase.

The often very gradual onset of symptoms can mean that individuals are unaware of how much their thinking and behaviour has
changed. Part of our ability to retain a sense of ourselves depends
on adapting our thinking and finding explanations for our actions,
however uncharacteristic they may appear to other people.

A further complication is that many people first experience the
symptoms during their teens and early adulthood, a time of considerable physical and psychological change. Lethargy, disturbed
sleep, difficulty in getting up in the morning, then suddenly coming
alive late at night, can be an early sign of mental disturbance. But
the same behaviour is not unusual in young adults who do not
develop serious mental health problems.

Similarly, a young person who is experiencing delusions may
withdraw and stay silent through fear of attack by imagined hostile
forces. Or, unbeknown to others, they may self-harm or attempt
suicide to obey the commands of voices. But withdrawn behaviour
might also appear as normal "teenage moodiness" or the effect of
taking drugs, such as cannabis.

Without treatment and support, however, disturbed thinking
may intensify to the point where someone completely loses touch
with reality and needs specialist support and treatment. This phase
is referred to as "acute" or "active".

Yet, even if someone's thinking is very disturbed, he or she may
be aware that they have a problem and need help. Initially, it is a

good idea for them to consult their GP. If they would rather see a different doctor, the Health Information Service (HIS) can put them in touch with other GPs in their area who might be willing to see them as a temporary patient. If the person is not registered with a doctor the HIS can give details of local GPs.

Other sources of information and local support include The Mental Health Foundation and the charities Rethink, formerly known as the National Schizophrenia Fellowship, SANE, the National Schizophrenia Fellowship (Scotland), Schizophrenia Association of Great Britain (SAGB), and Mind's information telephone service, MindinfoLine.

Individuals may worry that if they discuss their symptoms with a doctor they will automatically be thought mad and involuntarily admitted to hospital. This is likely if their symptoms are so severe that monitored treatment and care is considered vital to their health. Doctors and psychiatrists also take account of the risk that a person will endanger his/her own, or someone else's life. But the decision to "section" someone under the English or Scottish Mental Health Acts (See Appendix II) is not taken lightly. More often, relatives complain that their concerns about the person's mental health are not taken seriously and there are unnecessary delays before he or she is given treatment and support. Such delays are especially regrettable, since research suggests that the sooner individuals are treated the less likely they are to develop negative symptoms (Waddington, Youssef, & Kinsella, 1995).

Misdiagnosis

The stigma surrounding mental health problems may be a factor in someone rejecting the idea that they are unwell. However, schizophrenia may be confused with other conditions. For example, people with the comparatively rare condition of temporal lobe epilepsy may experience hallucinations and delusions. Therefore, since people can, and have been, misdiagnosed, anyone can ask for a second medical opinion. This is not a legal right, but a recommendation of The National Institute for Health and Clinical Excellence (NICE, 2002a), an independent organization which recommends which drugs and medical procedures should be available on the NHS.

A second opinion

There is advice on getting a second opinion on Rethink's website. They suggest that individuals should first contact their GP. Doctors sometimes refuse if a person has had several previous second opinions. However, people can then ask their psychiatrist for a referral to another psychiatrist although, if the psychiatrist is employed by the same hospital trust, some people may wonder if the second opinion will be truly impartial. If this is a concern, the person could ask to be referred for a second opinion from a psychiatrist working in another hospital trust. Alternatively, he or she could request a referral to a Second Opinion Clinic, such as The Maudsley Hospital in London, where a lengthy assessment will be given.

Rethink tries to put people in touch with psychiatrists who do second opinion work, but individuals still need a referral from their own psychiatrist. Rethink's Advice Line can give information.

It is possible that a person's psychiatrist will be offended by a request for a second opinion, but this is not common. However, Rethink advises putting the request in writing, as a letter is harder to ignore. If the psychiatrist still refuses, the person could contact his or her local Citizens Advice Bureau or Community Health Council. (See the telephone directory under the name of the local authority.)

What is the point of a diagnosis?

Generally, psychiatrists are sensitive to the problems that may result from a diagnosis of mental illness. For example, it can hamper someone's chances of getting a job, or insurance cover. The psychiatrist may also hope that someone will have just one episode of illness and, meanwhile, it is better not to "label" the person.

For a time it may also be unclear if the symptoms are caused by substance abuse, or another physical or mental health problem. In theory, symptoms can be treated without a diagnosis. But currently this will prevent a person from making a successful application for benefits, such as Disability Living Allowance, or being given the respect and support he or she is entitled to rather than being seen as difficult or lazy.

For many individuals it can be a relief to know that they have a recognizable and, usually, manageable problem. Philip says he would have preferred to be told straightaway that he had schizophrenia.

> My symptoms were pure textbook so when a nurse in the hospital gave me a book about mental illness I said to the psychiatrist: "I've got schizophrenia, haven't I?" His reply was: "We don't like to label people." I can't understand that. Why try to hide it like a guilty secret. That doesn't help improve the public perception of schizophrenia. It's a treatable illness. People can get violent, of course, but that's because they've not received proper care or have been let down by the authorities. Schizophrenia's not something to be ashamed of, it's an illness like any other.

However, because of the stigma and misconceptions that surround schizophrenia, receiving the diagnosis may be disturbing. Liz P explains:

> When I was told by my GP that I'd been diagnosed as paranoid schizophrenic it was a real shock. In my mind it meant that I had a split personality, a Dr Jekyll and Mr Hyde personality, and that there was an evil side to me that would come out. Even that I would do things that I wasn't conscious of. I was very scared. I also thought this is a really serious illness which I'll never recover from.
>
> At the time I was working at a university and had access to the library so I read up on schizophrenia and how lots of people don't even think it exists. That it's a psychiatric term for a cluster of symptoms and there's a real challenge as to whether it's a useful label or diagnosis anyway. So I felt a lot more positive then. Reading one of Peter Chadwick's books, *Schizophrenia: The Positive Perspective* (1997) about his experience of psychosis was very helpful. He was diagnosed as paranoid schizophrenic and he recovered and went on to become a lecturer in mental health issues. That gave me some hope.

Liz's experience of finding some hope after the initial devastation is echoed by other first-hand accounts in a study about how people recover (Andresen, Oades, & Caputi, 2003). Finding hope was one of the four key processes identified, along with re-establishment of identity, finding meaning in life, and taking responsibility for recovery.

These processes are vividly conveyed in Susan's poem, "Rules of Recovery". (Bobbi is the name of one of her favourite cats.)

Bobbi's Rules of Recovery

> I admit there's a problem I need to overcome
> So I face it head on, full force and then some
> I begin to meditate just on the positive
> With the strength of my hope I can live like I want to
> I work toward solutions that I can achieve
> Search for some answers that I can believe
> I draw my strength from my highest potential
> Knowing this action is truly essential
> I strive to be the best that I can
> Strive to respect my fellow man
> I live in the solution and not in the problem
> And when I do this my trouble's forgotten
> I never give up if I think I have lost
> Remembering that sometimes there must be a cost
> I forgive myself when I make a mistake
> And know true intentions are not to forsake
> I thank myself when I see sound results
> Cause I choose to take action in spite of my faults

There's more of Susan's poetry on her website: http://www. geocities.com/bobisoo. Anyone else who enjoys reading or writing poetry might also be interested in the poetry website www. moontowncafe.com.

Note

1. The first stage of meditation, as in the Ethiopian flag.

Useful organizations and addresses

Rethink (Severe Mental Illness) (England including Northern Ireland), Royal London House, 5th Floor, 22–25 Finsbury Square, London EC2A 1DX. Tel: 0845 456 0455; email: info@rethink.org; website: www.rethink.org

Rethink Hafal (Wales), Hafal Head Office, Suite C2, William Knox House, Botanic Way, Llandafrcy, Neath SA10 6EL. Tel: 01792 816600; Fax: 01792 813056; email:hafal@hafal.org; website: www.hafal.org

Rethink's advice line answers queries on symptoms, medicine, and Rethink groups and services. Tel: 0208 974 6814 (10 a.m. to 3 p.m. Mon–Fri); email: advice@rethink.org. Allow at least two days for a reply.

National Schizophrenia Fellowship (NSF) (Scotland), Claremont House, 130 East Claremont Street, Edinburgh EH7 DLB. Tel: 0131 557 8969 (9.00 a.m.to 5.00 p.m. Mon–Fri); Fax: 0131 557 8968. Helpline for Grampian region: 01224 213034; email: info@nsfscot. org.uk; website: www.nsfscot.org.uk

Rethink Northern Ireland (formerly the National Schizophrenia Fellowship), Wyndhurst, Knockbracken Health Care Park, Saint-field Road, Belfast, BT8 8BH. Tel: 02890 402323; Fax: 02890 401616; email: info@nireland.rethink.org.uk; website: www.rethink.org

Mind (National Association for Mental Health), 15–19 Broadway, London E15 4BQ. Tel: 020 8519 2122; Fax: 020 8522 1725; general enquiries email: enquiries@mind.org.uk. Mindinfo line: 0845 766 0163 (Mon–Fri 9.15 a.m. until 5.15 p.m). Calls are charged at local rates. For information, leaflets and publications on mental illness, including prescribed medications, therapies, and support groups contact your local Mind office (see telephone directory) or write to the address above.

Publications Line (10.00 a.m. to 3.00 p.m. weekdays), Tel: 0844 448 4448; Fax: 0208 534 6399; email: publications@mind.org.uk. Send a stamped addressed envelope for a free publications list, or visit the website: www.mind.org.uk/osb to order online.

Mind Cymru, 3rd Floor, Quebec House, Castlebridge, Cowbridge Road, East Cardiff CF11 9AB. Tel: 08457 660163.

The Mental Health Foundation Tel: 020 7803 1100 (Mon–Fri 10.00 a.m. to 5.00 p.m.). A free booklet *Understanding Schizophrenia* can be ordered or downloaded from the website: www.mentalhealth. org.uk, and a fact sheet which includes a list of organizations that offer support.

The Mental Health Foundation Scotland Office, Merchants House, 30 George Square, Glasgow G2 1EG. Tel: 0141 572 02125.

Schizophrenia Association of Great Britain (SAGB), Administration Office, Bryn Hyfryd, The Crescent, Bangor, Gwynedd LL57 2AG. Tel: 01248 354048; Fax: 01248 353659 9.00 a.m. to 3.00 p.m. most weekdays; email: info@sagb.co.uk; website: www.sagb.co.uk. Annual membership costs £5. There are twice-yearly newsletters and information packs are sent on request.

SANE, 1st Floor, Cityside House, 40 Adler Street, London E1 1EE. Tel: 020 7375 1002; Fax: 020 7375 2162. Helpline: 0845 767 8000 (1.00 p.m. to 11.00 p.m. every day of the year); website: www.sane.org.uk

Sharing Voices (Bradford), 99 Manningham Lane, Bradford BD1 3BN, Tel: 01274 731166, is a community development project for people from black and minority ethnic community groups. People living in Bradford who are experiencing pressure or stress can contact the project for help. Website: www.sharingvoices.org.uk

CALL (Community Advice and Listening Line) mental health helpline for Wales, 0800 132 737, can advise on UK agencies and organizations that support people with a diagnosis of schizophrenia.

CHAPTER TWO

What are the causes?

Despite being one of the most widely researched mental health problems, exactly what causes schizophrenia—if there is a definitive cause, or even if it is a specific illness—is not known, although throughout the ages there have been countless theories, some of which now appear ridiculous. For instance, the Greek physician Hippocrates, born in the fourth century BC and known as the Father of Medicine, attributed mental illness to organs which had taken to wandering around the body, or to defects in the body's fluids, or "humours".

In the Middle Ages, mental illness was often interpreted as a sign of demonic possession and the person might be cruelly punished, imprisoned, or sometimes put to death. Even today some religious sects believe that auditory hallucinations are caused by benevolent or, more usually, evil spirits.

People's sexuality has also been blamed. At one time it was thought that masturbation drove people mad. Kraepelin claimed that schizophrenia was due to poisons secreted from the sex glands that affected the brain. The psychologist Sigmund Freud (1856–1939) believed schizophrenia was due to repressed homosexual impulses.

In *Surviving Schizophrenia: A Manual for Families, Consumers and Providers* (2006), Fuller Torrey, an American psychiatrist, lists numerous similarly odd and unsubstantiated theories, including the notion that schizophrenia is caused by "bad parents".

Bad parenting

The myth that "bad parents" cause schizophrenia took hold in the 1960s. R. D. Laing, a psychiatrist, author of *The Divided Self* (1965) and, with A. Esterson, *Sanity, Madness and the Family* (1968) was a leading exponent of the theory. A founder of what came to be known as the "anti-psychiatry movement", Laing argued that schizophrenia was a response by sensitive people to the intolerable stress of dysfunctional family life.

Not surprisingly, a traumatic childhood involving physical, sexual, or emotional abuse may negatively affect someone's mental health. Parents often blame themselves or each other if their son or daughter is diagnosed with schizophrenia. Anecdotal and research evidence also indicate that there are families who feel that professionals blame them for their relatives' mental health problems (Shepherd, Murray, & Muijen, 1995; Tarrier, 1991; Winefield, 1996). However, from the 1950s onwards, research shows that the interactions and relationships within the families of people who are diagnosed with schizophrenia are not markedly different from the families of those who are not (Prout & White, 1951). More recently, a study of over four thousand participants, aged 18–64 (Janssen et al., 2004) concluded that early childhood trauma increases the risk of a person developing psychotic symptoms. Bebbington and colleagues (2004) also identified an excess of "victimising experiences"—many of which occurred in childhood—among people with "definite or probable psychosis". However, as noted previously, psychotic symptoms are not unique to schizophrenia.

Extensive clinical evidence has also identified an association between traumatic or victimizing experiences and mental illness, but this does not mean that such experiences actually cause schizophrenia. In fact, no research has identified a causal link between parenting practices and the illness.

What part does inheritance play?

Research suggests that a predisposition to develop schizophrenia is passed on through the genes a person inherits from their parents (Gottesman, 1991). One in ten people with schizophrenia has a parent with the diagnosis. If a person's "first-degree" relative, such as a brother or sister, has schizophrenia, there's the same ten per cent chance they will develop it too, whereas it is two per cent for a "second-degree" relative, like an aunt or uncle, compared to about one per cent for the general population (Gottesman, McGuffin & Farmer, 1987).

It does not automatically follow that if one or both parents have schizophrenia a son or daughter will develop schizophrenia. However, if both parents have schizophrenia there is a fifty per cent chance. There is the same chance that if one identical twin develops schizophrenia the other twin will also, as they share the same genes. As it is common for twins to have a largely similar upbringing, it was once thought that environmental factors might be the reason; however, twins born to parents who have schizophrenia, but who were fostered or adopted from birth, have much higher rates of schizophrenia than those in the general population (Heston, 1966; Kety, Rosenthal, Wender, & Schulsinger, 1968; Kety, Rosenthal, Wender, Schulsinger, & Jacobson, 1975).

More recent support for a genetic link comes from an ongoing ten-year study of people who are considered at high risk because they have close relatives with schizophrenia (Edinburgh High Risk Study). Johnstone, Russell, Harrison, & Lawrie (2003) identified similar structural differences in the brains of people with schizophrenia and their "high risk" relatives—some of whom later developed the illness. Specifically, there is a reduction of tissue in the temporal lobes, an area that is associated with auditory sensation, perception, and the integration and comprehension of speech and writing, which might account, at least partially, for both positive and negative symptoms. Apparently it is not, as once believed, that drugs prescribed to treat symptoms such as hallucinations and delusions might cause this sort of tissue loss. However, the underlying reasons for these structural differences, or how they might cause schizophrenia, have not been explained. For instance, research has not identified a "schizophrenic gene". It is emphasized that people appear only to inherit a predisposition. Environmental factors, such as major life events, or using recreational drugs might affect a person's chances of developing schizophrenia.

Stress

In 1968, two American researchers, Brown and Birley, identified a link between crises and life changes (such as bereavement, redundancy, marriage, or the birth of a child) and the onset of mental health problems, including schizophrenia.

A study by Malzacher and colleagues (1981), however, failed to find a causal link between stressful events and a first episode of schizophrenia. A review of the existing research by Malla (1993) concluded that people who are diagnosed with schizophrenia do not necessarily experience more stressful events, though they do appear to be more vulnerable to stress than people who develop depression, or other mental health problems, and that this increased vulnerability may be due to genetic factors.

More recently, a report from the Edinburgh ten-year study (Miller et al., 2001) found that among young people there was a link between "upsetting life events"—but not "less upsetting ones"— and developing psychotic symptoms, whether or not they were at genetic risk of developing schizophrenia.

It has also been suggested that less intense, but prolonged stress, from unemployment, racial discrimination, poverty, and social isolation, for instance, may be equally damaging and contribute to the high incidence of schizophrenia among the UK's African-Caribbean population (Bhugra, 2000; Boydell et al., 2001; Mallett, Leff, Bhugra, Pang, & Zhao, 2002).

This "prolonged stress" theory seems to be particularly true for second generation African-Caribbeans, compared to those who came to Britain in the 1950s and 1960s (Hutchinson et al., 1996). One possible explanation is that they have had longer exposure to this form of stress. However, currently, there is no consistent scientific evidence to indicate that stress alone causes schizophrenia, though it may trigger and worsen the symptoms.

Virus infection

A virus infection during the early months of pregnancy is another theory. Torrey (2006) stated that it is well known that some viruses, such as the herpes, cold sore virus, may remain inactive for years, so that someone who contracted the virus prenatally, or at an early age, may not experience any symptoms until their teens or later in life.

At least two studies lend support to the theory (Kendell & Kemp, 1989; Brown et al., 2004). In the latter study, of sixty-four people diagnosed with schizophrenia, it is suggested that for around fourteen per cent this could have been caused by influenza during the mother's pregnancy, possibly through her antibodies reacting with the baby's developing immune system and affecting brain development.

Seasonality

A statistical association between individuals born in the winter or early spring—when cold and flu viruses are prevalent—and schizophrenia has been shown (Bradbury & Miller, 1985). But whether or not a virus is involved, there are other seasonal factors, such as the weather, which might affect a mother's lifestyle during pregnancy (Torrey, 2006). Even if these do not definitely cause schizophrenia, they might add to other possible contributing factors, like birth complications.

Birth and pregnancy complications

The evidence for such a link is inconclusive. Lewis (1989) argues that there is sufficient data to establish an association between obstetric problems and schizophrenia, but many of the studies have been criticized as being poorly designed, as well as inherently weak, since all rely on "retrospective assessment"—mostly the mother's recollection.

None the less, one large, well-designed study (Jones, Ranta-kallio, Hartikainen, Isohanni, & Sipila, 1998) indicates an association. Drawing on over eleven thousand Finnish people (from the 1966 north Finland general population birth cohort), it found that a combination of low birth weight and a shorter pregnancy (thirty-seven weeks) was more common among people who developed schizophrenia, while six of the 125 adults who survived severe perinatal brain damage (4.8%) had developed schizophrenia.

An analytical review of the studies (Cannon, Jones, & Murray, 2002) also identified low birth-weight and complications during pregnancy and delivery among factors associated with schizophrenia. Even so, they noted that a lack of detailed information about the prenatal period and the difficulty of assessing typically small interactive effects were major problems in drawing any conclusions.

Torrey (2006) claims that the overwhelming majority of women who experience a difficult birth do not have children who as adults are diagnosed with schizophrenia. In the light of research (Torrey & Rawlings, 1996) he suggests that it is more likely that schizophrenia, like stillbirths and those attributed to seasonality effects, is linked to "un-observable events", such as an in-utero infection.

Brain damage

Some people with schizophrenia have been found to have slightly enlarged ventricles, the fluid-filled cavities in the brain. This may be due to hereditary, but, as mentioned, birth complications can cause brain damage. Following a head injury, people sometimes develop the symptoms associated with schizophrenia. However, the possibility that head injury may be a partial cause of schizophrenia has not been supported by a critical review of the evidence (David & Prince, 2005).

A related theory is that a deficiency of certain polyunsaturated fatty acids (PUFAs) causes brain damage and, ultimately, schizophrenia. These fatty acids are essential for healthy functioning of the body, including the membranes of the brain cells. Reduced levels of these PUFAs have been identified in people diagnosed with schizophrenia (Glen et al., 1994; Peet, Laugharne, Mellor, & Ramchand, 1996).

Studies by Malcolm Peet and his colleagues (1996, 1997, 2002a) have demonstrated that fatty acid supplements can significantly reduce the positive and negative symptoms of some people with schizophrenia. Since the body cannot make these fatty acids, it is theorized that a poor diet during a mother's pregnancy, or in childhood, causes membrane damage. Currently, no direct causal link between this and schizophrenia has been established. However, a systematic review of the research evidence (Joy, Mumby-Croft,

& Joy, 2003) concluded that some data supports the original hypothesis.

Illegal drugs

There is no question that the heavy use of marijuana can create severe psychological disturbance, when a person becomes highly delusional and possibly violent. Cocaine, crack, ecstasy, LSD, and amphetamines can cause hallucinations or delusions to the point that a person becomes psychotic (Farrell et al., 2002). Research from the Edinburgh High Risk study (Miller et al., 2001) has also identified a link between psychotic symptoms and the use of cannabis and other "street drugs" among young adults.

However, a questionnaire study with patients in a detoxification unit at London's Maudsley Hospital (Unnithan & Cutting, 1992) does not support the theory that such drugs cause lasting psychosis. The researchers also found that the hallucinations and delusions of drug users were experientially different to those described by people with schizophrenia, whose symptoms were not drug-induced.

Moreover, despite clinical evidence of a link between the widespread use of "street drugs", particularly by young adults, and a dramatic increase in mental health problems, there is no clear research data that illegal drugs cause someone to develop the major psychological disturbances associated with schizophrenia, who might not be predisposed to do so.

Biochemical imbalance

From the time it was first described as a specific illness, psychiatrists have speculated on the possibility that schizophrenia is caused by a chemical imbalance. Kraepalin believed poisons secreted from the sex glands caused the illness, the psychologist Jung thought that a mystery chemical he called "toxin X", would eventually be discovered as the cause. Since the 1970s, the excess activity of the chemical messenger (neurotransmitter) dopamine has been thought to be responsible (Matthysse, 1973).

Two studies (Angrist, Lee, & Gershon, 1974; Snyder, Banerjee, Yamamura, & Greenberg, 1974) showed that high doses of amphetamines, which increase dopamine levels in the brain, produced symptoms of paranoia. Also, when in the past people with schizophrenia were given L-dopa, a drug which the body converts into dopamine, it worsened their symptoms. Most persuasively, perhaps, antipsychotic drugs work by "blocking" the effect of dopamine in various parts of the brain. This may reduce dopamine to below normal levels, causing stiffness, tremors, and movement difficulties known as extrapyramidal symptoms (EPSs). EPSs are similar to those of Parkinson's Disease, which is caused by insufficient dopamine in the brain.

However, in the last decade or so, other neurotransmitters, particularly serotonin, have been linked with schizophrenia. Newer antipsychotic drugs that block some, but not all dopamine and serotonin in the brain, produce fewer EPSs. The antipsychotic drug Abilify seems to produce fewer EPSs and, it is claimed, works not by simply blocking, but by establishing a normal balance of these neurotransmitters.

Abilify is not, however, an effective treatment for everyone diagnosed with schizophrenia. It has also been pointed out that an imbalance might occur after, rather than before, the start of the illness, or may be due to hereditary factors.

A further challenge to the "dopamine hypothesis" comes from the efficacy of Clozapine, which has proved an effective treatment for people with "intractable schizophrenia". Yet, compared to the old-style drugs, is a "relatively weak" dopamine blocker (Frith & Johnstone, 2003, p. 88). Willner (1997) argues that "schizophrenia does not reflect primary abnormalities of dopamine transmission, but probably does reflect abnormalities in systems that have an intimate interaction with the dopamine system."

This might explain why some people do well on psychostimulants, such as L-dopa (Lieberman, Kane, & Alvir, 1987), as David Healy points out in his book *Psychiatric Drugs Explained* (2005). He also refers to his own brain imaging research (Healy, 1991), which found that the dopamine system in the brains of people with schizophrenia is normal.

The continuum theory

Although much effort has been concentrated on trying to identify a single cause for schizophrenia, some studies suggest that there is no clear dividing line between what are described as sanity and madness and that these merely represent the polar extremes of a continuum of different mental states.

A review of the research (Johns & van Os, 2001) concluded that "normal" human functioning comprises a continuum, extending from healthy functioning through eccentricity, depression, mania, and psychosis to schizophrenia. For instance, a study (van Os et al., 1999) with people attending a GP practice found that differences between "normal" people and those with anxiety/depression, psychosis, and delusional and hallucinatory experiences were not absolute, but simply a matter of degree.

According to continuum theory, social, environmental, emotional, and hereditary factors mean that anyone may experience the symptoms associated with these conditions—and that this ability is part of what makes us "normal", not "abnormal", human beings. This is one of the ideas explored in Richard Bentall's *Madness Explained: Psychosis and Human Nature* (2003).

Research also shows that people may repeatedly experience psychotic symptoms that do not increase in severity or prevent them from continuing with their daily lives (Frith & Johnstone, 2003, p. 43). Moreover, it is estimated that one in four people will develop at least one form of mental illness at some time in their life (Kessler, Chiu, Demler, Merikangas, & Walters, 2005).

Continuum theory fits well with Jeanette Simpson's view of normality. This is a shortened version of her article, which was published in *Voices* (Summer, 1997).

Who's normal?—I am!

> Looking back at the periods of "mental illness" in my life, the thing I remember most, even more than the confusion and fear, is the shame. What would I have given not to be "schizophrenic", not to be "manic-depressive" (different psychiatrists, different labels). If the idea of being "manic-depressive" frightened me, the information that I had inherited "schizophrenia" from my aunt who used to throw the contents of her chamber pot on the heads of passers by, terrified and saddened me almost to the point of despair.

I stuck even more labels on myself. I was a "head case", I was "round the twist", a "nutter". I was beyond the pale, hopeless, useless. How I admired and envied "normal" people and how hard I strove to prove that although I was a "nut-case", although I had to take the tablets to stop me feeling so bad about myself that I may be tempted to take my own life, I could in fact act like a "normal" person. Only those close to me knew my dreadful secret. I fooled everyone else. They believed I was normal . . . I longed to be normal.

Normal? What's normal? We're recognising now that it's perfectly normal to be angry with someone we love who dies. It's "normal" to experience unusual symptoms after an accident or severe shock. Post-traumatic stress disorder is now regularly diagnosed and treated. Some day, soon, perhaps, we'll accept that it's perfectly normal to be severely depressed, to hear voices, to see things, to stop eating, when life throws more pain or problems at us than we're able to cope with . . . We're all normal. But we're different and we react in different ways. Gazza doesn't behave like Jeremy Beadle, Julie Andrews doesn't have a lot in common with Margaret Thatcher. And none of them are like me. But we're all normal.

Creativity and madness

The idea that madness and creativity are linked dates back to the ancient Greek philosopher Aristotle. And in his book *The Madness of Adam and Eve: How Schizophrenia Shaped Humanity* (Bantam), the late David Horrobin, a former president of the Schizophrenia Association of Great Britain, advanced the theory that schizophrenia has played a vital part in human evolution.

There appears to be a genetic link between extremes of creativity and schizophrenia. We are clearly distinguished from our immediate pre-human ancestors by our exceptional creativity, whether it be in science or technology, in the arts, in religion or in political and military organization. These skills are typical of those seen commonly in the families of schizophrenic patients . . . If schizophrenia and bi-polar disorder, present before the races separated, are responsible for much of human creativity, madness may have played a critical role in the emergence of modern humans. [Horrobin, p. 3]

Horrobin gives examples of people whom he believes were touched with both genius and madness, including the scientist Sir Isaac Newton and the Nobel Prize-winning author James Joyce. The book also explores links between nutrition, fatty acids, and mental health.

How long will the symptoms last?

Psychiatrists may encourage people to view schizophrenia as a life-long condition, since it is not possible to predict if, when, or for how long they might be free of symptoms. As mentioned in Chapter One, statistics indicate that about one in six people recover from an initial episode and never have a recurrence of their symptoms, whereas for about ten per cent of people symptoms tend to worsen over time and, as yet, are unable to be effectively treated. However, people's symptoms can improve, even when they have been very severe (Harding, Zubin, & Strauss, 1987); for instance, the drug Clozapine has helped many previously "untreatable" people.

For most individuals, however, periods of stability, interspersed by a return or worsening of symptoms, are not uncommon. Almost invariably, people learn to recognize their own warning signs and take action, which often enables them to avoid or prevent lengthy relapses.

Is there a cure?

Being cured, in the traditional medical sense of the word, means a reduction or absence of symptoms, to the extent that someone needs little or no medication to stay well and can live without ongoing treatment or support. However, critics of this so-called "medical model" point out that this is not applied to all physical conditions, diabetes or hypertension, for example—and nor should it be applied to schizophrenia or other mental health problems.

In contrast to the medical model is what is known as the "recovery model" or the "recovery and self-empowerment model". The basic idea is that people should be viewed as individuals, rather than in terms of their symptoms or diagnosis. Instead of being passive recipients of treatment, it is recognized that they are able to take responsibility for their lives and, as someone with schizophrenia rarely is permanently ill, able to make the choices and fulfil the goals that are right for them. As Graham puts it: "Everyone has a right to their dreams and ambitions and so do we. We have that right and we want to achieve them."

The ways in which individuals with mental health problems define and achieve recovery, and how other people and policies may help or hinder the process, has generated considerable writing and research, much of it by people who have a diagnosis of severe mental illness. Among the numerous personal and research-based writings are those by Allott, Loganathan, and Fulford (2002); Deegan (1988); Harding, Zubin, and Strauss (1987); Leete (1989); Ralph (2000); Repper and Perkins (2003); and Tooth, Kalyanasundaram, Glover, and Momedzadah (2003).

This chapter has described the main theories of the cause of schizophrenia. However, the key question for many people is what treatments are available, and this is the subject of the next chapter.

Useful addresses/resources

The Second Opinion Clinic, The Maudsley Hospital, Denmark Hill, London SE5 8AZ. Tel: 0203 228 4418; Fax: 0203 228 4419.

CHAPTER THREE

Medication and other treatments

Medication is the first-line treatment for people with a diagnosis of schizophrenia. These drugs are called antipsychotics, neuroleptics, or major tranquillizers and described as "typicals" or "atypicals". (See Table 1.) Antipsychotics, like other psychiatric drugs, affect chemicals in the brain and other parts of the body which carry messages between the nerve cells. These chemical messengers are called neurotransmitters and act on sites in the nerve cells, known as receptors.

Research and personal accounts show that medication helps many people to manage their symptoms and is decisive in their recovery. A Mind survey, *Roads to Recovery* (2001) reported that forty-two per cent of respondents who felt recovered, or were coping, said psychiatric drugs first helped their recovery, and three-quarters of the people in a study by Sullivan (1994) also cited medication as the most important factor in their recovery.

However, these drugs do not necessarily make someone *feel* any better and it is not unusual for people to be unaware of just how much medication affects their behaviour, though it may be apparent to their relatives and friends (Kuipers & Bebbington, 2005). Even so, only about half the people with "schizophrenic disorders"

Table 1.   Antipsychotics: relative adverse effects—a rough guide

Drug	Sedation	Extra-pyramidal	Anti-cholinergic	Hypo-tension	Prolactin elevation
Amisulpride	–	+	–	–	+++
Aripiprazole	–	+/–	–	–	–
Benperidol	+	+++	+	+	+++
Chlorpromazine	+++	++	++	+++	+++
Clozapine	+++	–	+++	+++	–
Flupentixol	+	++	++	+	+++
Fluphenazine	+	+++	++	+	+++
Haloperidol	+	+++	+	+	+++
Loxapine	++	+++	+	++	+++
Olanzapine	++	+/–	+	+	+
Perphenazine	+	+++	+	+	+++
Pimozide	+	+	+	+	+++
Pipothiazine	++	++	++	++	+++
Promazine	+++	+	++	++	++
Quetiapine	++	–	+	++	–
Risperidone	+	+	+	++	+++
Sertindole	–	–	–	+++	+/–
Sulpiride	–	+	–	–	+++
Thioridazine	+++	+	+++	+++	++
Trifluoperazine	+	+++	+/–	+	+++
Ziprasidone	+	+/–	–	+	+/–
Zotepine	+++	+	+	++	+++
Zuclopenthixol	++	++	++	+	+++

Key: +++ high incidence/severity; ++ moderate; +low–very low
Table reprinted with permission from *The Maudsley 2005–2006 Prescribing Guidelines* (8th edn). Editors: David Taylor, Carol Paton, & Robert Kerwin (Taylor & Francis).

Note: the editors emphasize that the table is made up of approximate estimates of relative incidence and/or severity of side-effects based on clinical experience, manufacturers' literature and published research. Other side effects not mentioned in this table do occur and these are discussed in the *Prescribing Guidelines*.

will benefit from neuroleptics (Falloon, 2006). Many continue to experience psychotic symptoms, which result in increased anxiety, depression, and risk of suicide (Tarrier, 1987).

Antipsychotics can be taken orally, in tablet or liquid form, or by an injection. Drugs in tablet or liquid form are usually taken once or twice a day, while the effects of an injection are designed to last for between one and five weeks. These injections are called depots, and comprise antipsychotic medication suspended in, usually, a thin vegetable oil.

The first antipsychotics

Antipsychotic medication became available in the 1950s. Thorazine (Largactil) was the first drug, and belongs to a class of compounds called phenothiazines that, by accident, scientists found were very sedating. Subsequent research revealed that phenothiazines work by blocking the impulses of the neurotransmitter dopamine. Largactil modified some people's hallucinations, delusions, and paranoia and is often credited with enabling many individuals to leave hospital and live in the community. However, it has also been claimed that this resulted from changes in economic factors and social policy (Warner, 1994; Whitaker, 2004).

In the 1960s other drugs were developed, including haloperidol and fluphenazine. Like Largactil, these "typicals" block the effects of dopamine. Typicals are still prescribed and suit some individuals, but the side-effects can be very unpleasant (Awad & Hogan, 1994; Falloon, Watt, & Shepherd, 1978; Van Putten, 1974; Van Putten, May, Marder, & Wittman, 1981). Headaches, dizziness, blurred vision, and constipation are common, along with mind-numbing feelings that have been described as being "bombed out", "numb" or "out of it". In addition, several of these drugs raise prolactin levels, which may cause breast changes in women and breast development in men. Furthermore, up to forty-five per cent of people taking typical antipsychotics experience some form of sexual dysfunction (Smith, O' Keane, & Murray, 2002). Men, for instance, may lose their sexual desire, have problems getting an erection, or achieving a normal orgasm (Macdonald et al., 2003). Loss of sexual desire and enjoyment also affects women (Macdonald et al., 2003; Smith, 2003).

The most obvious side-effects, however, are disturbances in a person's muscle tone and movements. Collectively, they are known as extrapyramidal symptoms (EPSs) and individually as Parkinsonism, dystonia, dyskinesia and akathisia.

Parkinsonism

Dopamine is involved in the control of movement, so blocking its effects can cause tremors, especially of the fingers, muscle rigidity, and involuntary movements, such as twitching. These resemble the symptoms of Parkinson's Disease, which is caused by too little dopamine in the brain.

Dystonia

This includes muscle spasms, twitching, eye rolling, stiffness, and rigidity, particularly in the face and neck—sometimes to the point where both are twisted to one side, known as torticollis. People may be unable to speak or swallow properly and, in extreme cases, a sufferer's back arches involuntarily and the jaw is dislocated.

About ten per cent of people develop acute dystonia on typical drugs (American Psychiatric Association, 1977). It can occur within hours of starting on the medication and when withdrawing from it. At its worst, dystonia can be very painful and frightening. Some people find relief by using an anticholinergic drug, such as procyclidine or orphenadrine, although these drugs produce their own side-effects, typically dryness of the mouth, blurred vision, and constipation.

Dyskinesia

These are abnormal movements of the muscles, which can cause a twisted posture of the neck, arching of the back, or involuntary chewing or grimacing. These uncontrollable movements may develop only after many years of using antipsychotics, when they are called tardive (meaning late) dyskinesia.

A study by Kane and colleagues (1984) reported that tardive dyskinesia (TD) affects between ten and twenty per cent of people using typicals over a long period of time. Other research suggests that repeated, or lengthy "drug holidays" may possibly increase the risk of TD in individuals predisposed to develop it (Greden & Tandon, 1995; Jeste, Potkin, Sinha, Feder, & Wyatt, 1979).

Dyskinesia also occurs with atypical drugs (Zhang et al., 2004). Anticholinergics may be prescribed, though a systematic review (Soares & McGrath, 2000) found that there was insufficient data to reach any conclusions about their effectiveness for TD. However, a systematic review of research studies (Soares & McGrath, 2001) indicates that vitamin E may protect against its worsening, though there is no research evidence that it improves the symptoms of the condition.

Akathisia

This extreme restlessness is a very unpleasant side-effect. The person is unable to relax or sit down for more than a short time, but feels constantly agitated and compelled to restlessly pace up and down. About twenty to twenty-five per cent of people taking typicals experience akathisia (Halstead, Barnes, & Speller, 1994). In a review of antipsychotic drugs, Gardner, Baldessarini, & Waraich (2005) claim that this is often misdiagnosed as psychotic agitation and mistakenly treated with more antipsychotic medication.

Akathisia appears to be a persistent side-effect of neuroleptics, which may be relieved by anticholinergic drugs. However, a systematic review (Lima, Weiser, Bacaltchuk, & Barnes, 2004) found no reliable research evidence that they are effective.

High doses

If typicals are prescribed in very high doses and/or in combination with other antipsychotics—as often occurred in the past—they can cause premature death (Fisher & Greenberg, 1977) or, at the very least, be physically and psychologically disabling. James recalls his first experience of drug treatment:

Fifteen years ago I had a psychotic episode and was sectioned. They put me on chlorpromazine which sent me deeper into a psychosis. I didn't hurt anyone, but really took it out on the walls and tables and chairs. So they kept upping the dose till I was more or less zombified. I used to shuffle my feet to get from one place to another. My dad used to call it the Harlem shuffle it was that bad, though I can see the funny side of it now.

Around 20–50% of people on acute psychiatric wards are given high, "as required" doses of medication with the intention of calming them. (The doctor prescribes the frequency and upper limit of the dose and the drug is then given at the discretion of clinical staff.) A systematic review (Whicher, Morrison, & Douglas-Hall, 2002) found no randomized trials comparing "as required" medication regimes to regular ones. The authors concluded that, as the practice was based on clinical experience and habit rather than high quality evidence, it was difficult to justify.

The Royal College of Psychiatrists (2006) has also stated that there is no firm evidence that high doses of antipsychotics are more effective than standard ones, and that this holds true for their use in "rapid tranquillisation, acute psychosis and chronic aggression management".

Greden and Tandon (1995) recommend avoiding "megadoses" of antipsychotics during acute stages as they may not offer any advantage over more modest doses, and also avoid the need for subsequent dose reduction. But even after being discharged from hospital, people may still be taking too high a dose of the old drugs and suffering unduly from the side-effects (Baldessarini, Cohen, & Teicher, 1988; Davis & Chen, 2004; Marder, van Putten, & Mintz, 1987). When this is remedied, conventional antipsychotics might not cause more EPSs than the new drugs, according to a systematic review and meta-analysis of previous research (Leucht, Wahlbeck, Hamann, & Kissling, 2003). Jan says that she has never experienced severe side-effects.

I've been on Stelazine (trifluoperazine) for 15 years. There are times when I get a bit stiff or restless, but it's nothing too serious. Usually taking a procyclidine tablet helps. Or having a cup of camomile tea or a soak in a hot bath does the trick. I've no wish to try one of the new drugs.

These drugs, the atypicals, were made available in the UK in the 1990s. Like the first antipsychotics, atypicals block dopamine and also the neurotransmitter serotonin and are said to be better targeted to the nerve receptors. A systematic review of atypicals (Geddes, Freemantle, Harrison, & Bebbington, 2000) reported that there was no clear evidence that they are more effective or better tolerated than the old neuroleptics. Even so, anecdotal and research evidence suggests that many people tend to experience fewer and less "intolerable" side-effects on atypicals and, unlike typicals, they seem to relieve at least some negative symptoms, such as social withdrawal, as well as positive ones, like hallucinations. Csernansky and Schuchart (2002) reported that they are more effective in preventing relapse than typicals. Mind (2005a) point out that people who have used typicals for years may do better on atypicals, or might at least like to give them a try.

The first atypical was Leponex, known in the UK as Clozapine or Clozaril. Stephen describes the difference the drug has made to his life.

Stephen's story—"Now I am recovered. I am not psychotic"

I am in a top security hospital. I've been on Clozapine for 20 months and it's like a new life—as the Christians say—"born again". I am no longer hearing those hellish torturous voices. I no longer believe my room to be bugged by transmitting and receiving devices. I don't believe the staff do torture, as the medication cured the voices hours after taking the first dose.

I used to think there was an intercom device in my room so the staff could wind me up and torture me, because of my crimes of 27 years ago. Well, my room isn't bugged, and probably never was—it was psychosis. There's the conspiracy theory of course, but most times that is paranoia.

Before being admitted to a medium secure unit 17½ years ago, I was very suicidally depressed and grossly psychotic. I just knew that I was an addict of Valium and Mogadon, which could have been treated in an addiction therapy unit rather than being neglected and eventually led to my being charged with two actual bodily harm charges.

I was blacklisted by the local mental hospital as violent, so could not receive psychiatric help. I just went to my GP's every few days for repeat scripts of Valium and Mogadon and to inject my own thigh with the drug Modecate. None of that stopped the voices, as I thought the voices were part of me—my mind, so therefore were not illness.

During the 17 years on Modecate I denied that I was hearing voices to have the drug gradually reduced—after all the voice was my guardian angel, or part of me that was looking after me. Actually, it was severe schizophrenia paranoia. And if I had not committed the ABHs, I would have died via an overdose. I even jumped out of a train travelling at 60 miles per hour and another time lay on the main railway line with two GPs searching for me.

Now I am recovered. I am not psychotic and hardly get any depression. I started studying and have passed my GCSE Maths and English and plan to do more studying in the future, though I do get tired on the drug. For the past eight months I have also attended group therapy three mornings a week and my profile is now low risk, not dangerous. I am always kept very busy so that I don't have time to think about psychosis.

When occasionally I can't sleep in the early hours I listen to the silence—very precious. I assumed I would never recover from suicidal tendencies. I thought my illness would kill me. Now I love living and every day is a God given gift of new life. I live life to the full as much as I can because really I am living on 20 years borrowed time from the psychiatric system.

For all those who help me and have helped me get to how I am now, I thank God and Clozapine. Some meds helped, like Risperidone and Olanzapine, but for me it's Clozapine which wins the star prize.

All the staff say that I am doing well and will probably be transferred to a low secure unit later this year. I visited there a few years ago and there are no bars on the windows! Well, recovery isn't just a bed of roses. It's going to be more therapy and in the new unit will include an anti-violence group and individual sessions for drug abuse and, hopefully, help so that I can quit smoking. It will be five years of treatment and then in the sixth year putting what I've learned into practice. As I say, recovery isn't a bed of roses and nor is it freedom, but it is a better quality of life than I have ever known.

Atypicals may produce fewer and less severe side-effects, such as EPSs but they cause other problems. Some are associated with rapid or irregular heartbeat (Healy, 2005). Like typicals, they may cause sexual problems. This has been Liz P's experience.

> Risperidone has helped me, but one serious side-effect is its affect on my sex drive and that's quite a big issue for me. It's a barrier to having a relationship with someone--and that can really affect your quality of life, though it's not necessarily something you feel comfortable discussing with your psychiatrist or GP.

Questions about medication

The following questions from Rethink's free booklet, *Only the Best*, are designed to help people use consultations with their GP or psychiatrist to the best effect and become more knowledgeable about their medication and treatment options.

- Why have you prescribed this particular medication for me?
- Why have you set the dosage at this level?
- What are the most common side-effects of this treatment?
- Would a different drug be less likely to make me tired/cause tremors/increase my weight/etc?
- When will there be a decision as to whether this is the best treatment for me?
- How does this drug interact with smoking/alcohol/the contraceptive pill/etc?
- In choosing this treatment, have you taken my family history into account (eg diabetes, etc)?
- How often will you be reviewing my medication?
- How often will you measure the effects of medication on my physical health?
- Will you refer me to a psychologist/arrange a course of talking therapy/etc?
- Why are you prescribing more than one antipsychotic for me?
- Are there any financial considerations which affect what you can prescribe?

(Reprinted with permission from Rethink)

While sexual problems have been reported as a side-effect of all atypicals (Segraves, 1989), research indicates that Quetiapine has the lowest risk (Bobes et al., 2003; Byerly et al., 2004; Knegtering et al., 2004) and, despite there being little data, sexual problems are not anticipated with Abilify (Taylor, Paton, & Kerwin, 2005, p. 100).

Clozapine and Olanzapine have been linked to diabetes mellitus, hyperglycaemia (high blood sugar) and ketoacidosis, an over-acid condition of the body fluids or tissue. Being male, non-white, around forty and obese, or having recently gained weight, are the particular risk factors for these conditions (Taylor, Paton, & Kerwin, 2005, p. 10). Clozapine has also been associated with the painful condition of pancreatitis, which can cause diabetes and digestion problems (Bergemann, Ehrig, Diebold, Mundt, & von Einsiedel, 1999).

Even more seriously, for about three per cent of people Clozapine prevents the body from producing sufficient white blood cells, thereby undermining the immune system and its ability to fight infection and disease. Consequently, Clozapine is only prescribed when other antipsychotics are ineffective. People on the drug have their white blood cell count monitored with weekly or fortnightly blood tests. (At the time of writing, the makers have reportedly identified a gene which may enable them to determine which individuals are likely to be affected, so that some people using Clozapine will not need such tests.)

Taylor, Paton, & Kerwin (2005) state that though Clozapine can cause serious, life-threatening adverse effects (Munro et al., 1999), it has, however, reduced the rate of suicide among people with schizophrenia (Melzer et al., 2003; Walker et al., 1997). Healy, however, claims the evidence for this is minimal (2005, p. 38). Nevertheless, Clozapine is linked with fewer suicides than Olanzapine.

Obviously, any concerns a person might have about the side-effects of their medication, especially suicidal thoughts, need to be discussed straightaway with a doctor or psychiatrist.

Another commonly reported side-effect of the atypicals is weight gain. In some people it may be moderate, but others experience massive increases that are difficult to control (Bryden & Kopala, 1999). Obviously this causes numerous health problems and possibly diabetes. Clozapine has the greatest potential for weight gain, followed by Olanzapine, Quetiapine, Risperidone, Amisulpride and Ziprasidone (Gardner, Baldessarini, & Waraich, 2005). Abilify is the least likely to increase weight, if at all (Taylor, Paton, & Kerwin, 2005).

A trial with people in hospital (McQuade et al., 2004) found that at the end of twenty-six weeks, compared to those taking Olanzapine, who had a mean weight gain of almost 9½ lbs, those on Abilify had a mean weight loss of just over 3 lbs.

When Abilify became available in the UK in 2004 the makers described it as the first dopamine system stabilizer. They claim it both restricts and increases dopamine activity in the brain to a more "normal" level, thereby reducing positive and negative symptoms and improving cognitive functions, like thinking, planning, and concentration. Modell and co-researchers (2004) found that Abilify could be effective for people who do not benefit from other atypicals, including Risperidone and Olanzapine.

Anecdotal evidence indicates that, compared to other antipsychotics, Abilify's side-effects are generally no worse, and sometimes much less. Headaches, nausea, and insomnia are reportedly the main problems, although, as with many antipsychotics, these seem to lessen or cease as tolerance to the drug develops. Abilify does not appear to inhibit a person's sex drive, cause erection problems in men, or the adverse heart rhythms found with some atypicals (Pigott et al., 2003; Potkin et al., 2003).

However, the long-term effects of using Abilify, or any of the atypicals, cannot be known. Nor, based on previous evidence, will there be an antipsychotic that works for everyone. Finding a suitable drug may involve trying several over a period of time, but in some instances the "right" drug can be life-changing, as James explains.

James' story—"I got my life back"

I've been on lots of drugs, but not until I went on Abilify did I really get my life back. I got a new psychiatrist who put me on Clozaril. If you've seen the film *Awakenings* with Robert De Niro—it was like that. I was getting my thoughts back, but it was too much. I couldn't stop running—up and down the corridors—and then I thought I was Superman, tied sheets together and tried flying out of the windows.

Next I went on Olanzapine for two years and was able to work, but I really piled on the pounds. I've also been on Risperidone which wasn't a bad drug. It kept me stable and wasn't as sedating as

Olanzapine, but it tended to numb my motivation. I didn't seem to have any "go". But Abilify is a really good drug. A lot of the trouble with some of the medications is that they tend to put a lot of weight on whereas this one doesn't. The worst side-effect is just a metallic taste in your mouth, but everything else is fine with Abilify. It's superb—the best drug I've been on.

I'm at college now and got a distinction in brickwork so I'm doing a second year. I want to be a bricklayer and then go travelling. Abilify's been fantastic for me. I feel a bit more positive about myself every day. It's given me a new start in life.

Managing side-effects

Side-effects are often the reason people stop taking antipsychotics (Van Putten, May, Marder, & Wittman, 1981). Mind's report *Coping with Coming Off* (2005) gave side-effects as the reason most people wanted to come off medication—this included antipsychotics, mood stabilizers, and antidepressants.

The right dose

Side-effects are dose-related, so that a high dose is likely to produce more side-effects than a lower one. As with any drug, it is advisable to read about possible side-effects in the accompanying leaflet and share concerns with a pharmacist, GP, or psychiatrist

Taking a correct dose of a drug is important. Every drug has a therapeutic range. Before it is licensed for use, clinical trials will have indicated the lowest dose at which the drug is effective, as well as a recommended upper limit. Using less than a therapeutic dose increases the risk of someone's symptoms worsening, while taking more than the upper limit does not make it more effective.

People's metabolisms vary and so does the amount of medication they need to manage their symptoms. It is sometimes believed that the higher the dose, the more ill the person is, but this is not necessarily the case. One person may absorb the drug so poorly that little gets into his or her bloodstream. Another person may be a fast metabolizer and the enzymes in his or her blood will rapidly destroy the drug.

When taken orally, a drug interacts with the body's hormones, food, or other drugs. (This is the reason neuroleptics are more effective when injected into a muscle rather than taken in tablet or liquid form. Bypassing the stomach ensures that the drug goes more directly into the bloodstream.) By contrast, someone's symptoms may be managed by a low dose if he or she is a "poor excretor", so that the drug is eliminated slowly and also accumulates in the blood. Elderly people also often manage successfully on smaller doses.

Prescription guidelines do not distinguish between men and women, but drug metabolism may vary between the sexes. The normal fat ratio of women's bodies can affect how drugs are distributed to different organs. Hormonal fluctuations due to the menstrual cycle, pregnancy, or the period following childbirth, may involve a woman needing to adjust her dose to avoid symptoms recurring or becoming more severe.

Other factors that may affect medication needs include additional stress, sickness, changes in weight, diet, exercise, and other medication. For instance, antacids such as Gaviscon or Rennie tend to interfere with the absorption of some antipsychotics and may lessen their effectiveness. It is recommended, therefore, that they are taken an hour before, or after, antipsychotics.

Low doses

After a period of feeling well and, relatively symptom-free, it is not unusual for someone to reduce their medication. While this decision seems perfectly reasonable, if it means using less than a therapeutic dose it may increase the risk of the symptoms returning or worsening. There is no research to suggest that less than a therapeutic dose is effective in preventing relapse (Taylor, 2006) and very low doses are associated with relapse (Baldessarini, Cohen, & Teicher, 1988; Marder, van Putten, & Mintz, 1987).

Omega 3 fatty acids

The research findings are inconsistent, but studies have reported that, taken in addition to medication, Omega 3 fatty acids improve some people's symptoms and lessen side-effects. These fatty acids are found in oily fish, such as mackerel, salmon, pilchards, and sardines, though not in tinned tuna. Fish make Omega 3 from algae, and the body can make it from linseed/flax oil, rape seed oil, and walnuts.

Omega 3 comprises two fatty acids: EPA and DHA. Studies have reported that oils with a high EPA to low DHA ratio may effect a significant improvement in people's symptoms (Mellor, Laugharne, & Peet, 1995). People using Clozapine reported significant symptom improvement with two grams of EPA daily as the most effective dose (Peet & Horrobin, 2002a) and a significantly greater reduction in symptoms and tardive dyskinesia (Emsley, Myburgh, Oosthuizen, & van Rensburgh, 2002).

However, eighty-seven patients with a diagnosis of schizophrenia or schizoaffective disorder who took three grams daily showed no improvement (Fenton, Dickerson, Boronow, Hibbeln, & Knable, 2001). The researchers concluded that this might have been because the people were older and had been ill for longer, compared to participants in earlier studies who improved with Omega 3 fatty acid supplements.

Kirunal fish oil has an EPA to DHA ratio of 3:1 compared to proprietary brands of cod or halibut liver oil that have a less effective 3:2 ratio. Neither of these, therefore, are a recommended source of EPA, since to obtain a therapeutic dose would mean taking an excessively high and potentially damaging amount of fish oil.

Based on case reports (Puri & Richardson, 1998; Puri et al., 2000; Richardson, Easton, & Puri, 2000; Su, Shen, & Huang, 2001), *The Maudsley Prescribing Guidelines* (Taylor, Paton, & Kerwin, 2005, p. 69) "very tentatively" recommends EPA "for the treatment of residual symptoms of schizophrenia, but particularly in patients responding poorly to Clozapine".

Professor Basant Puri, a consultant psychiatrist and researcher in this field, recommends specially formulated VegEPA as a purer and more effective source of EPA than fish oils. VegEPA oil is available in capsule form by mail order from Igennus Ltd (0845 1300424), website: www.vegepa.com

(A systematic review of fatty acids (Joy, Mumby-Croft, & Joy, 2003) reported that one small study that compared Omega 6 with a placebo for tardive dyskinesia found no clear benefit.)

A case study

In a letter entitled "Sustained remission of positive and negative symptoms of schizophrenia following treatment with EPA" (1998), psychiatrists Basant Puri and Alexandra Richardson reported a dramatic remission of positive and negative symptoms in a patient who had been diagnosed with schizophrenia twelve years earlier. Periodic follow-ups have shown normal levels of fatty acids in the patient's blood, and brain scans indicate that the previous brain tissue loss is being reversed.

Changing medication

If it seems that someone may benefit from using a different drug, the usual procedure is to reduce the current medication by about a half for at least a week and then, in addition, take the lowest therapeutic dose of the new drug. Provided there are no serious adverse effects (described in the leaflet accompanying the drug) the person continues on the new medication alone, with the starting dose adjusted as necessary. This fine-tuning may take several weeks until the person's metabolism adjusts to the effects of withdrawing from the old drug and the side-effects of the new one.

Severe side-effects may be the reason someone gives up on a new drug. Initially, these are difficult to distinguish from the withdrawal effects of the former drug, so during this period it may be helpful to involve the GP or psychiatrist for advice and reassurance.

Coming off antipsychotics

A person's symptoms may return or worsen if they reduce or stop taking antipsychotics. One study (Crow, MacMillan, Johnson, & Johnstone, 1986) reported that fifty-seven per cent of people who did not take medication relapsed after a year. Although it is not possible to predict if someone will relapse, individuals who have previously relapsed when they stopped using medication, and those who have had symptoms on and off for many years are thought to be the most vulnerable. This seems to be the case for John E, as he describes.

Like many other people I know with a diagnosis of schizophrenia, I have experimented with trying to stop my antipsychotics or, at least, to cut them down. Some time ago, I read a book with a series of self-help exercises. One was to draw a graph of your life, with its high and lows, peaks and troughs, plateaux, valleys and plains. Then to mark significant events in your life on the graph, to see if there was any pattern. One event I marked was when I cut down or stopped my antipsychotics. This proved very significant.

I discovered that it was at a peak when I was feeling good about myself and life, that I quite often decided to stop or cut down my tablets. When I did, I noticed that later I dropped into a trough. After a while, I'd decide to go back on the medication. Even so, I found that I stayed in the trough, feeling depressed. It then took one or two years until I gradually climbed out of it to another peak, where, if I decided to come off my tablets, the whole process was repeated.

Once when I was off tablets for six months, I ended up in a mental hospital, seriously ill for two months. I went back on my tablets at other times because I was having a relapse. I couldn't see that at the time, but everyone was telling me to go back on my tablets, and in the end I did. During my later experiments in coming off, I went back before I had a full-blown relapse, as I saw the danger signs myself more clearly.

This had occurred several times before doing the exercise made me realize that I was following a pattern. After that I decided to end my tablet experimentation once and for all, and follow the doctor's orders. I have met people who have successfully come off their antipsychotic medication, and they said that it was extremely difficult, and were loathe to recommend it. Though I do realize that some lucky people have successfully come off their antipsychotics, I, unfortunately, like many other people, am not one of them.

Studies show that, like John, many people learn to become aware of their own "warning signs" (Breier & Strauss, 1983; Kumar, Thara, & Rajkumar, 1989; McCandless-Glimcher et al., 1986). This may prevent the disruption to their lives that a relapse inevitably brings—and reduce the risk of further relapses (McGlashan, 1988), since it seems that every relapse increases the chance of another occurrence. Also, each relapse might require larger doses of neuroleptics to be taken for a longer period for someone to regain stability (Wyatt, 1991).

Using antipsychotics continuously may be the best way for some people to stay well. However, as John pointed out above, some people manage to come off their medication and avoid relapse, and research shows that schizophrenia is not necessarily a life-long condition.

Bockoven and Solomon's (1975) five-year follow-up of 100 randomly selected patients "unexpectedly" reported that antipsychotics might not be indispensable to people's recovery. The authors stated that antipsychotics might actually prolong the social dependency of some discharged patients. Moreover, other research suggests that people permanently on antipsychotics tend to have longer periods of hospitalization (Epstein, Morgan, & Reynolds, 1962).

These findings are supported by the results of a five-year follow-up study by the World Health Organization (WHO). People with schizophrenia living in poor and less developed countries, where antipsychotic drug treatment is not widely available, had significantly better outcomes compared to people in developed countries (Leff, Sartorius, Jablensky, Korten, & Ernberg, 1992). A second, ten-country study by WHO confirmed the earlier finding and concluded that: "being in a developed country was a strong predictor of not attaining a complete remission." (Jablensky et al., 1992).

However, there is considerable evidence that antipsychotics help some people to recover, regardless of where in the world they live. For instance, a two-year follow-up study of people with schizoprehenia in a rural Chinese community (Ran, Xiang, Huang, & Shan, 2001) reported that, compared to participants using antipsychotics, three-quarters of the others who had not used them remained symptomatic and their illness had become more serious over time.

While it is impossible to know how coming off medication might affect someone's quality of life, discussing the possibility beforehand with friends, relatives, and members of their self-help or support group, if they have one, may help people to weigh up the pros and cons.

It is known that people coming off antipsychotics are more likely to be successful if they feel well-supported, particularly by a mental health professional, such as a psychiatrist, or someone who has successfully helped people come off medication. Writing in the magazine *OpenMind*, Holmes and Hudson (2003) make the point that workers from substance abuse charities often have personal as well as professional experience of drug withdrawal and may be able to offer help. Even so, some people have successfully managed to stop using medication without support (Crepaz-Keay, 1999).

It is not a good idea, however, for people to reduce or stop using medication if they feel excessively stressed, but to wait until such difficulties have been resolved. If a person experiences signs of relapse during withdrawal, it is sensible to discontinue reducing their medication for a while.

Rapid reduction

Too rapid a reduction can trigger a relapse and/or acute withdrawal symptoms. A study by Green and colleagues (1992) found that a slow tapering off from antipsychotic medication over an eight-week period resulted in only eight per cent of people relapsing, compared to fifty per cent who relapsed with more rapid withdrawal over two weeks.

After rapid withdrawal, the relapse rate in the first six months is twice that of gradual withdrawal (Viguera, Baldessarini, Hegarty, van Kammen, & Tohen, 1997), whereas Baldessarini & Viguera (1995) found that only one third of patients with schizophrenia relapsed within six months if they withdrew from drugs gradually. Those who reached the six-month point without becoming unwell had a good chance of remaining so indefinitely.

Relapse also seems to be associated with the amount of antipsychotic the person is using. A study by Prien, Cole, and Belkin (1968) of people who abruptly stopped using antipsychotic medication reported that the higher the dose before withdrawal the greater the chances of their relapsing. People who have used antipsychotics for several years, therefore, may need at least a year or more to come off safely.

Even after long-term use people may be able to reduce their dose safely if the reduction is slow. Smith's (1994) study with sixteen patients who had chronic psychotic symptoms and had been in hospital for an average of over eleven years, describes medication being reduced very slowly, by one fifth to one third, every one to two months. This enabled them to achieve an approximate sixty per cent reduction with an accompanying lessening of symptoms.

For people taking tablets, the general rule is to reduce the dose at monthly intervals by up to one fifth of the starting dose. A rough guide is one month for every year, although, of course, this does not apply if someone has been taking neuroleptics for twenty years or more. But again, it is important for people not to hurry the process.

Depending on the original dose, it tends to take longer to come off depot injections—two to three years is not uncommon. Usually, this is achieved by extending the length of time between injections and at the same time reducing the dose. For instance, instead of fortnightly, a person has injections every three weeks and then once a month and so on, until they are finally discontinued. At the same time, the depot dose is very gradually reduced, say by up to a third, every three months. In their booklet *Advice on Medication* (2003), Philip Thomas, a psychiatrist, and Rufus May, a psychologist, state that a ten per cent reduction of the total dose is a good starting point.

Individuals using injections and oral medication are recommended to reduce and completely stop oral medication before starting to reduce the injections. If someone is using anticholinergic drugs to combat side-effects, the advice is to continue using them until the antipsychotics have been largely reduced.

Withdrawal effects

Apart from lessening the risk of relapse, coming off drugs slowly helps avoid or lessen withdrawal effects. Just as with "hard drugs", like heroin, these may include anxiety, insomnia, restlessness, nausea, vomiting, disturbed sleep, runny nose, extreme salivation, sweating, diarrhoea, and high blood pressure. Involuntary muscle movements and twitching may also occur, though they tend not to last for more than a few days. More persistent is tardive dyskinesia, which may worsen or be experienced for the first time.

People coming off antipsychotics may experience hallucinations and delusions because they are relapsing. However, these symptoms are not necessarily a sign of the underlying illness, but may be what is known as tardive psychosis or supersensitivity psychosis.

Supersensitivity psychosis

Research suggests that after years of having the neurotransmitter dopamine blocked by antipsychotic drugs, the body responds by increasing the number, and possibly the sensitivity, of dopamine receptors. This causes an over-activity of dopamine, which may cause psychosis (Chouinard & Jones, 1980; Chouinard, Jones, & Annable, 1978; Muller & Seeman, 1978; Viguera, Baldessarini, Hegarty, van Kammen, & Tohen, 1997).

Joanna Moncrieff is a psychiatrist with a research interest in supersensitivity psychosis. In her research paper (2006a) she refers to a study by Baldessarini and Viguera (1995), which suggests that withdrawal from antipsychotics may induce or bring forward relapse, and to studies which show that while psychosis does occur after withdrawal from drugs, it tails off thereafter (Gilbert, Harris, McAdams, & Jeste, 1995; Viguera, Baldessarini, Hegarty, van Kammen, & Tohen, 1997).

In Moncrieff's opinion, in some cases the speed of the onset of psychosis—typically within days of stopping medication—suggests that the symptoms, which usually include auditory, and occasionally visual, hallucinations, paranoid delusions, and hostility, may be a reaction to long-term treatment with antipsychotics, rather than simply a sign of the underlying disorder and relapse.

Linda experienced severe psychosis when she abruptly stopped taking antipsychotics.

I'd been on very high doses of old style drugs for almost forty years, lots of them, but mainly Depixol. I'd tried Clozapine, but it didn't work for me—nor Risperidone—and one day I decided I'd had enough. I was sick of feeling tired, with no energy and unable to think straight and so I just stopped taking everything. I was okay for a week or so and then went completely bonkers and was admitted to an acute ward.

Fortunately, my new psychiatrist recognized that it was withdrawal effects and didn't suggest I go back on the medication. But for a year I was really ill. It took about two years before I started to feel more like myself. The old drugs had a very damaging effect on me. It's not only tardive dyskynesia, but the brain scans show severe and deteriorating abnormalites and now I have to use a wheelchair.

Throughout this I've had a lot of support from my psychiatrist, which is essential if you want to withdraw from medication. I think more doctors and psychiatrists are coming round to the realization that people do want to try to live without drugs, but often there just isn't enough support. I've been lucky that there was a rehabilitation and treatment unit where I could stay, and which I still use at times. It would be a great help to people wanting to withdraw from drugs if there were more places like that, but my impression is there are very few and the one I use is also under threat because of funding cuts.

According to Moncrieff (2006b) a person's ability to manage their symptoms with low or even no medication is crucially affected by the attitudes of their relatives and carers and of mental health professionals. Negative attitudes may act as a "nocebo" (Hahn, 1997) whereby individuals become physically and psychologically distressed simply through suggestion. (Thus the nocebo is the opposite of the placebo effect, when individuals feel better because they believe that they will.)

Based on her clinical experience, Moncrieff states that psychological—as well as physical—withdrawal symptoms can occur when medication is reduced. Like physical symptoms, these may be mistaken for relapse, or may themselves contribute to relapse.

One study found that Valium, if taken at the first sign of symptoms recurring, can be as effective as the antipsychotic Modecate in preventing withdrawal symptoms getting worse without the need for antipsychotics (Carpenter, Buchanan, Kirkpatrick, & Breier, 1999). The researchers stated that benzodiazepines, such as Valium, might also be helpful for people who become ill while using antipsychotics and thus prevent the need for increased doses of medication.

A review of studies of the use of benzodiazepines (Wolkowitz & Pickar, 1991) concluded that 30–50% of people benefited from a combination of antipsychotic medication and benzodiazepines. People with more severe psychosis showed improvements in positive and negative symptoms, some within 24 hours (Paton, Banham, & Whitmore, 2000). However, since these drugs cause dependence and rebound psychosis when stopped (Wolkowitz, Turetsky, Reus, & Hargreaves, 1992), the recommendation is that their use is kept under review.

Understandably, individuals, their relatives, and others involved in their care, may worry that without substantial doses of medication they will inevitably become ill and relapse. But several major research studies show that this is not necessarily the case. For example, a pioneering American project, Soteria, found that a drug-free treatment environment was as successful as antipsychotic treatment in reducing psychotic symptoms within six weeks (Mosher, 1999).

The Soteria approach—important therapeutic ingredients

The therapeutic ingredients of these residential alternatives, ones that clearly distinguish them from psychiatric hospitals, in the order they are likely to be experienced by a newly admitted client, are:

1) The setting is indistinguishable from other residences in the community, and it interacts with its community.
2) The facility is small, with space for no more than 10 persons to sleep (6 to 8 clients, 2 staff). It is experienced as home-like. Admission procedures are informal and individualized, based on the client's ability to participate meaningfully.
3) A primary task of the staff is to understand the immediate circumstances and relevant background that precipitated the crisis necessitating admission. It is anticipated that this will lead to a relationship based on shared knowledge that will, in turn, enable staff to put themselves in the client's shoes. Thus, they will share the client's perception of their social context and what needs to change to enable them to return to it. The relative paucity of paperwork allows time for the interaction necessary to form a relationship.
4) Within this relationship the client will find staff carrying out multiple roles: companion, advocate, case worker, and therapist—although no therapeutic sessions are held in the house. Staff have the authority to make, in conjunction with the client, and be responsible for, on-the-spot-decisions. Staff are mostly in their mid-20s, college graduates, selected on the basis of their interest in working in this special setting with a clientele in psychotic crisis. Most use the work as a transitional step on their way to advanced mental health-related degrees. They are

usually psychologically tough, tolerant and flexible and come from lower middle class families with a "problem" member (Hirshfeld et al., 1977; Mosher et al., 1973; 1992). In contrast to psychiatric ward staff, they are trained and closely supervised in the adoption and validation of the clients' perceptions. Problem solving and supervision focused on relational difficulties (eg "transference" and "counter-transference") that they are experiencing is available from fellow staff, onsite program directors and the consulting psychiatrists (these last two will be less obvious to clients). Note that the MDs [psychiatrists] are not in charge of this program.

5) Staff are trained to prevent unnecessary dependency and, insofar as possible, maintain autonomous decision making on the part of clients. They also encourage clients to stay in contact with their usual treatment and social networks. Clients frequently remark how different the experience is from that of hospitalization. This process may result in clients reporting they feel in control and a sense of security. They also experience a continued connectedness to their usual social environments.

6) Access and departure, both initially and subsequently, is made as easy as possible. Short of official readmission, there is an open social system through which clients can continue their connection to the program in nearly any way they choose; phone-in for support, information or advice, drop-in visits (usually at dinner time), or arranged time with someone with whom they had an especially important relationship. All former clients are invited back to an organized activity one evening a week. [Mosher, 1999, reprinted with the permission of *The Journal of Mental and Nervous Disease*]

Many people at Soteria were experiencing a first episode of illness. (Some people may only have one, or possibly two episodes of illness.) However, at centres where so-called long-term "frequent flyers" received the "Soteria approach" they were also found to be as clinically improved as patients who had conventional hospital treatment.

Other clinicians using the Soteria approach have reported equally positive findings. Robert Whitaker, in his book *Mad in America: Bad Science, Bad Medicine, and the Enduring Mistreatment of the Mentally Ill* (2002), refers to research findings that support the minimal use of medication for people with first episode psychosis (Ciompi et al., 1992; Cullberg, 1999, 2002).

While a two-year Finnish study of people treated "according to an integrated model involving teamwork, patient and family participation and basic psychotherapeutic attitudes" (Lehtinen, Aaltonen, Koffert, Rakkolainen, & Syvalahti, 2000) showed that little or no medication for people experiencing a first episode of illness resulted in their having a significantly better outcome than those receiving conventional treatment. After five years, eighty-eight per cent of the former patients had not been re-hospitalized (Lehtinen, 2001).

These participants received considerable ongoing support, which is not always available when people become ill or after they leave hospital. But although not widely practised, this holistic approach has obvious appeal, especially to people who found their conventional hospital treatment insufficiently supportive. Rachel explains:

> Much of the hospital environment is focused on medication. The doctors prescribe it and the nurses often suggest it when you are distressed, anxious or need to calm down. Some nurses do encourage you to relax or distract yourself, but without proper support we often begin to resent this. Instead of hiding in the office, mental health workers could spend more time listening and talking to their patients and, rather than handing out clichéd advice, treat people as individuals.

> Having contact with a therapist might also provide an opportunity to deal with some of the factors that contribute to a person's mental health problems. In acute wards this would be short-term and, if found to be supportive, extended after discharge. Medication, useful as it sometimes is, can't listen to you and doesn't try to understand.

Sheila said,

> I wasn't given a lot of information and the doctors don't see you enough. Perhaps they thought I wasn't well enough, but I would have liked more input from the staff. Half the time they're doing paperwork and the other half they're in the office. I wanted to be talked to and listened to more.

Similarly, Carole's view was that "Psychiatrists should listen to us patients. We can tell them how we're feeling. Doctors need not just to treat the illness, or the mind, but the whole person."

Liz P said,

Inside and out of the hospital setting, mental health professionals need to listen to us service-users more. When I was doing research into their views, one of the big pleas from service users was *Please listen more*. That applies to the interpretations of the causes of our mental distress. People have quite thought-out and complex analyses of how they became unwell, but none of that will ever be recorded by psychiatrists.

Just as people can learn to become questioning of the medical model, so can doctors and psychiatrists, not just slap on a diagnosis and prescribe medication. There is a lot more to mental distress than that and a lot more to recovery, too. Research by the psychiatrist Marius Romme—which inspired the hearing voices network—and his partner Sandra Escher, shows that the professionals need to take a broader perspective.

A Rethink report, *Future Perfect* (2005), based on the views of mental health service users and their carers, advocates replacing psychiatric hospitals with crisis centres, retreats, and therapeutic sanctuaries. The sanctuaries would have "open spaces and gardens, complementary therapies available, and private rooms with ensuite facilities" (p. 4).

Managing without antipsychotics

Dr Moncrieff believes that the serious physical and psychological effects of coming off antipsychotics give a misleading picture of how many people genuinely relapse without this medication and, therefore, the number who might be able to manage their symptoms without being permanently on drugs. Jo feels her quality of life has improved considerably since she stopping using medication continuously.

Jo's story—"Using medication when I need it"

If I hadn't instigated it, no one would have suggested it, but I was determined to try. I gradually reduced the dose, cutting tablets in two if necessary. I informed my mental health SHO doctor that I was reducing my dose with a view to stopping. It wasn't particularly recommended, but I explained that I would start taking the antipsychotic medication if I noticed any of my warning signs. These are:

- Become suspicious of people (paranoia).
- Dwelling on things that have happened in the past.
- Smoking and drinking more than usual.
- Not looking after myself very well—not eating well and neglecting personal hygiene.
- Waking up in the night with racing thoughts.
- Feeling stressed.
- Loss of sense of humour.
- Starting to see "messages" in papers or on the TV or radio.

I did pretty well for two years. I wasn't always totally symptom free. I did get stressed out sometimes. I have a habit of jumping to conclusions and can be paranoid at times. On the other hand I felt really strong mentally the majority of the time and did not have the "fuzzyhead" from medication.

Then I ignored my own warning signs. Moving house, starting a new training course, Christmas—it all got on top of me. I became ill and needed to go back on the medication. Stress has always been a big factor in my becoming unwell. I've realized that and always thought if I just did enough to keep that at bay I'd be able to avoid it. In the past, I've left it far too late to bring medication into the picture, whereas now I'd say, well, I might be getting unwell so if I bring in medication then I definitely won't become unwell.

I suppose I've felt it was a failure if I couldn't cope without medication. Now it's sort of treating it as more of a friend, using it when I need it—and it's there to be used after all! I take Quetiapine, which is not one of those which makes you put on a lot of weight, and it works well for me. Even so, for the past year I haven't used anything and have been able to stay well. But I wouldn't hesitate to use medication again if I thought I needed it.

Using drugs "cleverly", as Healy describes it (2005, p. 6) works well for Jo and for some others. Healy refers to his research, which found that people adopting this approach were no more likely to be readmitted to hospital than people who use antipsychotics continuously (Healy, 1990).

Healthy eating, exercise, and stress management, complementary therapies, and counselling may help someone cope with withdrawal symptoms and to stay well (see Chapters Five, Seven, and Eight). The Mind booklet *Making Sense of Coming Off Psychiatric Drugs* (2005b) can be bought or read online at their website.

Electroconvulsive therapy (ECT)

Like antipsychotics, ECT has been used as a treatment for schizophrenia. ECT involves placing electrodes on both temples, or one, through which, for a fraction of a second, a current of electricity is passed. This causes the person to have a seizure and then become unconscious.

ECT was developed by an Italian psychiatrist and neurologist, Ugo Cerletti (1877–1963). After experimenting on animals, in 1938 he and a colleague, Lucio Bini, first used ECT on a human patient who had been diagnosed with schizophrenia and was experiencing delusions, hallucinations, and confusion.

They reported that after a series of shocks their patient returned to a normal state of mind. Celetti's method made him world-famous. However, ECT is not a cure for schizophrenia and can have harmful side-effects, chiefly memory loss, in particular long-term, autobiographical memory. Although in some cases ECT is used as a treatment for severe or unremitting depression, NICE (2003) does not recommend it as a treatment for schizophrenia.

ECT review

A review of twenty-four randomly controlled trials by Dr Prathap Tharyan, Head of Psychiatry at Christian Medical College in Tamil Nadu, India, concluded that for twenty per cent of patients who did not respond to antipsychotics, the addition of ECT helped relieve symptoms more effectively. These findings can be read on the April 2005 update of the Cochrane Database of Systematic Reviews (www.tinyurl.com/dsyn7).

However, according to Lucy Johnstone, a clinical psychologist and researcher, the review did not include data that compared ECT with psychological treatments, such as cognitive behaviour, individual, or family therapy, which have been shown to be effective and long-lasting in helping people to manage their symptoms (see Chapter Eight).

> A Cochrane review (Tharyan & Adams, 2002) found only limited evidence to support its [ECT's] use in schizophrenia. It is also widely acknowledged by psychiatrists that the relapse rate is high (The Royal College of Psychiatrists, 1995) and that there is no evidence that benefits last more than four weeks. [Johnstone, 2003, p. 237]

Johnstone's own research confirmed her belief that it is unethical to administer ECT, a view echoed by some of those who spoke to her about their experiences. "It is not justifiable to give people something that harms their brains and gives them an epileptic fit on the NHS. It's just not, in my view, an ethical way to proceed." And: "It is inhuman and inhumane" (Johnstone, 1999, p. 81). (This research can be read online at www.ect.org.)

ECT Anonymous provides listening support and information for those contemplating ECT or who have been affected by it. They also sell a booklet that includes the issues involved in ECT and alternatives.

Depression and medication

Depression affects about one in six people at some point in their life (The Mental Health Foundation, 2005). It is not regarded as an "identifying" symptom, but depression is common among people with a diagnosis of schizophrenia (Taylor, Paton, & Kerwin, 2005). There are several treatments for depression, discussed in Chapter Five, but the most common is antidepressants.

Antidepressants cannot cure depression, but they do alleviate the symptoms and, therefore, may enable individuals to begin to deal with depression themselves, by having counselling, for instance. Usually, it is suggested that someone takes antidepressants for at least six months, or longer if they have a previous history of depression. There are three main types: tricyclics, monamine oxidase inhibitors (MAOIs) and serotonin selective re-uptake inhibitors (SSRIs).

The tricyclics are named after the three linked "rings" of their molecular structure. These drugs principally affect the neurotransmitter noradrenaline, as well as serotonin. The anticholinergic effects can cause drowsiness, dry mouth, blurred vision, constipation, rapid heartbeat, tremor, skin rashes, difficulty in urinating, sweating, increased appetite, weight gain, and loss of sexual desire and orgasmic difficulties, though some trycyclics are less associated with some of these side-effects.

For instance, studies show that imipramine (Tofranil) is less sedating than amitryptyline, (Trypitzol) as is lofepramine (Gamanil), which also has fewer anticholinergic effects, though constipation is commonly reported (Taylor, Paton, & Kerwin, 2005). However, in the case of an overdose, the effect on the heart can be particularly dangerous (Kuipers & Bebbington, 2005), and immediate medical attention is essential.

Like the tricylics, MAOIs affect the noradrenaline and serotonin neurotransmitters and cause many of the same side-effects. In addition, oedema (swelling of the legs), insomnia, dizziness, and postural hypotension (feeling faint or dizzy after standing up) may be experienced.

MAOIs interact badly with a number of foods, mainly dairy products, yeast and beef extract, and pickled foods. Strictly speaking, people should not drink alcohol while taking MAOIs, but many people are able to drink in moderation.

In line with the NICE (2004) recommendation, the SSRIs are the most commonly prescribed antidepressants. These drugs work by selectively blocking the re-uptake of serotonin so that it stays around the receptor sites. Two of the best-known SSRIs are Prozac (fluoxetine) and Seroxat (paroxetine).

The SSRIs are very effective in treating moderate to severe depression. In the case of the latter, NICE recommends a combination of cognitive behaviour therapy and antidepressants. Sometimes ECT is given for depression. NICE recommends that it is only used to treat very severe depression with life-threatening symptoms and when all other treatment options have failed.

SSRIs have many possible side-effects. Among the main recorded ones are nausea, vomitting, dyspepsia, abdominal pain, diarrhoea, rashes, sweating, restlessness, anxiety, headaches, insomnia, tremors and dystonia, loss of appetite, bleeding disorders of the skin and a less than normal concentration of sodium in the blood, which in severe cases can lead to convulsion, confusion or collapse.

Clinical and research evidence link SSRIs to sexual problems (Ashton, Hammer, & Rosen, 1997; Montejo-Gonzalez et al., 1997; Piazza et al., 1997). For example, SSRIs can cause orgasm problems (Labatte, Grimes, Hines, & Oleshansky, 1997), in particular delayed or unsatisfactory orgasm, which is the reason they are sometimes prescribed for premature ejaculation. Anafranil (clomipramine) is associated with the highest rates of sexual dysfunction (Gitlin, 1995).

Anecdotal and clinical reports link SSRIs to panic attacks, suicide, aggression, and mood swings. Obviously, as with any drug, unusual or disturbing reactions should be discussed with a doctor straightaway.

In addition, there have been claims that SSRIs are addictive. While these have been rejected by the manufacturers, it is recognized that people may experience "discontinuation symptoms" with these and with other antidepressants. The term describes symptoms that are experienced on stopping drugs that are not classified as drugs of dependence, such as heroin or cocaine.

Discontinuation effects may be new, or similar to some of the original symptoms of the illness (Taylor, Paton, & Kerwin, 2005, p. 176) and are experienced by at least a third of people (Lejoyeux, Ades, & Mourad, 1996). As it may be very difficult for people to come off these antidepressants, a rapid withdrawal is inadvisable, and especially not without ongoing support. Withdrawing from more than one drug at a time, such as an antipsychotic as well as antidepressants, is not advisable either (Holmes & Hudson, 2003).

MAOIs' discontinuation effects include anxiety, agitation, paranoia, headaches, low blood pressure when standing, muscle weakness, shivering and tingling, burning sensations, and mania. Even catatonic states have been reported (Mind, 2005a). With tricyclics, depression, panic attacks, excessive anxiety, restlessness, insomnia, nausea, fast or irregular heartbeat, stomach pains, and diarrhoea are common.

Coming off SSRIs can cause flu-like symptoms, "shock-like" sensations, dizziness, diarrhoea, muscle spasms, insomnia, excessive, vivid dreaming, irritability, depression, confusion, and feeling "unreal". Anecdotal accounts suggest that Robert's experience is not unusual.

> I'd been on Seroxat for about six months when I decided to come off. It was affecting my libido and I was lacking in energy. I was also worried that I might get addicted. First of all I cut down. I was taking 30 mg and I halved that to 15 mg a day. Then I began to take 15 mg every two days. At this point, I felt very depressed, that my life wasn't worth living, and had thoughts about killing myself. Because my emotions were still a bit blunted by the Seroxat I felt I might act on those thoughts and got very worried. If I hadn't had someone to talk to about it, I don't know what I would have done.

> I also had vertigo type nightmares. Every night I dreamed that I was falling from a great height. These were very scary and made me more nervous. I also had vertigo feelings during the day. I've always been a bit afraid of heights, but this was a lot worse. It was quite a while before I dare go out.

> I had to use all my willpower, but I was determined to come off and about a week later I stopped taking them altogether. The withdrawal effects gradually got less, but it took a long while.

Some antidepressants are usually more of a problem to come off than others. This is related to the "half-life" of a drug: how long it takes the quantity of a drug in a person's bloodstream to drop by half. Drugs with a long half-life may be easier to withdraw from than those with a short half-life because withdrawal is more gradual. For this reason SSRI discontinuation effects are most often experienced with Seroxat and Efexor (venlafaxine), which have a short half-life (Taylor, Paton, & Kerwin, 2005, p. 176).

Mind (2005a) suggests that anyone having difficulty coming off a drug with a short half-life might first change to one with a long half-life. For example, someone could change from Seroxat to Prozac (fluoxetine). Mind's booklet *Making Sense of Coming Off Psychiatric Drugs* lists the half-life of almost all psychiatric drugs.

As with antipsychotics, the advice is to withdraw gradually, though this is not thought necessary with Prozac (Rosenbaum, Fava, Hoog, Ashcroft, & Krebs, 1998). MAOIs may be very difficult to come off (Taylor, Paton, & Kerwin, 2005, p. 177). The risk of discontinuation effects are increased for someone who has taken antidepressants for eight weeks or longer and is also taking antipsychotics. Someone who has been on antidepressants for many years, therefore, may find it takes several years to come off them completely.

SSRIs and suicidal behaviour

In recent years, concerns have been expressed about a possible link between the use of SSRIs and suicidal behaviour. In June 2006, the Medicines and Healthcare Products Regulatory Agency (MHRA) stated:

> The Medicines and Healthcare products Regulatory Agency (MHRA) continually reviews and monitors the safety of all medicines. The Committee on Safety of Medicines (CSM) and its Expert Working Group concluded in December 2004 that SSRIs are effective medicines in the treatment of depression and anxiety conditions, and that the risks and benefits of all SSRIs in adults remains positive in their licensed indications. However, they advised that prescribers should be more aware of the side effects of SSRIs and the need to closely monitor patients taking SSRIs.

> Recently, GlaxoSmithKline published further analyses of suicidal behaviour from their clinical trial database in adults. These analyses are being considered by the MHRA in conjuction with other European regulatory authorities. [p. 1]

Drug development

The development of more effective antipsychotics is the goal of several pharmaceutical companies. Abilify has been described as a "smart drug" because it claims to regulate imbalances in brain chemicals. At the time of writing, one focus of research is the design of antipsychotics that, instead of mimicking the generalized actions of current psychiatric drugs, would be able to repair damaged brain cells. These are seen as a further improvement on those that simply rebalance brain chemicals, but which may cause unforeseen imbalances in other parts of the brain as well.

Medication information

The Cochrane Schizophrenia Group (CSG) produces objective information and "plain language", updated reviews of drug treatments. Summaries and full reports of these are published on their website.

Information on prescription drugs can be found in the British National Formulary. This is available in the reference section of libraries and online at www.bnf.org. *The Maudsley Prescribing Guidelines* (Taylor, Paton, & Kerwin, 2005) is also consulted by pharmacists and clinicians. The latest (eighth) edition, may also be available in reference libraries.

The Maudsley Hospital's Psychiatric Helpline gives confidential advice about medication and side-effects. Tel: 0207 919 2999 (Mon–Fri, 11.00 a.m. to 1.00 p.m., 1. 00 p.m. to 5 p.m.). After an initial discussion, callers can fax (0207 919 3448) a detailed medication history, including side-effects, for comment and further advice from the hospital's clinicians.

Drop-in centres, like those run by Mind, often have medication support groups with someone from the community pharmacy team available to discuss individual concerns. www.schizophrenia.com has a notice board where people share their first-hand experience of antipsychotics and managing side-effects.

Summary

Medication is the mainstay of treatment for schizophrenia. Clinical and anecdotal evidence shows that antipsychotics help many people to manage their symptoms and enjoy a better quality of life, though all these drugs cause side-effects and possibly long-term problems.

Accumulating research suggests that continuous neuroleptic treatment may not be necessary for everyone diagnosed with schizophrenia. A supportive "therapeutic environment" and minimal or no medication may be effective both with "first episode" and chronic illness. Other people with an awareness of their "warning signs" may be able to use antipsychotics "cleverly", as and when they need them. None of these approaches inevitably results in increased relapses and re-hospitalizations.

Reduction and/or withdrawal from antipsychotics is, therefore, a safe and realistic option for some—but not all—individuals, especially if done gradually and with the support of a psychiatrist or others with appropriate experience. This might relieve the concerns of relatives, carers, and health professionals whose attitudes will influence the outcome.

Depression is a common problem for people with a diagnosis of schizophrenia and antidepressants are often prescribed, although non-drug treatments, such as exercise, diet, counselling, or complementary therapies may also be effective.

Acknowledgement

I should like to thank Dr David Taylor for his helpful comments on the first draft of this chapter.

Useful addresses/resources

Only the Best, Rethink guide to choosing and getting the most out of medication. Contact the Rethink National Advice Service on 020 8974 6814, or email advice@rethink.org

Kirunal fish oil capsules are available from Nutri-Link Ltd, Nutrition House, Unit 24 Milber Trading Estate, Newton Abbot, Devon TQ12 4SG. Tel: 0870 405 4002; Fax: 0870 405 4003. (There is a 10% discount for SAGB members.)

Igennus Ltd., St John Innovation Centre, Cowley Road, Cambridge CB4 0WS. Tel: 0845 1300424; website: www.igennus.com

Advice on Medication by Philip Thomas and Rufus May, The Hearing Voices Network (HVN), 79 Lever Street, Manchester M1 1FL. Tel: 0845 1228641.

The Second Opinion Clinic, The Maudsley Hospital, Denmark Hill, London SE5 8AZ Tel: 0208 776 4418; Fax: 0208 776 441.

ECT Anonymous, c/o Una Parker, Flat 5, Quaker House, St Mark's Street, Leeds LS2 9EQ. Tel: 0113244 5454; website:

www.patient.co.uk (Ring 9.00 a.m.–11 a.m. only. BT call minder may operate, so leave a message.) *Shock Treatment: Things you you need to know before having ECT* (£2 incl. p & p).

NICE guidelines on depression are available on their website: www.nice.org.uk/page.aspx?o=cg023 Or they can be ordered on the NHS Response Line 0780 1555 455; email: doh@prolog.uk.com

The Cochrane Schizophrenia Group (CSG). Academic Unit of Psychiatry and Behavioural Sciences, Institute of Health Sciences and Public Health Research, University of Leeds, 15 Hyde Terrace, Leeds LS2 9LT. Tel: 011343 2706; Fax: 011343 2703; website: www.leeds.ac.uk/csg

Sexual Dysfunction Association, Windmill Place Business Centre, 2–4 Windmill Lane, Southall, Middlesex UB2 4NJ. Tel: (Admin) 0870 7743 3571; Fax: 0870 774 3572; email: info@sda.uk.net; website: www.netdoctor.co.uk

Brook (sexual advice for people up to the age of 25), 421 Highgate Studios, 53–79 Highgate Road, London NW5 1TL. Tel: 0207 284 6040; Fax: 0207 284 6050; email: admin@brook-centres.org.uk; Helpline 0800 0145 023 (Mon–Fri, 9.00 a.m. to 5.00 p.m.). 24-hour information line: 0207 950 7700. Questions can be sent form the Ask Brook section of the website: www.brook.org.uk

CHAPTER FOUR

Sources of support

Support is the cornerstone of recovery from severe mental health problems. If someone has been diagnosed with schizophrenia, NHS support will be provided by a multi-disciplinary team, known as the community mental health team (CMHT), although the first person people tend to contact with concerns about their mental health is a general practitioner (GP). Usually, it is by appointment at the surgery, though a doctor will sometimes make a home visit if the person has been a patient for some time. If GPs think that someone has a serious mental health problem they will refer him or her for a psychiatric assessment. This may take between two and three weeks. However, a home visit from a psychiatrist, or one of the mental health team, can be arranged within a day or two if a GP considers a person's symptoms require urgent attention.

When someone is diagnosed with schizophrenia their GP will be kept informed of their treatment by the person's psychiatrist. In addition to providing repeat prescriptions of medication, the GP will continue to take care of the person's general health. The leaflet "Getting the most from your GP practice" gives information on how people can receive help for their physical and mental health. It is available from GP surgeries and can be downloaded from the Rethink website: www.rethink.org/publications

GPs are well-placed to liaise with others in the mental health team if someone is dissatisfied with their treatment, such as their medication. If a person wants a second opinion on their diagnosis a GP can request this from their psychiatrist.

Although GPs have a role in a person's care, essentially it is the CMHT's responsibility to arrange ongoing treatment and support. Being aware of the team members' specific responsibilities can help people make the best use of their expertise. The team will be under the overall charge of a psychiatrist.

Psychiatrists

Psychiatrists are doctors who have qualified in medicine before undertaking additional training in mental health. Consultant psychiatrists are those who have passed the membership examination of The Royal College of Psychiatrists and are entitled to use the letters MRCPsych after their name.

During their two to three year training in psychiatric units and outpatients clinics they are known as junior psychiatrists or registrars. Their official title will be either Specialist Grade Registrars (SpR) or Senior House Officer (SHO). Often people with an outpatient appointment will see an SpR or an SHO who confers with the consultant psychiatrist about their treatment.

It is a consultant psychiatrist who makes final decisions about someone's treatment. This will almost certainly include prescribing medication and monitoring the person's general and mental health at regular appointments. Depending on the psychiatrist's assessment, and someone's care plan (see below), these appointments may vary from around once a month to twice a year.

Ideally, people will feel able to talk frankly to their psychiatrist, but complaints that psychiatrists give them too little time or don't "listen" aren't unusual. However, many people have a good relationship with their psychiatrist. When Graham couldn't cope with the side-effects of medication his psychiatrist was wholly supportive.

I'd been put on haloperidol in hospital. I wanted something that would allow me to take part in daily life, which haloperidol didn't—it just kills you. When I told my psychiatrist, he didn't argue. He accepted that it might mean going through several new antipsychotics to find the one that was right for me, which it did, and the fourth drug I tried, Risperidone, was okay.

NICE (2002) recommends that mental health professionals discuss medication options with their patients and clients. This should involve explaining the benefits and side-effects and, when at all possible, making decisions jointly with the person about the drugs being prescribed. As David Healy, author of *Psychiatric Drugs Explained* (2005, p. 16) points out, research shows that people who do not like a particular drug do not do well (May et al., 1976). Although this finding may sound obvious, Healy, who is director of the North Wales Department of Psychological Medicine at the University of Wales College of Medicine, says it is not always taken into account by health professionals.

Working together

Sharon used to run a support group for people with a mental health diagnosis. Based on her own and group members' experiences she compiled these guidelines to help people voice their treatment concerns and get the most from appointments with their psychiatrist.

- Psychiatrists aren't mind-readers. You need to ask for what you want.
- Don't worry about wasting the psychiatrist's time. Voicing your concerns is an important part of helping you to stay well. That can only make life easier for both of you.
- Note down the issues you want to discuss and take them with you to appointments. Be specific about the action you'd like taken. For example, if it's for the psychiatrist to make changes to your medication that's what goes on your list—not something on the lines of "discuss medication".
- Being clear about your requests doesn't mean you have to hold out for them come what may. The intention is to talk about

them—and be open to compromise. However, first and foremost you need to ask for exactly what you want.

- Well before your appointment, write to let your psychiatrist know the issues you want to discuss and request a sufficiently long appointment.
- If you feel nervous or worried about expressing your wishes, consider asking a friend, relative or community support worker to accompany you.
- Don't be fobbed off! If you don't feel that your concerns are being taken seriously put them in writing—possibly with the help of a friend or relative—and post it well before the next appointment.
- It's not a failure if by the end of your appointment not all of your requests have been fully addressed. But you need your concerns to be acknowledged and a mutually-agreed time set to discuss them in the near future.
- Whatever changes are agreed to, you need to know what action you or your psychiatrist will take to ensure they're carried through.

In Sharon's opinion, the main advantage of these guidelines is that they enable individuals and their psychiatrist to work together more effectively, though changing to a more collaborative relationship may involve a period of adjustment on both sides.

Being this assertive is not always easy. Some people are not comfortable at the thought of asking for what they want, perhaps for fear of offending their psychiatrist and then being penalized in some way. Of course, most people tend to feel more vulnerable when they are unwell and psychiatrists occupy a powerful position, but someone may simply feel insufficiently articulate to put across their case. Whatever the reason, contacting an advocate might be helpful. (See below.)

Psychiatric Social Worker/Approved Social Worker (ASW)

These are social workers who have specialized in mental health. Some have been trained to be "approved" to apply parts of the Mental Health Acts. For instance, ASWs carry out independent assessments of people's psycho-social needs. Based on social and medical factors, should they think it necessary, they can apply for someone to be compulsorily admitted to a psychiatric unit, although this is always done in consultation with the person's nearest relative, a GP, and other mental health professionals. Also, under the English and Scottish Mental Health Acts, social workers are required to consider alternatives to involuntary admission, such as home treatment.

Anyone who is involuntarily detained in a psychiatric unit—rather than receiving treatment as a voluntary patient—will be assigned a psychiatric social worker. At this stage, he or she may take on the role of the person's care co-ordinator, often referred to as a key worker.

Care coordinator/key worker

Their job is provide the support people need to live successfully in the community. Initially, they carry out an assessment of people's needs and, in consultation with the person and their carer(s), develop a care plan. This is written down and a copy given to the person to keep. Care coordinators are also responsible for implementing the plan; for example, by encouraging people to participate in activities outside their home or to take advantage of appropriate training and employment opportunities. This could be permitted work, previously known as therapeutic work, or a "community link/bridging" course designed for people with mental health needs. Such courses aim to build confidence and enable individuals to learn skills such as IT, first aid, assertiveness, or English and maths.

Care plans

These were introduced in the early 1990s as part of the Care Programme Approach (CPA). Both the CPA and care plans have been updated. Currently, there are Standard and Enhanced plans. Both are an assessment of the health and social care needs of anyone in contact with specialist mental health services. Plans are agreed with members of the CMHT, the person's GP and carer(s) and are meant to be reviewed regularly and, with the individual's input, amended to cater for changes in their circumstances, health and social care needs.

Standard care plan

This is designed for a person whose needs can be met by one agency, such as social care, and who does not need the support of the entire CMHT. Someone who has a standard care plan is not considered to pose a risk to themselves or to others if they lose contact with services.

The person will probably continue to see the community mental health nurse regularly and he or she might well be appointed as the care coordinator. Appointments with a psychiatrist are likely to be every three to six months. Should someone think that more frequent appointments are needed, this can be included in the care plan.

Advanced care plan

An advanced care plan is recommended if it seems that a person's mental health needs are best served by support from both health and social services—for example, if they have more than one clinical condition, or if he or she has had difficulty maintaining contact with these services in the past and it is thought that if this happens again it could pose a risk to themselves or to others.

People with an advanced care plan will also be given a risk assessment and a plan for what to do and who to turn to in a crisis: for example, ringing their care coordinator or a home care team.

Community mental health nurse (CMHN)

These nurses have trained in psychiatric nursing and community care. Still generally called CPNs (community psychiatric nurses), he or she is the team member people tend to have most contact with. Community nurses usually see people every two to four weeks, in the person's own home, at the local health centre, or hospital outpatients departments, but these meetings can be more frequent if someone requests additional support. CMHNs administer injections, which is an opportunity for people to discuss the side-effects of medication or minor physical ailments.

CMHNs are responsible for maintaining links with everyone involved in a person's care and are expected to convey any concerns or requests to the appropriate professional. If someone has remained well for some time after being in hospital, his or her CMHN may take over from a social worker to become the care coordinator and main source of support. This has been Carole's experience.

> I've had two community mental health nurses and they've both been good and really listened to me. My present nurse visits me every two to three weeks—when I'm unwell it is more frequent. It was my nurse who told me about the Disability Discrimination Act and that I was covered. I then felt able to come out about my disability at work and approach my employer for a more flexible working arrangement and thereby manage my condition more effectively.

> I trust my nurse and can be open with her about my illness, which is important as I'm on my own with no family close by. Having regular visits from her is a preventative measure. When I got very paranoid last year she advised me to take time off work before my condition worsened. I could have ended up having a complete breakdown as I'm not always able to gauge how ill I am. However, she is, so it's very good knowing that she is there.

Disability Discrimination Act (DDA)

Discrimination is defined as someone with a disability being unjustifiably treated less favourably than others, for a reason which relates to the disability.

The Act covers discrimination by employers, providers of services, landlords and people selling property, transport services, schools, universities, and other educational establishments. It applies to anyone who has a "mental impairment" which has a substantial and long-term adverse effect on his or her ability to carry out normal day-to-day activities, and schizophrenia is a qualifying condition.

An illness is considered long-term if it has lasted for a year, or is expected to last for a year, or for the rest of a person's life—and this does not necessarily mean someone has to be continuously experiencing symptoms.

Community support worker (CSW)

Strictly speaking, support workers are not part of the CMHT, but they work out of local social services departments to help people live as independently as possible in the community. CSWs undertake practical tasks, like cooking, cleaning, shopping, and accompanying people to appointments. They can also give emotional support by listening and getting to know a person's particular concerns and so act as an unofficial advocate should someone feel that other mental health professionals or agencies are not addressing their needs.

To apply for a CSW individuals complete an application form— or a social worker or friend can do it on their behalf. A home visit is arranged and, depending on people's needs, they are assigned a CSW for a period of time, for instance, three or four months or so, to help them over a difficult period, or possibly on a longer-term basis. Carol lives with her widowed mother and has had a community support worker for almost a year.

> My mother had a mild stroke last year. She's getting better, but still can't do as much. My CPN knew that things were getting on top of me and now Jean comes and helps with the washing and shopping. Sometimes when my mother's friends visit her the support worker and I go to see a film which makes a nice change for me.

Chris welcomes the regular visits of a CSW. He also found his social worker and CPN a great help when he first became ill.

Chris's story—"Without him I wouldn't have known where to start"

> I was visited by a social worker throughout my time in hospital, but mostly it was towards the end of my stay that constructive stuff happened. This was mainly because I was too ill and delusional to

make much sense before then. Before my first breakdown I'd been living with my parents and they insisted I get a place of my own on leaving hospital. I told my social worker and we discussed housing options whilst I was on the ward. I could, if I'd wanted, have gone to a hostel or halfway house for a while. However, after six weeks on a rehabilitation ward I felt quite confident and was looking forward to having my own space.

The social worker enabled me to get a really nice council flat. Without him I wouldn't have known where to start. He did all the paperwork and liaised with the housing department, even taking me to view it a couple of times, and arranged a date for me to move in. He came round a few times after to make sure I was coping okay and told me that there would be a place in hospital for me should I need it.

At the same time I had regular visits from a CPN who chatted about things in general and made sure I was keeping to my medication regime. I told the CPN that I was getting a little bored and lonely, so between him and the social worker they arranged for me to attend a day centre nearby. The CPN took me there the first couple of times and introduced me to some of the staff and clients. It was a good break being able to go to the day centre and I joined in with some of the groups such as art, pottery and going swimming. It was good to meet new friends there as well, who had various, though similar problems.

Recently, after a second breakdown and a stay in hospital, I was offered the option of a support worker from a private agency coming to see me three times a week. This helper has proved very helpful in keeping my meds stocked up, helping with everyday chores, getting me to appointments, shopping (both grocery and clothes), days out and quite simply being a nice friendly face and a bit of welcome company.

I have been told that both my CPN and social worker are available still and I only need to phone, plus of course my support worker will make them aware if there's any deterioration in my health. In fact, my support worker attends my psychiatrist's appointments with me, by my choice, so that she can give her perspective on how I'm coping.

Clinical psychologist

Clinical psychologists have a psychology degree and a minimum of three years training in clinical psychology. Often they work along-

side psychiatrists in mental health units and outpatient departments. Most are not medically qualified, so they cannot prescribe
medication. Their main job is to assess people's psychological
health. They may give advice on how someone can make the best
use of their intelligence and skills when looking for work or educational opportunities, but principally they recommend, and sometimes provide, non-medical treatments. These include stress/
anxiety management, social skills training, family therapy, and
cognitive–behavioural therapy (CBT).

Counselling psychologist

In addition to a psychology degree, these psychologists have
undertaken further study, including research, and have gained
a doctorate in counselling. They may work in GP practices as well
as NHS clinics. Like clinical psychologists, many are qualified to
teach CBT.

Home care/rapid response/crisis team

As with most illnesses, there is no guarantee that a person's symptoms will not worsen, possibly to a point when they are becoming
seriously unwell. But if someone has a crisis outside the usual office
hours, or at weekends, no one in the CMHT will be available to give
support. To avoid this sort of situation, ideally, a home care—also
known as a rapid response, or crisis—team can be contacted to provide support and any necessary treatment in a person's own home.

Theoretically, the teams are on call twenty-four hours a day,
seven days a week, but in practice the service is patchy. For
instance, in some areas of the UK there is none, while in others the
team does not cover evenings or weekends, times when people are
often most in need of support (Allott, 2005). A national survey by
the Healthcare Commission (2006) of over 19,000 people using
community health services reported that only forty-nine per cent
had the phone number of someone from their local NHS service
whom they could contact out of office hours.

Individuals who are aware that they are having a relapse may worry that contacting the home team will automatically lead to their being hospitalized. However, home-based care and support should be regarded as the norm for the delivery of mental health services, according to the National Institute for Mental Health and Care Services Improvement Partnership (2006). The aim is to help people through a crisis in their own home and so minimize disruption to their daily life. This has been Liz P's experience.

> What's good about receiving support in the home it is that you don't have a big break with your life. In the past I've been taken out of my home and put in an unreal environment. In hospital you don't have responsibility for anything. Your food's cooked for you, your medication's given and you can get sleeping pills if you need them. You don't need much motivation—you just lie about and do what you want. So when you come home it's very difficult to rehabilitate yourself and get back into the domestic routine of shopping, washing and keeping your house clean.

> It's always been a big struggle, that jump from being cared for in hospital. Luckily, I share a house with someone so I've been able to take on more responsibility gradually. But if I'd been living on my own it would have been impossible. Though there are support workers who will come and help. A friend who lives on her own hasn't had to go into hospital this time and is able to function on her own with the support of the home team.

> When I was ill they came once a day, initially—they can come twice a day. A lot of it is about checking that you take your medication, but also there's someone to talk to if you feel able to talk about what you're experiencing. That can be very beneficial. Though one problem was that pressure on resources meant they sent lots of different people who I'd never met before. That was difficult to adjust to when I was very paranoid. It's hard to say anything when you're dependent on people for your care. But a friend did mention it and now they just send my key worker and a couple of other people I know and I feel happier about that.

A systematic review of crisis home care (Joy, Adams, & Rice, 2004) reported that it was a more satisfactory form of care than hospitalization, for both the people themselves and their families, and that it might help to avoid repeat hospital admissions.

Crisis centres

Like crisis teams, these centres provide a less formal alternative to hospital. Individuals can be referred by a social worker, a doctor, or refer themselves. The centres are staffed by specially trained social workers. As a general rule, people stay for about three weeks. They are assigned a social worker, a care plan is drawn up, and ongoing support is arranged before they leave.

Occupational therapist (OT)

Anyone who has spent any time in a psychiatric unit will almost certainly have come in contact with an occupational therapist. After a three-year training, OTs are attached to "rehabilitation" wards and involved in the coordination of practical projects designed to help people gain or regain useful skills, such as cooking and managing their finances. OTs also provide group and individual activities like pottery, relaxation classes, art, music therapy, and computer skills. These take place in the hospital's "therapy" unit or as part of community-based schemes in day and drop-in centres.

Other sources of support

A good supportive relationship with mental health professionals invariably helps a person stay well and move on with their life, but, of course, there are other people who can provide support.

Family

Studies estimate that between forty and sixty per cent of people diagnosed with schizophrenia live with their families (Fadden, Bebbington, & Kuipers, 1987; Kuipers, 1993) and benefit greatly from their support. *Roads to Recovery*, a survey by Mind (2001b) of almost 1,000 people with a serious mental health diagnosis, reported that "talking to friends and family" was a key factor in their recovery and remaining well. This has been Narinder's experience.

My family are very understanding. They listen to me when I go on about my problems and support me. I really cringe when I think of the things I've done to my mum and dad, like insulted, even threatened them when I was psychotic. But they've always stood by me and tried to get me the best treatment. If it wasn't for my dad I'd still be on the old drugs which were doing me in. It's only because he kept insisting that something else was tried, which turned out to be Risperidone, that I started to get better and felt life was worth living again.

Research suggests that when parents learn of their son or daughter's diagnosis they may feel grief-stricken by what they experience as a "loss", though these feelings do not necessarily last. A study by Veltman, Cameron, & Stewart (2002) found that, despite negative feelings about being a carer, families felt love and a sense of pride and gratification at the opportunity to "be there" for their relatives.

But, however close the family bonds, sharing a home with other adults can be stressful. It is important, therefore, to establish ground rules and decide how individual preferences and priorities can best be accommodated. Obviously, no adult wants to be treated like a difficult child. By the same token, parents and other family members do not want to feel dictated to or bullied.

Family therapy has helped families to negotiate more harmonious ways of getting along. By involving all the members everyone has the chance to express his or her views and needs, while the family as a whole learns to work collectively to resolve difficulties. (There is more information on family therapy in Chapter Eight.)

Carers groups, run by local authorities and mental health charities, such as Making Space, provide similar practical advice. These groups often arrange breaks for people who are designated carers, which involves an assessment by Social Services.

Self-care for carers

- You will feel less stressed if you try to handle situations calmly and consistently—and so will your relative.
- Support your relative, but know your limits. Do not aim to be a superman or superwoman.
- Try not to fit your entire existence around your relative.

- Avoid being intrusive. You both need time and space to live your own lives.
- Take regular breaks apart. Tourism for All has information on holidays that are tailored to the needs of people with physical or mental health problems. Tel: 0800 444000; email: info@tourismforall.org.uk; website: www.holidaycare.org.uk.
- Do not try to cope alone. Ask for help if you need it—from family members, friends and the professional support services. The Department of Health (1999, Standard 6) recognizes that carers are entitled to help with problems, though it can some-times be difficult to access it. However, local councils often have carers support projects. Carers UK has information on all aspects of caring on their website: www.carersuk.org.
- Make time to relax and recharge, with leisure interests and socializing.

Friends

Friends may be a lifeline in difficult times, but simply on a day-to-day basis friendships can help people to stay well (Breier & Strauss, 1984). Martin says that friends have been crucial to his recovery and ability to cope with stress.

> I'm a bit up and down, but luckily I have good friends, like Lyndon. We met in the hospital smoke room. That was the place to share experiences and have a group hug and we've kept in touch ever since. Now when we meet we're like old soldiers, reminiscing about our time in the trenches!

> Since getting on the Internet I've made new friends. Twice a day I visit a chat room for people who have similar problems to me. It's usually six or seven of us chatting about our lives and venting our frustration if we need to. I get a lot out of that and really look forward to the sessions.

The chat room Martin visits is the limbic system at: http://groups.yahoo.com/i? There are discussion groups on mental health topics, among other things, at the website: www.schizophrenia.com.

A study of people discharged from acute admission wards by Reynolds and colleagues (2004) showed that support and encouragement from other former patients was a key factor in their remaining well. At a five-month follow-up the researchers reported a significant improvement in the participants' symptoms and "functional ability", and a fifty per cent reduction in re-hospitalization rates.

Advertisements from people seeking penfriends and partners appear in *Voices*, *The SAGB Newsletter*, and *Perceptions,* the magazine of the National Voices Forum (NVF). The NVF, which is a UK network of people who have experienced severe mental illness or distress, also has regular group meetings for its members.

Such groups may be less stressful for people who have got out of the habit of socializing. There is not likely to be the usual social pressure to "perform" or even to talk to others unless, or until, a person feels ready. It is one reason Tony attends a film club at his day centre.

> I wanted to meet other people, but I was scared of not being able to be interesting or chatty enough for "normal" people. Mixing with people who've had similar experiences there's not that stress. You're all in the same boat so you don't have to worry what people think of you, or whether they're judging you. It's good to be with other people and enjoy doing something together, even if it's just watching a DVD.

Mixing with people who have similar mental health problems also avoids what some people see as the dilemma of whether or not to "come out" about their diagnosis. Says James:

> There's a stigma attached to having schizophrenia. It's hard to go out there and meet people and make new friends, especially women. If you do get into a relationship, you have to disclose that you're schizophrenic and you don't know how someone will react. Will they want to know you any more? Might they reject you? Dare you risk saying you're schizophrenic? It's a hard decision.

Other people, like Nicholas, may simply follow their instinct as to whether or not to tell others about their diagnosis.

> Some friends know I have schizophrenia and others don't. I play it by ear how much or who I tell about myself and that applies to lots

of things. We all speculate about other people, their background, their sexuality and if they have a physical or mental health problem. But they don't have to tell us everything about themselves— even if we ask. Sometimes you just know that if you did tell someone you have schizophrenia they'd be embarrassed or ask a lot of questions. I don't want that and I certainly don't feel I need to explain or apologize for myself or my illness.

Shyness and poor social skills often add to people's difficulty in making friends. Social skills training has been shown to be useful for some people (see Chapter Eight), while regular meetings with a befriender may reduce feelings of isolation and help someone to develop a wider social network.

Befrienders

Befrienders are volunteers who are carefully selected and trained by organizations and mental health charities, such as Mind and Making Space, to provide support and companionship to people who are lonely or emotionally distressed through mental health or other problems. Befrienders are the same sex as the person and visit someone for an hour or so every week. This can be at the place where they live or an agreed venue. The visit is meant to meet the person's individual needs, so it can involve going shopping, for a walk, or simply having a chat. While the schemes try to match people with others they can get on with, this might not happen straightaway. Anne's experience is not that unusual.

> I didn't really get on with any of my befrienders and after a year I'd practically given up hope. But now I see Cass and we get on like a house on fire. I've usually recorded a nice film, though I talk through most of it, and she listens. I enjoy seeing her very much.

Some befriending schemes include social events, creative classes, as well as self-help groups, for those who hear voices or have agoraphobia, for instance. The overall aim is to encourage people to come into their own—by developing a social network and gaining new skills, often through individual coaching and mentoring.

Having been mentored themselves, individuals may want to mentor others. But no one is a client, everyone is a member, and befrienders do things *with* members, not for them.

A research study with fifty-seven participants reported that gaining this sort of active sense of themselves was an important factor in people's continuing recovery, coupled with their determination to get better and manage their illness (Tooth, Kalyanasundaram, Glover, & Momedzadah, 2003).

Members of befrienders groups are also encouraged to devise and achieve their own goals. This may be entering or re-entering the job market. In Tally's case it was to feel sufficiently confident to use public transport again.

> The first time I took a bus ride alone I cried most of the way I was so het up. I'd not gone out for a very, very long time I'd been so frightened to leave the house. My befriender got me out. At the start it was just a few steps down the road and even then I'd stand at the front door for ages beforehand. I got panicky lots of times and didn't think I'd ever make it. A year later, almost to the day, I did the journey on my own.

As yet there is no national befriending network, but care coordinators are likely to know of local groups. *A Practical Guide to Befriending* (Beside) has advice on setting up a befriending scheme.

Schizophrenia Update is a free internet newsletter (www.schizophrenia.com) published by Brian Chiko, "in memory of my brother John who suffered from schizophrenia and who, to my infinite regret, took his own life." *Update* has articles on the latest treatments and research. Letters to the Editor can be emailed to: news@schizophrenia.com.

Advocates

Advocates speak on behalf of people to ensure that their views are expressed and listened to. Alternatively, they may support people to become their own advocate and speak for themselves. Difficulties in accessing essential services in the community or a hospital setting, feeling that decisions about their lives are being made for them against their wishes or consent, are some of the issues advocates help people with.

Although they rarely have legal training, advocates tend to have specific knowledge of services and systems, such as housing and employment, and therefore can help people get a fair hearing and obtain their rights.

Most advocacy services are voluntary organizations. Some are small and independent while others are local services linked to larger national organizations such as Mind. Action for Advocacy (A4A) supports dozens of advocacy groups and individuals. The United Kingdom Advocacy Network (UK-AN) is a network of groups involved in advocacy within the mental health system. User Voice is a service user involvement project. Based in Birmingham, it aims to encourage participation and improvement in mental health services and can also refer people to advocacy organizations which help individuals.

Liz S's story—"My advocate helped me regain my self-respect"

I was in hospital, ill, confused—definitely not stupid, although there were days when I didn't have the confidence to realize it. I felt that the people around me weren't really listening to me. I was afraid to complain in case it would somehow add to my difficulties, although it was a member of staff who suggested that I needed the help of someone from a new advocacy project. I didn't even know what the word advocate meant, but was willing to try anything that might help sort out what felt like a total mess.

The first thing my advocate did was listen to me. He also assured me that he was independent, which made me feel safe about saying exactly how I felt. I knew that I needed the help of professionals, but was afraid if I said too much it might annoy them and their help would be withdrawn. He also helped me differentiate between the problems I had as part of my illness and those that had arisen as a result of my treatment.

While I was in hospital a doctor had diagnosed me as suffering from paranoid schizophrenia. He didn't bother telling me this, but when I routinely attempted to renew my bus driver's licence I discovered mine had been suspended, following a medical report from the hospital. My advocate helped me to make a formal complaint, which ran the full course of the NHS complaints procedure. Sadly, this process is long and complicated, but I was helped to carry it through. Despite my fears this didn't "compromise" my treatment. I was supported by both the advocacy project and the hospital staff.

My advocate also acted as my representative, talking to doctors, nurses and managers on my behalf. He gave me clear information about my options, like having a second opinion about my illness, or seeing different staff if I thought it would help. He was there during a ward round so that we could identify which aspects of my treatment I was unhappy about. The result was that the hospital started to acknowledge my concerns.

Recovery from mental illness is unpredictable; some people may get over it quickly in a few weeks, others take months or even years and for some it never goes away. What is really important, however, is that even when people are ill, they are still seen as individuals with rights, beliefs, and abilities. Throughout his contact with me, my first advocate treated me with a respect that is often lost when someone is considered mentally ill. My advocate didn't "take over" my life, he gave support when it was needed, at the same time allowing and encouraging me to do what I was capable of for myself.

Today I still have mental health problems and at times have needed hospital treatment. This doesn't mean that I can't do things, it means that sometimes I need support to use my abilities to their best advantage. For example, although one year I spent four months in hospital I still managed to pass an honours degree. I know that not everyone who has a mental illness can do this, some people who are perfectly healthy can't, but one of the biggest problems I had was being told by people that I had to accept the limitations of my illness. Mental illness doesn't restrict people nearly as much as people's attitudes towards it.

Despite good intentions, sometimes the services provided to help people with mental health difficulties can result in control of the individual rather than control of the illness. Without that first advocate I'd probably still be wandering around in a "medicine" induced haze, believing myself too ill to do anything. Since then I've gone from the written-off wreck who fifteen years ago was told by a psychiatrist that I'd never work again, to holding down a responsible job, acting as an adviser and consultant—and having regained my self respect.

Liz went on to work as an advocate herself. Her positive experience of advocacy is shared by Graham, who is also an advocate and involved in supporting and training other people with mental health problems to move on with their lives.

> I'd just come off an acute ward and basically didn't want to do anything. My advocate listened to me. He was very knowledgeable about different aspects of mental health and came up with suggestions that were well within my scope, such as light admin work, but wouldn't be massively demanding. That work option was a reason for me to get out of the house and not sit in a corner, constantly listening to my voices for hours on end.

> But my key worker was also an advocate. She too listened, advised, gave me information and encouraged me when there was something I needed to do—but which I didn't necessary want to do! An advocate doesn't have a specific job description, it's a person who speaks up for people, advises them and helps them get to where they want to go. That's how it worked for me.

This chapter has looked at the sources of professional, personal and voluntary support which may be helpful to people's recovery. The next chapter describes some of the ways in which individuals can improve their physical and psychological health and well-being.

Useful addresses/resources

Making Space arranges carers breaks for people in the north of England, 46 Allen Street, Warrington, Cheshire WA2 7JB. Tel: 01925571680; Fax: 0192523 1402; website: www.makingspace.co.uk

A Practical Guide to Befriending, Beside, 1 Merchant Street, Bow, London E3 4LY, Tel: 0208 980 9787; email: besidecre@aol.com

Action for Advocacy (A4A) PO Box 31856, Lorrimore Square, London SE17 3XR. Tel: 0207 820 7868; Fax: 0207 820 9947; email: info@action-foradvocacy.org.uk; website: www.actionforadvocacy.org.uk

United Kingdom Advocacy Network (UK-AN), Volserve House, 14–18 West Bar Green, Sheffield S1 2DA. Tel: 0114 275 8171; email@u-kan.co.uk; website: www.u-kan.co.uk

Scottish Independent Advocacy Alliance, 138 Slateford Road, Edinburgh EH14 1LR. Tel: 0131 455 8183; website: www.siaa.org.uk

The Independent Advocacy Service (London Borough of South-wark). Tel: 0207 703 0261.

The Mental Health Project (London Borough of Brixton). Tel: 0207 274 4490.

Project for Advocacy, Counselling and Education (PACE), 34 Hartham Road, London N7 9LJ. Tel: 0207 700 1223; Fax: 0207 609 490; email: pace@dircon.co.uk; website: www.multikulti.org.uk. For lesbians and gay men in greater London.

User Voice, Ten Acres Centre, Dogpool Lane, Stirchley, Birmingham B30 2XH. Tel: 0121 678 2106; Fax: 0121 678 2107; email: user. voice@bsmht.nhs.uk

Voices Noticeboard: info@hearing-voices.org

Perceptions, the magazine of the National Voices Forum, perceptions@rethink.org, voicesforum@rethink.org, or Perceptions at Rethink, 28 Castle St, Kingston on Thames KT1 1SS. Tel: 0208 547 9226; website: www.voicesforum.org.uk

The Independent Complaints Advocacy Services (ICAS) supports patients and their carers wishing to pursue a complaint about their NHS treatment or care. Tel: 0773 892 8492; Minicom: 01268 722 505; email: pohwericas@pohwericas.net. A UK areas map and telephone numbers are on their website: http//www.dh.gov.uk

Mind's bi-monthly magazine *OpenMind* is for people who use and provide mental health services and is a forum for complaints, analysis, opinions, and news on medication, legal, and welfare issues. It is available on subscription or in libraries.

Psychminded is an online magazine for those who work in psychology, psychiatry, and mental health. It has a research and news archive and members' forum. Psychminded Ltd, Chorlton, Manchester M21 0TG. Tel: 0161 881 8036 (9.00 a.m. to 5.00 p.m.); Fax: 0161 881 8036; email through website: www.psychminded.co.uk

The American scientific journal *Schizophrenia Bulletin* reports the latest research and medical treatments and has first-person accounts by people with the diagnosis. It is available in reference/medical libraries.

CHAPTER FIVE

Health and well-being

P eople with a diagnosis of schizophrenia are more than aver-
agely unhealthy. Their symptoms and the effects of medication often result in a tendency to exercise little, eat
unhealthily and smoke heavily, meaning that many individuals are
unfit and vulnerable to physical illness (Connolly & Kelly, 2005).
One study (Harris, 1988) indicates that they are more prone to infections, heart disease, Type II diabetes (adult onset) and female breast
cancer.

There is also evidence (Torrey, 2006, p. 115) that some people
with schizophrenia have a higher than usual pain threshold. They
are not so likely, therefore, to seek medical advice until a particular
illness has reached a less easily treatable stage, or to get treatment
for problems such as backache or asthma, which can undermine
their morale and even lead to depression.

A possible first step for someone to improve their health is to
have a medical check-up with their GP, who can also give dietary
advice and support in tackling unhealthy habits such as excessive
drinking and smoking, and ways to manage stress.

Stress management

People experience stress differently and vary in their tolerance of stressful events and situations. But it is well known that stress undermines physical and psychological health and causes numerous problems, including headaches, backache, dizziness, panic attacks, muscle tension and pain, insomnia, and loss of appetite or food cravings.

Stress contributes to and worsens many chronic long-term conditions, such as irritable bowel syndrome (Bennett, Tennant, Piesse, Badcock, & Kellow, 1998) and heart attacks (Sheps et al., 2002), as well as the symptoms associated with schizophrenia (Leff, Kuipers, Berkowitz. Eberlein-Vries, & Sturgeon, 1982).

Causes of stress

Worries about work, money, or personal relationships are a common source of stress. Certain situations are inherently stressful, such as travelling on an overcrowded commuter train in the rush hour, which raise people's blood pressure and may trigger panic or anxiety attacks. Once at work, a stressful environment can cause individuals to become anxious and depressed (Health and Safety Executive, 1999).

Environments and interactions high in "expressed emotion" (EE) are also especially stressful to people with schizophrenia and are associated with poor short-term outcomes (Bebbington & Kuipers, 1994; Butzlaff & Hooley, 1998; Kavanagh, 1992; Vaughn & Leff, 1976).

Enthusiastic, talkative, demonstrative or over-protective carers, relatives, friends, or medical professionals generate stressful levels of EE. So do conversations marked by cold, critical comments and hostile accusations, whereas conversations and environments which are characterized by low EE contribute to a person remaining less stressed and calm.

However, even a low EE relationship can be stressful if it is felt to be distant, cold, or negative, as are "neutral" ones—which might be the intention of a health professional—if they are experienced as being negative, and are significantly associated with poorer outcomes (Tattan & Tarrier, 2000).

Identifying stress

Feeling unaccountably angry, tense, irritable, or anxious are obvious signs of stress. Less difficult to pin down is a sense of hopelessness, overwhelming tiredness, or the desire to eat, sleep, or drink alcohol much more than usual. Many people's stress shows itself in heartburn, indigestion, insomnia, or sexual difficulites.

Once the stressors have been identified, and whatever their cause, the aim is to develop effective management techniques. For instance, loud, unwanted noise is a major stressor. Using earplugs, a personal stereo or I-pod may help block the worst excesses. Neighbourhood noise can be reported to the local authority's confidential noise nuisance line—most councils have one—or the environmental health officer. Council or housing association tenants in accommodation with poor sound insulation can request improvements or a transfer. (A supporting letter from the person's psychiatrist may increase their housing points and speed the process.)

Of course, it's sensible to avoid potentially stressful stituations whenever possible, like especially busy times at the supermarket and volatile or argumentative people. Refusing requests that feel like pressure may mean having to be very assertive, such as when faced with over-protective friends or relatives.

Releasing stress

- Pummelling a pillow or cushion may help to relieve tension.
- Closing the eyes can be calming as it encourages the brain waves that promote relaxation and detachment.
- Yawn! Stretching the facial muscles is a quick relaxant and stimulates less shallow breathing.
- Smile broadly to lift the corners of the mouth. This help reduce stress—even if the smile is forced.
- Breathe! Three slow in-breaths through the nose to the count of three—exhale through the nose to the count of three.

Ideally, individuals learn to recognize their signs of stress and do not allow it to build up. If people have become overwhelmed by household tasks, money worries, or emotional problems their care coordinator can liaise with the mental health team to arrange additional support.

At the same time, trying to prioritize what is important and to be more laid back about the "what might happen" is important. Being time, rather than task, orientated often pays dividends. For example, instead of trying to do everything in one go, allocate a set amount of time for chores—and then stop! Learn to switch off and relax. The exercise below can help.

Relaxation

1. Get settled in a comfortable chair with eyes closed and breathe slowly and evenly for a couple of minutes.
2. Focus on any areas of tension in your body and mentally tell those muscles to relax.
3. Tighten and then relax each part of the body in turn, from the top of your head to the feet. As you focus on each part of the body, think of warmth, heaviness, and letting go.
4. After 15–20 minutes, stand up and stretch your arms above your head and allow yourself to yawn a few times.

Mind's *Guide to Managing Stress* (2005c) can be read or ordered on their website or from their publications department.

Pets

Pets can have a powerful effect on people's health. Stroking a cat promotes a sense of calmness and relaxation and simply keeping a pet lowers blood pressure (Allen, Shykoff, & Izzo, 2001; Allen, Blascovich, & Mendes, 2002). Strange as it may sound, people with a diagnosis of schizophrenia who had a dog in attendance at a psychotherapy session derived added psychological benefit, a study suggests (Nathans-Barel, Feldman, Berger, Modai, & Silver, 2005).

The individuals who had psychotherapy sessions with a dog in the room showed a reduction in clinical symptoms and felt that their quality and joy of life were significantly improved, compared to individuals who attended sessions alone. The participants who had "dog therapy" also showed an improved use of their leisure time.

Similarly, a study of "animal assisted therapy" with elderly patients who had a diagnosis of schizophrenia found that structured companionship sessions with cats and dogs significantly improved people's mobility, socializing, self-care, and general well-being (Barak, Savorai, Mavashev, & Beni, 2001).

Personal accounts suggest that pets make people feel better by providing non-judgemental companionship, as Suresh explains:

> I've got a gerbil, Double Dragon, named after one of Bruce Lee's films. Gerbils are very hardy animals—their natural habitat is the desert. They're also very social animals and want company so DD enjoys me playing and talking to him. I don't have much family support and when I got schizophrenia my friends disappeared. If I feel lonely, or on the days when I hear voices, I talk to the gerbil and that helps.

James also finds comfort knowing that his cat, Smudge, is always there for him.

> Smudge's not a pedigree, but he's been superb. You get that loving feeling when you come home and he turns up and rubs himself against you. You feel you're wanted and needed. He jumps up on your knee and you feel more at ease. Then he wants feeding and you have to do that. You can talk to a cat and in its own way it'll talk back to you.

Of course, it would be irresponsible for people to get pets unless they can care for them properly. But animal refuges and charities always need good foster and permanent homes for unwanted animals.

Bullying

There is considerable anecdotal and some research evidence that people with a mental health diagnosis are often the targets of bullying (The Mental Health Foundation, 2002). Martin recalls his experience.

> After I was discharged from hospital the first time I was put on a run-down 60s estate where I stuck out as someone different. I'd get followed by a huge gang of kids, mocking and taunting me. My place was broken into six or seven times, once when someone put their shoulder against the door. After these incidents I'd be really tense for quite a long time. One night I came home and found super

glue had been put in the door lock and I couldn't get inside. The harassment went on and on. It was a nightmare. I needed acceptance and got only hostility. With the stress of it all I was re-hospitalized for three months.

Obviously, bullying or harassment undermines a person's confidence and health, but hoping that the bullies will eventually get bored and give up is not a realistic option. Martin endured eighteen months of harassment before eventually speaking out. He was re-housed and the bullying stopped.

Experts on bullying advise people to keep a record of the incidents and immediately report them. Those who can help to resolve the problem include the police, the local authority, local counsellors, MP, neighbourhood watch coordinator, advocacy services, and the person's care coordinator.

Eating for health

Despite how often it is recommended, there is sometimes confusion about what constitutes a well-balanced diet. Essentially, it contains sufficient protein, carbohydrates, and fats to enable the body to maintain itself and function efficiently, as well as the vitamins and minerals necessary to help the immune system ward off and fight infection.

Protein is essential for the body's growth, repair, and normal metabolism. Meat, fish, eggs, milk and dairy products, as well as beans and lentils, known as pulses, and Quorn are good sources. Soya is excellent for vegetarians and vegans as, like meat, it contains the eight essential amino acids which the body can't make. Men need about 55 g (just over 2 oz) of protein a day and women, 45 g. That's roughly equivalent to a small size portion of chicken or fish, one thick slice of meat, or a large egg.

Carbohydrates comprise natural sugars, starches, and fibre. Carbohydrates provide most of the body's energy, and starchy foods like pasta, rice, or baked potatoes encourage production of the calming chemical serotonin. Cereals such as oats and wheat and fruits and vegetables are other good sources of carbodydrates. High protein/fat slimming diets advise "cutting out carbs", but a mainly carbohydrate, low-fat diet is a healthy way to lose excess weight.

Fats provide insulation and protection within the body and form part of the cell membranes. Reserves of fat are energy sources if other food is in short supply. Vitamins A and D are stored in the body's fat, as well as the liver, but a diet need contain only a very small amount of fat to be healthy.

The polyunsaturated fats in unprocessed, non-hydrogenated vegetables oils and margarines are healthier than the saturated fats in meat and dairy products, which clog up the arteries and contribute to heart disease and strokes. High levels of saturated fats in the diet of people with schizophrenia are also associated with poorer outcomes than if their diet contains plenty of fruit and vegetables as well as fish oils (Christensen & Christensen, 1988).

The body derives the sugar it needs from fruit and other foods, whereas refined sugar contains no nutrients, only fattening calories. The nutritional advice is to reduce or, ideally, eliminate added sugar from the diet. The sugar content of many processed foods is hidden behind the words glucose or sucrose.

Fresh food is healthier than processed, which tends to be high in additives, salt, sugar, and saturated fat. Eating fresh fruit and vegetables reduces the incidence of certain forms of cancer. Raw apples are rich in antioxidants and reduce the growth of human liver and colon cancer cells (Eberhardt, Lee, & Liu, 2000). Apple-rich diets are also linked to lower risk of diabetes, cardiovascular disease, cataracts, and Alzheimer's Disease.

Eating a variety of foods will provide a wider range of nutrients. To obtain a healthy amount of vitamins, minerals and fibre, WHO recommends eating at least five 80 gram (3 oz) portions of fruit and/or vegetables (excluding potatoes) a day. These can be tinned, fresh, or frozen, preferably without added sugar, salt, or syrup, or as unsweetened juices. Baked beans, lentils, red kidney beans, and dried fruit each count as one portion.

Home cooking

Home-cooked meals are invariably less expensive and healthier than ready meals and takeaways. Dozens of cookery books are published every year and most libraries have a good selection. Delia Smith's *How to Cook Book One* and *How to Cook Book Two* (BBC Books) are excellent for anyone who literally does not know how to boil an egg.

Cookery classes at a further education college or day centres can be arranged through a person's care co-ordinator, as well as an appointment with a nutritionist if someone wants specialist dietary advice, about a vegetarian or gluten-free diet, for instance.

Help to lose weight

Compared to the general population, people with schizophrenia are more likely to be overweight (Meyer, 2001; Thakore, 2005). This is a side-effect of several medications, particularly the atypicals, and is the biggest risk factor for Type II diabetes for people with schizophrenia.

Excess weight may also lessen people's motivation to look after their health by adding to negative feelings. In turn, these may lead to an even unhealthier lifestyle as, when stressed, individuals tend to eat foods that are higher in fat and to exercise less (Cartwright et al., 2003; Greeno & Wing, 1994).

The latest fad or celebrity diet may lead to fast weight loss, but maintaining it is less easy. GPs can give advice and the practice will very likely have a nurse who can devise a weight loss plan that includes regular weigh-ins and the ongoing support that research suggests can produce good results (Ohlsen, Treasure, & Pilowsky, 2004).

Studies also show that slimming organizations, such as Rosemary Conley, Slimming World and Weight Watchers, can help people achieve and maintain a healthier weight, despite their taking medication which stimulates the appetite (Ball, Coons, & Buchanan, 2001; Pendlebury & Ost, 2002).

Switching to a drug which is not associated with excessive weight gain is another option (Taylor, Paton, & Kerwin, 2005). These include Aripiprazole (Casey et al., 2003); Risperidone (Ried, Renner, Bengtson, Wilcox & Acholonu, 2003) or Quetiapine (Gupta et al., 2004).

Caffeine

Caffeine is in tea, coffee, colas, and chocolate. People with schizophrenia often consume large amounts of caffeine-containing drinks (Rihs, Muller, & Bauman, 1996). By stimulating the brain caffeine aids concentration, and low to moderate amounts are associated with pleasant effects (Clementz & Dailey, 1988). But excessive amounts (600 mg daily) can cause or increase agitation, restlessness, irritability, anxiety, rambling speech, raised blood pressure, and even psychosis (Sawynok, 1995).

A mug of brewed coffee contains about 100 mg, instant coffee, 60 mg, tea 45 mg, soft drinks 25–50 mg per can. Caffeine is a drug and reducing its intake is best done gradually, to minimize withdrawal effects. Herbal teas do not contain caffeine, or sufficient herbal extract to undermine the effects of medication. Camomile, especially, is known to be calming.

Vitamins, minerals and dietary supplements

Whether it's vitamin C to stave off a cold, or a "fortifying nutritional tonic", some people have great faith in the ability of certain vitamins, minerals, or food supplements, not only to maintain good health and prevent illness, but, in some instances, to cure health problems such as schizophrenia.

Such claims are notoriously difficult to prove—although a daily multivitamin pill may make some people *feel* better. However, in Britain—as in the rest of the developed world—people generally derive sufficient vitamins and minerals from their diet. Possible exceptions are very restricted vegetarian or vegan diets, or ones consistently lacking sufficient protein, fruit, or vegetables.

Before taking supplements people are advised to consult their GP or psychiatrist, if only to learn whether research evidence indicates that they are likely to be effective. For example, high doses of vitamins were once advocated as a cure for "schizophrenic symptoms". This has not proved to be the case, and more than recommended doses of any vitamin can cause discomfort, constipation, nausea, diarrhoea, and, more seriously, increase the risk of liver problems and cancer.

As mentioned in Chapter Three, Omega-3, comprising the fatty acids EPA and DHA, which is found in certain fish, walnuts, rape seed oil, and linseed/flax seeds, may improve some people's symptoms. A 120 gram can of sardines or pilchards contains a sufficient daily dose.

A correspondent to the SAGB newsletter (No 27, 1998) recommended Linseeds (Brown) as the highest source of Omega-3, with advice to grind the seeds and keep them refrigerated, ready for sprinkling on food, especially cereals. Other recommended sources were golden linseed, "cracked" for easy absorption, and bottled linseed oil.

Ginkgo biloba

This herbal supplement is typically marketed as an aid to concentration and memory and research shows that it can improve cognitive function in people with Alzheimer's Disease (Oken, Storzbach, & Kaye, 1998). Ginkgo biloba may also benefit people whose symptoms are resistant to antipsychotics (Zhang, Zhou, Su, & Zhang, 2001; Zhang et al., 2001; Zhou et al., 1999). In these studies one group was given the antipsychotic haloperidol and ginkgo biloba. Compared to another group who received the antipsychotic and a placebo, those taking ginkgo biloba showed a significant decrease in positive symptoms such as hallucinations and delusions.

The improvements were attributed to ginkgo biloba's ability to mop up free radicals. The researchers concluded that it might be an effective addition to antipsychotics for people with "untreatable schizophrenia". Another study (Zhang et al., 2001) found that ginkgo biloba enhanced the treatment of "resistant schizophrenia" and reduced the extrapyramidal side effects of antipsychotics.

Vitamin deficiencies

Clinical evidence suggests that many of the people hospitalized for psychiatric problems have low levels of vitamin B12 and folic acid, B9. Folic acid (folate) is needed for cell replication and growth, and is found in beans, leafy green vegetables, citrus fruits, wheat germ, and meat. A study by Goff and colleagues (2004) identified low concentrations of folic acid in patients with predominantly negative symptoms (see Chapter One). The researchers theorized that this might reflect a low dietary intake, cigarette smoking, and the involvement of folic acid in the synthesis of neurotransmitters.

Significant improvements in social and clinical recovery in patients who took folic acid and vitamin B12 supplements for six months, in addition to antipsychotics, have been reported (Godfrey et al., 1990). The study's participants, which included people with depression, had previously shown a definite, or borderline folate deficiency. Both folic acid and vitamin B12 are reduced by medications such as chlorpromazine. However, the authors suggested that the deficiency may have resulted from difficulties in the participants' ability to metabolize folic acid. A study of outpatients with schizophrenia suggests that they, too, may have a greater tendency to be deficient in folic acid (Herran et al., 1999).

Allergies

A possible genetic link between coeliac disease and schizophrenia has also attracted research. Coeliac disease is caused by eating gluten, a protein from wheat, some other grains, and, to a lesser extent casein, a dairy protein. It has been suggested that people with schizophrenia are more likely to have immune reactions to these proteins than the general population (Reichelt & Landmark, 1995). This results in damage to the lining of the gut, which deprives the body and brain of essential nutrients. In a letter published in the medical journal *The Lancet* (2004), Gwynneth Hemmings, director general of SAGB, refers to studies which support the theory.

Post mortems have identified damage to the gut and evidence of colitis, enteritis, and gastritis in people with schizophrenia (Buscaino, 1978). Dohan (1978) reported that the highest incidence of schizophrenia was found in the wheat- and rye-eating areas of the world. More recently, a Danish population-based case control study (Eaton et al., 2004) concluded that a history of coeliac disease is a risk factor for schizophrenia.

Research indicates that a gluten-free diet may benefit people with schizophrenia. Singh and Kay (1976) found that participants on a milk- and cereal grain-free diet showed a reversal when this was interrupted and subsequent improvement when the diet was reinstated. A preliminary trial found that patients with schizophrenia improved on a gluten- and dairy-free diet and had shorter hospitals stays than those eating normal diets (Dohan & Grasberger, 1973).

Yet Storms, Clopton, and Wright (1982) reported that patients eating food containing gluten for ten days showed considerably greater improvement than those eating a cereal- and milk-free diet.

However, the authors stated that a longer time on the latter diet may be required for any beneficial effects to appear.

Apart from research evidence, first-hand accounts suggest that a gluten- and dairy-free diet may dramatically improve some individuals' physical and psychological symptoms, as described in a letter to the SAGB Newsletter (Winter, 2002).

> I react to all obvious gluten-containing foods, i.e. those that have wheat, barley, rye and oats in them, getting stomach bloating, diarrhoea and "voices" if I eat them. What may be of interest are the "hidden" ways of having wheat/gluten ... in shampoos and cosmetics, which are absorbed through the skin ... a powerful medium for drug administration.

> I live in a rural area and during the harvest months of July until the beginning of October, I inhale gluten dust. I can feel drugged and very slow. Each time my "voices" have started has been in August, the peak grain harvest month. Dairy foods also affect me to a lesser degree.

A list of gluten-free foods are available on the American website http://www.gicare.com/pated/edtgso6.htm

Nutrition therapy

Carl Pfeiffer was a leading exponent of the idea that mental health is linked to nutrition. Since his death, Pfeiffer's work is being continued by a former colleague, Patrick Holford, with whom he wrote a two-in-one-book, *Mental Illness The Nutrition Connection: How to Beat Depression, Anxiety and Schizophrenia* and: *How to Enhance your Mental and Emotional Well being* (1996). Reading the book at a particularly low point, John E decided to give nutrition therapy a try.

> I have a diagnosis of schizophrenia and got so depressed some time ago I tried to kill myself. Luckily, I failed and afterwards decided I had to do something about my illness. A good friend got me to read a book by Carl Pfeiffer which I was really taken with. I began buying large doses of vitamins and minerals. I felt marvellous, but on the advice of the same friend, I decided I needed specialist advice.

I found it at the Institute for Optmium Nutrition in London, which was founded by Patrick Holford. This was one of the best things that happened in my life. There I saw a nutritionist who specialized in schizophrenia. She corrected the amount of vitamins and minerals that I was taking, but it was remarkably similar. She also advised me to eat sensibly and cut down on caffeine, sugar and nicotine. I had given up alcohol and street drugs long ago. But at that time I was drinking twenty cups of tea a day, each with two teaspoons of sugar, plus smoking forty cigarettes. The previous five winters I'd suffered from sucidal depression, but that freezing cold and dark winter it was fantastic simply to be alive.

Switching to a healthy nutritious diet has had an enormously beneficial effect. I feel so much better, I can think more clearly and I came to realize that my voices came from me. With that realization, I was able to simply ignore them if they came back, which was much rarer. Now I'm capable of doing many more things: writing, sculpture, art, voluntary work, classes and other hobbies. I still take antipsychotic medication, but feel much healthier and happier than I did. I'm sure that it's mainly the good nutrition which has helped me in my recovery and to move on with my life.

While there seems to be no concrete evidence that the symptoms associated with schizophrenia may be dramatically improved by nutrition. Elaine Gottschall's book *Breaking the Vicious Cycle: Intestinal health through diet* (1994) explores possible links between "schizophrenic" symptoms and diet. *Treat Yourself with Nutritional Therapy* by Linda Lazarides (2002) has diets and recipes for specific conditions, including schizophrenia.

Mind's *Guide to Food and Mood* details the most commonly known associations between the two and can be ordered on their website.

Alcohol and "street"/illegal drugs

A high proportion of people diagnosed with schizophrenia misuse alcohol or illegal drugs (Duke, Pantelis, McPhillips, & Barnes, 2001; McCreadie, 2002). Research by Menezes and colleagues (1996) indicates that thirty-six per cent of people in South London with severe mental illness, including schizophrenia, and symptoms of psychosis, misused drugs or alcohol and that the in-patient rates among these individuals were almost twice that of people with psychosis alone. One survey suggests that half of all patients with schizophrenia have a "substance abuse disorder" (Regier et al., 1990).

Alcohol and drug use is associated with increased risk of psychotic symptoms among "vulnerable" individuals—those with a personal or family history of psychosis (Tien & Anthony, 1990). In addition to positive symptoms, drug use increases the risk of depression, suicide, and rates of hospital admission (Linszen, Dingemans, & Lenior, 1994), and is linked to poorer social and occupational outcomes (Drake, Osher, & Wallach, 1989; Pristach & Smith, 1990).

However, one study (Cantwell, 2003) found that, specifically among young men who had been ill for a relatively short time, drug misuse had only a minor effect on their symptoms, social functioning, or use of support services. None the less, depending on the amount, and other drugs they are used with, street drugs can cause temporary psychosis and unpredictable or dangerous behaviour. Since these drugs are invariably "cut" with dubious substances, they are an additional health risk. Also, once the "high" wears off, amphetamines (speed), cocaine, crack, heroin, LSD, and ecstasy can leave users feeling so depressed and exhausted that they feel driven to take other drugs to make them feel better.

Cannabis (marijuana, dope, hash, grass, weed, puff), by contrast, is often viewed as a safer drug and less harmful than alcohol. Again, this seems to depend on the quantity and the quality (skunk, for example, is a very strong variety of cannabis), whether it is taken with other drugs, and a person's degree of susceptibility to its effects. Cannabis may help someone to relax, but even small amounts impair judgement and concentration. Larger amounts can cause confusion, restlessness, hallucinations, or paranoid feelings.

A review of nearly sixty studies published between 1990 and 2002 indicates that cannabis use is high among people with psychosis (Green, Young, & Kavanagh, 2005). Heavy use by people who habitually use the drug, or those using cannabis for the first time, may trigger a "schizophrenic-like" episode (Thornicroft, 1990). However, Thomas (1993) states that acute psychotic episodes following drug use are not common and that there is no convincing evidence that cannabis causes chronic psychosis. Even so, as with any drug, people can become physically and psychologically dependent on cannabis.

Frank About Drugs freephone helpline 0800 77 66 00 (daily, twenty-four hours); website: www.talktofrank.com, gives confidential advice and information about drugs, including help with detox and rehabilitation.

People can become addicted to alcohol, of course. Individuals with a diagnosis of schizophrenia are at least three times as likely to be alcohol-dependent than others in the general population (Graham et al., 2001). Clinical evidence indicates that excessive drinking reacts badly with most medications. Alcohol also contributes to depression (World Health Organization, 2004) and exacerbates undetected or underlying depression (Merikangas et al., 1998). For these reasons Chris decided to give up alcohol altogether.

I have been teetotal for over ten years now. It wasn't initially my choice. I just found that my latest medication, Olanzapine, didn't mix very well with alcohol. Even small amounts of booze would give me hot flushes, headaches and an overwhelming sense of tiredness, so, reluctantly I had to go on the wagon. It took several attempts to totally abstain, 'cos of peer pressure to drink and a genuine desire to join in with my mates. I used to enjoy my drinking sessions and it was a terrible blow to have it taken away from me—I felt I was losing out on a major part of life.

Now, with the benefit of hindsight, I can see it's for the best. My mental state is fragile anyway and I'm not having drunken outbursts anymore, some of which were embarrassing and others dangerously ill-thought-out by a sozzled mind. Also I used to feel suicidally depressed a lot while drunk and even for a day or two after a binge. I don't miss either of these things at all!

I still go out to the pub occasionally and am happy drinking anything non-alcoholic. I tend to choose nights when there is a band, quiz or other entertainment on 'cos being sober in a pub can be really boring otherwise. But far from dying of boredom, I have looked to new interests, such as guitar lessons, target shooting and computing. Without the weekly beer bill I find I have more, not less options—and better mental health as a bonus.

The original guidelines on healthy alcohol consumption set a maximum of twenty-one units a week for men and fourteen for women. A unit equals a small glass of wine, half a pint of ordinary strength beer (half a pint of strong lager counts as two units), a single measure of spirits, or a small measure of sherry. However, as the serious health risks of binge drinking (more than eight units in a session) have become recognized, the advice is to aim for at least two alcohol-free days a week and set a limit of three to four units on any one day.

Anyone who suspects that they are using alcohol to "self-medicate", such as to take the edge off difficult situations, to blot out painful memories or feelings of depression, fear, loneliness or low self-esteem, is at risk of being dependent on alchohol and would benefit from professional help. GPs can give advice and possibly refer someone to an addiction counsellor.

Depression

Alcohol and drugs are often used to combat feelings of depression. These might stem from personal, social or financial problems—or, as is often the case, a combination of all three. Depression is the chief reason for people taking their own lives. Approximately fifty per cent of people with schizophrenia or schizoaffective disorder attempt suicide (Meltzer et al., 2003) and the suicide rate is 10–13 times higher than in the general population (Torrey, 2006, p. 311).

In addition to, or instead of antidepressants, practical support can be an important factor in people's recovery from depression. Counselling or psychotherapy with someone who will listen and be supportive—and, possibly, "work through" unresolved issues may be helpful. NICE (2004) recommends cognitive–behaviour therapy (CBT) for people with mild depression. It has also approved a self-help computer package, *Beating the Blues*, for mild to moderate depression. It comprises an introductory video, eight one-hour inter-active CBT-based computer sessions, and homework exercises. The NICE guidelines can be downloaded from their website: www.nice.org or are available in a leaflet.

CBT can be effective in reducing delusions which often reduces depression. Chapter Eight has information on CBT and other forms of counselling and psychotherapy.

Physical activity

Personal accounts suggest that physical activity has a positive effect on depression. Sixty-five per cent of respondents to the Mind survey, *Exercise Your Mind* (2001a), reported that it helped relieve their depression. This finding is supported by extensive research (Department of Health, 2004) and applies to people of all ages (Babyak et al., 2000; Blumenthal et al., 1999).

Some forms of exercise can also lead to meeting new people and so reduce isolation and loneliness. Possibly just as helpful is the fact that exercise takes time and attention which otherwise might get swallowed up by depressed thinking. This can break the cycle of someone becoming further depressed about the depression, which is a common feature of the problem.

In some parts of the UK people with depression, heart disease, diabetes, obesity, or high blood pressure can be referred by their GP to schemes where they will be helped to develop their own exercise programme, supervised by a qualified trainer. The programmes comprise a wide range of exercise, including gym sessions or structured classes with other people on the scheme. Usually the schemes last for three to six months and are provided at no or low cost.

Links between high levels of depression and low fish consumption and vice versa have been identified in several countries (Hibbeln, 1998), leading to the suggestion that people with depression may have an Omega-3 deficiency. For example, a study with over 3,000 Finnish adults (Tanskanen et al., 2001) found that the likelihood of their having depressive symptoms was signficantly higher among those who ate fish infrequently than among frequent consumers. Seasonal mood change, the so-called SAD syndrome, and its absence has also been linked to levels of fish consumption (Cott & Hibbeln, 2001).

However, toxins released by the burning of fossil fuels and incinerated waste, found in some oily fish, have been linked to birth defects, cancers, and depression. According to a systematic review of the research (Hooper et al., 2006) these pollutants might cancel out any benefits derived from the Omega 3 fatty acids in fish. As previously mentioned, walnuts, linseed/flax/rape seed oil, and Igennus vegetable oil capsules are a rich source of the Omega 3 fatty acids EPA and DHA and can be considered as an alternative source. These may be taken in addition to prescribed medication.

A study by Peet and Horrobin (2002b), with seventy depressed people who were taking antidepressants, found that after twelve weeks those receiving one gram of EPA a day were significantly less depressed than those receiving a placebo. Smoking may cancel out these benefits (Brown, Morrice, & Duthie, 1998).

Depression is also thought to be associated with severe folic acid deficiency (Carney et al., 1990; Reynolds, Carney, & Toone, 1984). A diet rich in folic acid might, therefore, help to reduce depression.

St John's Wort (SJW)

SJW (*hypericum perforatum*) is a traditional herbal remedy for depression and, like other such treatments, may be thought of as less harmful and more "natural" than antidepressants (Ernst, Rand, Barnes, & Stevinson, 1998). Test tube studies suggest that SJW works by blocking the re-uptake of serotonin, norepinephrine, and dopamine (Muller, Rolli, Schafer, & Hafner, 1997).

Clinical trials of SJW suggest that it may be effective for mild to moderate depression (Gaster & Holroyd, 2000; Linde et al., 1996; Voltz, 1997), though Taylor, Paton, and Kerwin point out (2005, p. 179) that none of these trials lasted longer than eight weeks and, despite claims that it is better tolerated than non-herbal antidepressants, SJW has not been extensively tested against newer anti-depressants like the SSRIs.

However, several drug interactions have been identified (*ibid.*, p. 80). It can adversely affect medications for HIV, the combined contraceptive pill, and possibly some anticonvulsant and migraine drugs. Common side-effects include dry mouth, nausea, constipation, fatigue, dizziness, headache, and restlessness. In addition, it may make the skin more sensitive to sunlight (Bore, 1998).

Help for depression

Depression Alliance is a charity offering help to people with depression. CALM (The Campaign Against Living Miserably) is targeted at 15–35-year-old men, whose rates of depression are higher than in the general population. Callers to the freephone helpline receive professional counselling and advice. Tel: 0800 58 58 58 (5.00 p.m.to 3.00 a.m., 365 days a year); website: www.thecalmzone.net. *Use Your Brain to Beat Depression: The Complete Guide to Understanding and Tackling Depressive Illness* (Illman, 2004) includes useful ideas and self-help exercises.

Whatever strategies are adopted, self-blame is not useful. People do not get rid of depression by "pulling themselves together". More effective than clichés and criticism are supportive and encouraging messages that remind the person that there are ways in which they can improve their situation and recover.

Trials and Tribulations

> I like enthralling literature,
> And popular music, most recently Frank Zappa, though I don't
> Think he can be counted as popular,
> I like the coolness of cats,
> Warm spring days,
> The smell of petrol stations,
> End to end football,
> Doctor Who,
> And I prefer free-verse over rhymes
>
> I dislike bullies: the sort at school and the sort than run
> Countries;
> Also soap operas (too many arguments),
> Evil spirits: the ones you drink and the ones that haunt me;
> Long dark winter nights,
> And the brevity of life.

This poem was written a month before Adrian Holohan died, aged thirty-four, on Christmas Eve 2002, and was originally published in the SAGB Newsletter. It is reprinted with the permission of his mother, Janice.

The Samaritans

The Samaritans are trained to listen to people experiencing despair or suicidal feelings. They do not criticize or belittle a person's problems, or offer instant solutions or advice. But they are experts at supporting people through a personal crisis of whatever nature and are available to listen twenty-four hours a day. Tel: 0845 90 90 90; email: jo@samaritans.org. They aim to respond to emails within twenty-four hours and most often will reply 10–15 hours after receipt. Or send a text to 07725 909090 (from the UK) or 0872 609090 (from Ireland).

Insomnia

Insomnia is very common. Most research studies estimate that between ten and thirty per cent of the population have persistent difficulties—lasting more than four weeks—with falling asleep, waking often in the night, early morning wakening, daytime sleepiness, or loss of well-being through feeling they have not had enough sleep (Hajak, 1999; Kales, Soldatos, & Kales, 1987).

Insomnia is more common among people with medical or mental health problems (Shapiro, 1993), particularly anxiety and depression (Nutt & Wilson, 1999), but may also contribute to such feelings. Anecdotal evidence from people with schizophrenia suggests that sleeplessness often signals that they are becoming unwell.

Antipsychotics can cause insomnia. While some are sedating, others are experienced as too "alerting". Anecdotal reports of Risperidone, for example, include complaints of feeling tired, but unable to "switch off" or sleep. However, as Healy (2005, p. 35) points out, a drug that causes sleeplessness in one person may be sedating in another.

Benzodiazepines, known as short-acting hypnotics, such as Valium, have often been prescribed for insomnia, but are addictive and quickly tolerated, so that increasingly higher doses are required to produce the same effect (Moller, 1999). Long-acting drugs, however, may cause "rebound insomnia" and "next-day sedation". According to Taylor, Paton, and Kerwin (2005, p. 202) Zopiclone and Zolpidem and other non-benzodiazepine medications are becoming more widely prescribed, but research suggests that these may be just as likely to cause dependence.

Herbal sleeping remedies have more appeal for some people. Valerian (*Valeriana officinalis*), often used in traditional Chinese medicine (TCM) and Western folk remedies, is usually the chief constituent. Controlled trials suggest valerian is a mild hypnotic with minimal side-effects (Beaubrun & Gray, 2000; Leatherwood, Chauffard, Heck, & Munoz-Box, 1982; Wong, Smith & Boon, 1998), though individuals may still become dependent.

Before using medicinal remedies, it might be worth trying the following strategies.

- Aim to get up and go to bed at a set time.
- Exercise can lead to increases in the deepest form of sleep (Loughborough Sleep Research Centre, 2006). Aim for a minimum of thirty minutes' exercise a day, but not in the evening.
- Cut down or cut out caffeine, cigarettes, alcohol, and street drugs.
- Avoid late-night eating and TV. Gentle soothing music can help people to unwind and get in the mood for sleep.
- Relaxation tapes, meditation, aromatherapy, The Alexander Technique, and other complementary therapies have been shown to reduce anxiety and encourage relaxation and sleep. (See Chapter Seven.)
- Count sheep—giving the mind an undemanding task prevents it slipping into worry mode.
- Stop daytime and evening catnaps and use the bed only for nightime sleeping.
- Try not to worry about not getting enough sleep. The traditional seven or eight hours a night is not essential to good health (Horne, 1998).

Smoking

Up to ninety per cent of people diagnosed with schizophrenia are smokers (Goff, Henderson, & Amico, 1992), nearly three times the rate in the general population (Hughes, Hatsukami, Mitchell, & Dahlgren, 1986). People with schizophrenia are heavy smokers—twenty-five or more cigarettes daily (Kelly & McCreadie, 2000) and more likely to smoke high-tar cigarettes—though low tar brands are very harmful too.

It is difficult to overestimate the health risks—heart disease, bronchitis, cancer, thrombosis, emphysema, and strokes are just some of the many. But the myth persists that at least smoking reduces stress. It is a fact that the nicotine in cigarettes stimulates the brain to release dopamine, which is associated with pleasurable feelings. But, once hooked, smokers need increasing amounts and feel stressed when the nicotine drops below a certain level in their bloodstream.

Cigarette smoke also contains cancer-causing polyaromatic hydrocarbons that can affect the metabolism and efficacy of antipsychotics, lowering the blood levels of some drugs by up to fifty per cent (Edward & Lyon, 1999). Consequently, some smokers need to use significantly higher doses of medication to manage their symptoms (Goff, Henderson, & Amico, 1992) The antipsychotics most likely to be affected by smoking are Clozapine, Olanzapine, fluphenazine, haloperidol and chlorpromazine.

Despite being counterintuitive, there is also research evidence that people who use medication that blocks dopamine derive more enjoyment and become more addicted to nicotine than other smokers (Laviolette & van der Kooy, 2003), although one study (Kelly & McCreadie, 2000) found that ninety per cent of people with schizophrenia had taken up smoking before they became ill.

The nicotine in cigarettes might lessen the side-effects of some neuroleptics, in particular tremors, muscle rigidity, involuntary muscle movements, and twitching (Kelly, 1998). But smokers are invariably financially worse off than non-smokers (McCreadie & Kelly, 2000). They also experience more akathisia (Goff, Henderson, & Amico, 1992), and since the newer drugs often produce fewer such side-effects and the health hazards of smoking are so severe, it seems worth trying to give up.

Stop smoking tips

- Consider the reasons why any previous attempts have failed and aim to overcome the difficulties.
- Don't be disheartened by past failure. Invariably people make several attempts before finally giving up.
- Set a relatively stress-free day to stop smoking rather than just trying to cut down.
- It is not unusual to feel temporarily depressed, but involve your GP or psychiatrist and he or she may be able to prescribe supportive medication.

- Giving up may affect antipsychotic medication needs, which is another reason for keeping a GP or psychiatrist informed.
- Nicotine replacement therapy comes in patches, chewing gum, microtabs tabs (tablets which dissolve in the mouth), nasal sprays and inhalators (plastic cigarettes which contain nicotine capsules). These all can lessen withdrawal symptoms—which may be confused with an increase in the symptoms associated with schizophrenia.
- Self-help groups or cognitive behaviour therapy encourage people to think of themselves as non-smokers. In the same way, getting rid of items connected with smoking, such as lighters and ashtrays, can be helpful.
- Be wary of therapists who advertise hypnosis or acupuncture as a cure for smoking. While some people find them helpful, there is no scientific evidence to support such claims.
- Many people have found meditation, relaxation exercises, and chewing sugar-free gum helps them to reduce the stress of giving up.
- Concentrate on the pros, rather than the cons of quitting, such as the health and financial benefits.
- Don't let your diagnosis—or any other health problems—be an excuse for not trying to give up.
- Remember the anti-smoking motto: don't give up trying to give up! Over eleven million people in the UK have succeeded. The NHS Smoking Helpline helps people take the first step (Tel: 0800 169 0 169, daily from 7. 00 a.m.–11.00 p.m.), as does the charity Quitline (Tel: 0800 00 22 00, daily from 9.00 a.m.–9.00 p.m.).

Exercise

Exercise helps lower blood pressure and cholesterol levels and so lessens the risk of heart disease and strokes. It can also help combat the weight gain associated with some antipsychotics. As mentioned, the Mind survey, *Exercise Your Mind* (2001a) found that a high percentage of people who exercised felt it lifted their mood and reduced stress. Fifty-seven per cent reported that exercise improved their motivation, fifty per cent their self-esteem, and twenty-four per cent their social skills.

It is important to note that anyone who has not exercised for some time and/or is overweight, or has any physical health problems, should check with their GP before taking up an exercise programme.

Whatever type of exercise is chosen, running, swimming, cycling, aerobics, belly dancing, or yoga, the experts advise building up slowly. Even individuals pronounced sufficiently fit by their GP may get breathless at first and feel their heart pounding. But this is normal and need not be a reason to stop. As little as five minutes exercise a day, gradually increased to ten, fifteen, and twenty minute sessions over a fortnight or so is recommended, until someone feels ready to do thirty minutes five times a week, which is the recommended minimum for maintaining fitness, though just ten minutes of exercise is sufficient to lift the spirits and increase energy (Hansen, Stevens, & Coast, 2001).

Walking

This is one of the easiest and cheapest ways to stay fit. Walking does not require special equipment or gym fees and can be done anytime and anywhere. A brisk one-hour walk four times a week could enable someone to lose up to 1½ lbs a week. (The exercise is equally effective if taken in ten or fifteen minute chunks.) William says he feels fitter and has lost weight since he started walking regularly.

> I do a few stretching exercises and press-ups in the morning, but when I started getting overweight I didn't want to ignore it. I began trying to get out and about more and thought I'd start walking regularly. I go to Sainsbury's almost every day and just by walking the twenty minutes there and back I've lost almost half a stone in five months. I feel much better for it and that's without making any changes to what I eat.

Alternating walking with a minute or so of jogging will further boost circulation and increase stamina. Anyone who enjoys walking might want to join others for town or countryside rambles. The Rambling Association can advise on local groups. Swimming, cycling, dancing—and any exercise which makes you feel warm and out of breath—are excellent for increasing flexibility, muscle tone, and stress relief.

Exercises that build bone, such as weight or load-bearing exercise, may help to prevent low bone density. This is a risk-factor for osteoporosis and a side-effect for men using prolactin-increasing atypicals—but not for women (Hummer et al., 2005). Muscle tone exercise includes weight-lifting, jogging, hiking, stair climbing, step aerobics, dancing, and racquet sports.

Exercise that is enjoyable and can be incorporated easily into a daily routine or carried out with a companion helps maintain motivation. Consistently using the stairs instead of the lift, for instance. Walking instead of taking the bus for short hops, or getting off a few stops short of your destination can become a healthy habit. Using a pedometer can be an added incentive to break previous records—a realistic goal might be 10,000 steps a day.

Try to be aware of opportunities and new interests that will get you moving rather than sitting still and becoming sluggish. *Effortless Exercise*, by Caroline M. Shreeve (2003), has ideas on how to become accustomed to regular exercise—gradually, safely, and enjoyably.

Naturally, there will be times when someone feels too ill to exercise or needs to take a break, but it is worth getting back into the routine as soon as possible.

Housing

Everyone wants somewhere decent to live. Social workers or care coordinators can liaise on people's behalf with the local authority or independent housing organizations to help them find a home in which they feel secure and comfortable.

Appropriate accommodation often helps people to recover and to stay well. For instance, supported and sheltered accommodation has been linked to fewer crises and hospitalizations (Brown, Ridgway, Anthony, & Rogers, 1991; Burek, Toprac, & Olsen, 1996), a reduction in symptoms (Dixon, Krauss, Myers, & Lehman, 1994), and increased confidence, coping skills, and feelings of self-worth (Parkinson & Nelson, 2003). Before leaving hospital, people may be offered the chance to live for a time in a halfway house, with individuals who have experienced similar mental health problems.

Halfway house

These houses or hostels aim to combine supported and independent living. They provide people with the chance to re-learn taking care of themselves and decide which sort of living arrangement best suits them. Everybody has their own room, with access to a shared sitting room, bathroom, and kitchen. Residents are able to come and go as they please and are expected to shop and cook for themselves. Generally, there is a caretaker/support worker living on the premises to provide practical help. Residents also have regular visits from their care coordinator and, possibly, others from the mental health team.

Supported housing

This accommodation gives people a high level of support and at least one study indicates that it is linked to "stable mental health" (Parkinson & Nelson, 2003). Residents have a room of their own and are encouraged to cook for themselves. Their day-to-day needs, such as laundry and cleaning, are taken care of, with the cost deducted from their benefits. There are regular group activities, outings, and holidays.

Local authorities and charities, such as Making Space and the Richmond Fellowship, have supported housing schemes. The Scottish Association for Mental Health and Rethink can also give advice on supported and sheltered housing.

Sheltered housing

This typically comprises self-contained flats in an individual block or large house. Residents live independently, but there are communal facilities, such as a laundry, lounge, and games room, and a variety of community activities. Support is provided by on-site managers and a twenty-four-hour careline service. A systematic review of supported housing schemes (Chilvers, Macdonald, & Hayes, 2006) reported that they might increase the chances of someone becoming dependent on professional help and "prolonging exclusion from the community", but at the same time such housing could provide a "safe haven" for those in need of stability and support. This was Philip's experience.

Philip's story—"A place of my own"

Living in the care home was a good experience. Before that I'd been in a bedsitter and wasn't too happy. I'm a bit of a loner, but there I felt lonely and isolated which you can easily do with this illness. At the home run by the charity Making Space there were people to talk to and I could go to my room if I needed to be on my own. The facilities were good and absolutely everything was provided out of my benefit, right down to my shaving soap and razor blades.

The home also organized holidays and outings and during a trip to the Lake District I met Sheila. We hit it off straightaway and began a relationship. By then I'd lived in the home for six years and had begun to feel trapped by the rules and regulations. Little things maybe, but like when I woke early and wanted to go outside for a breath of fresh air it meant waiting for the doors to be opened at 7.30—and at night, having to be in by a set time.

I'd just turned 60 and thought it was time I lived in the community. I got a flat with a housing trust. I have more space and it's sheltered accommodation so there's a warden and a cord by the door to pull in case of emergencies. A friend I made in the home lives nearby and so does Sheila. Love blossomed between us and we obtained flats just minutes apart. We have our problems, but look out for each other and are living in the community very well.

My life is very different now. I feel more independent and I'm happy about that. I buy what I can afford and come and go as I please. Living in the home was good for me. It gave me a breathing space to work out a lot of things in my life and after that I was ready to move on.

Stigma and self-esteem

People with mental health problems often say that the misunderstanding, prejudice, and isolation they experience is far worse than their symptoms, whereas greater understanding and awareness of mental health issues by society, including among mental health professionals, helps them feel supported (Faulkner & Layzell, 2000).

A Mind survey, *Counting the Cost* (2000) reported that seventy-three per cent of people with mental health problems felt that unfair, unbalanced, or very negative media coverage adversely affected their mental health. It also seems to affect public perception of mental illness. For instance, Thornton and Wahl (1996) found that simply reading a newspaper reporting a violent crime committed by a person with mental illness increased the participants' negative attitudes towards people with such problems.

Understandably, the sense of being stigmatized reduces people's self-esteem and self-confidence (Link et al., 1991, 1997). Believing that more needs to be done to tackle stigma and discrimination, The National Institute for Mental Health set up Shift, an initiative to monitor and review how the media treats mental health issues. The ultimate aim is to end stigmatizing portrayals. Meanwhile, people can read and discuss the Shift's "media alerts" on positive and negative coverage by email through the website: www.shift.org.uk.

The charity Mind has long campaigned against negative media coverage and makes an annual award to the journalist who has reported most responsibly and sensitively on mental health issues. They also believe it important that people complain about stigmatizing coverage. As well as Shift, complaints can be made directly to the publication or programme maker, via Ofcom (which replaced the Broadcasting Standards Commission), the Advertising Standards Authority, or The Press Complaints Commission.

A survey on stigma and discrimination, *Pull Yourself Together!* (The Mental Health Foundation, 2000a), recommended that the media should recognize their social reponsibility to portray positive real life stories and encourage inclusion rather than exclusion. Seven years on, however, stigmatizing language and negative portrayals of people with mental illness remain common. Marie thinks there is little hope of changing public perception of schizophrenia while this continues.

> Since getting involved with Rethink I feel less stigmatized by my illness. Close friends know about it and two have even become Rethink members to help with campaigning. But I still draw the line at telling my next-door neighbour, though I know if mental illness was more accepted in society I wouldn't have a problem.

> Some people, like my mum and dad, think there's no point talking about this, but I don't know how else public opinion is going to change—and it's got to. It's wrong to continually portray people

with schizophrenia in a bad light. We need more positive images, but also a change in the language that's allowed to be used. Why is it okay for someone with mental illness to be described as a looney, a headcase or a nutter when it's against the law to use stigmatizing language about people with other disabilities? If things are ever going to improve for people with schizophrenia, it's got to stop.

A month-long pilot campaign by Rethink to raise public awareness of the discrimination faced by people with mental health problems in 2006 in Norwich reported positive results. After the campaign thirty per cent of people said they had experienced a mental health problem, compared to the pre-campaign figure of fifteen per cent.

Before the campaign, forty per cent of people agreed strongly that they wouldn't want anyone to know they had a mental health problem. This decreased to twenty-two per cent. Fewer people held strong views that people with mental illness are often dangerous after the campaign (twenty-one per cent compared to thirty-three per cent) and should not be allowed to do important jobs (fourteen per cent compared to twenty-four per cent). Rethink plans further antistigma campaigns.

It is not surprising that people with schizophrenia commonly worry about being viewed unfavourably and avoid being open about their diagnosis (Dickerson, Sommerville, Origoni, Ringel, & Parente, 2002). But self-support groups and advocacy organizations may enable them to cope better with stigma (Dickerson, 1998; Frese, 1998). For Rachel, attending a Hearing Voices Group was a turning point in her recovery.

> The buzz I got from my first voices group was amazing—for the first time in a long time I didn't feel alone or crazy. Knowing that there were other people in a similar position to me was worth a thousand therapy sessions: it gave me back some confidence.

Some people's recovery involves a refusal to be stigmatized by their diagnosis. This may be linked to their regaining an active sense of themselves (Tooth, Kalyanasundaram, Glover, & Momedzadah, 2003). A refusal to be ashamed of their illness may also enhance individuals' self-esteem and enable them to be more resilient in the face of stigma (Dickerson, Sommerville, Origoni, Ringel, & Parente, 2002). This is Carole's approach.

Carole's story—"Why should I be ashamed?"

> Basically, I do not bother about what other people think of me. It is my opinion of myself that matters, though it's taken me a long while to get to that way of thinking. Schizophrenia destroys your ego, you have to find it again to get well. Previously, I never told anyone what I had. When I got ill I'd explain it as a breakdown which I thought was more socially acceptable.

> But five years ago my mother was killed in a terrible accident—my father was dead—and then my brother died from a heart attack. I was very ill and I sort of said, quite frankly: "Why should I be ashamed of this illness?"

> About this time the SANE newsletter was asking for personal experiences and I wrote mine. They published it and I agreed to be a spokesperson for their work, which I still am. I have had numerous contacts with the media but one issue that consistently pops up is schizophrenia and violence. Madness and murder make riveting press, but also a damaging and inaccurate picture of the mentally ill. We are not all unpredictable and dangerous. In fact, mentally ill people living in the community are more than twice as likely to be victims of violence.

Self-esteem

While it is a relief to some, for other individuals a diagnosis of schizophrenia is a serious blow to their self-esteem, as Charles recalls.

> When I learned that one in 100 people had schizophrenia and I was that one, it was a terrible blow to my self-esteem. I thought it was unfair and bad luck. It was hard to get over it, especially because it would probably mean I'd be excluded from employment. I was very depressed for a time and felt that I was worthless. What helped my self-esteem was setting myself realistic goals and achieving them, like getting an IT qualification and later a university diploma in computer programming.

Few people find studying easy and obviously it is more difficult if someone is also trying to cope with their symptoms and, possibly, the debilitating side-effects of medication. Under the Disability Discrimination Act (DDA), however, students are entitled to support from educational institutions. This may involve a person having access to study aids or being assigned a support tutor. Before committing to a course of study it is worth asking what support is available and making known any specific needs. Charles says he received good support from the Open University.

> I did my computer programming course part-time, which was just as well because it was very difficult to concentrate until the evening when the effects of the previous night's medication had worn off. Even then I couldn't do more than a couple of hours at a stretch, but with an understanding tutor and a few extensions I completed all my assignments and got good marks.

> Probably I'd have found sitting in a large examination hall very stressful, but the DDA meant that I was able to sit the exam at home under supervision. I was also allowed several short breaks. It took a lot of determination and willpower to complete the course, but I managed it and passed the exam with a very good grade.

Personal successes may boost someone's self-esteem. At the same time, it may lead to it being dependent on what a person can acquire, achieve, or prove, so that anyone unable to compete in this sort of status game may feel demoralized, or useless. Better then, it has been argued, to love, respect, and value ourselves simply because we are who we are. To view ourselves with *unconditional positive regard*, as the psychologist Carl Rogers put it. Turning that message into a positive self-affirmation, such as: "I like you unconditionally"; "I love you unconditionally"; "You are worthy of respect", may help to reinforce the message. This is Alistair's philosophy.

Alistair's story—"Learning to be kind to myself"

> I was first admitted to a psychiatric hospital in 1998 when I was forty-seven years old in a "florid psychotic state". During my psychosis I had visual and auditory hallucinations, flight of ideas,

paranoid delusions concerning the "star people", who I thought ruled the earth and controlled humans to their advantage, delusions of grandeur, thought broadcasting, depersonalization, tremendous elation and finally catatonia.

After about a fortnight I'd recovered my thought processes sufficiently and wondered whether to inform people/friends of where I'd been for so long. I live in a small community and an absence of a month or longer would be quite noticeable. After much thought I decided that I would tell the truth. If anyone had a problem with my having a mental illness then that was their problem, not mine.

Although I didn't realize it, this was the first step towards acceptance of my Self. My mental illness was the catalyst that made me evaluate my life, but it didn't happen overnight. Following the first admission to hospital I began a very difficult period; I was very unstable and also suicidal—on three occasions only just surviving a determined attempt to take my life. At that time I had thought my life was finished and underwent a lengthy period of bereavement for the person that I had once been.

As I was no longer working I had time to think. At first I found it so difficult to marshal my thoughts due to lack of concentration and even now, seven years later, I can only do one thing at a time—the days of multi-tasking are long gone. But gradually I began to realize that even though I had a mental illness and was economically inactive I was not totally useless, and felt somehow that I could contribute to society in some way. Obviously, I had recovered some of my self-esteem and I came to realize the importance of being kind to myself and would urge others to do the same.

Accept yourself as you are unconditionally—you are not perfect and neither is anyone else in this world. Love yourself unconditionally. When you have a quiet moment or are in bed at night, or look in the mirror, in your mind tell yourself that you love yourself. Do this regularly. Approve of yourself unconditionally—you are unique. Recognize your strengths and achievements. Don't be critical and judgmental of yourself—be kind, and whenever possible give yourself a treat.

Considerable clinical evidence suggests that creating and maintaining self-acceptance helps people to counteract negative or unkind messages and encourages healthy feelings of self-worth and confidence.

Self-acceptance exercise

- Stand tall or sit upright in front of a mirror. Make eye contact with your reflection.
- Look deep into your eyes and repeat your chosen affirmation at least ten times. Don't be deterred by feelings of embarrassment. In time you *will* feel more positive about yourself.
- Use any opportunity to boost your efforts, such as when you catch sight of your reflection in a bus or shop window. Again, however shy or silly you might feel at first, regular practice, several times a day, will fix the self-acceptance message.

Positive Thinking by Susan Quilliam (2003) includes ideas on developing an optimistic and self-confident outlook.

Sheila finds affirmations enable her to overcome setbacks, though she doesn't always choose to adopt a positive approach.

> There can be a lot of pressure from some people, like social workers, for you to stay positive all the time. It can get stressful, particularly when you start putting the same pressure on yourself. But you can accept yourself without always being positive. Though I aim to stay positive, sometimes I find it's better just to go with the flow and not strive to be upbeat.

Tony shares Sheila's opinion that positive thinking should be an option and not an obligation.

> With this illness you have to think positively or most days you'd never get out of bed in the morning. But it's not possible to be optimistic all the time and I don't always want to be. Why shouldn't you let yourself feel down or depressed over things. If you get miserable—and everyone does—I don't think you should blame yourself or force yourself to be cheerful.

Findings from a life-long study of over 1,200 people (Martin et al., 2002) support Tony and Sheila's view. While acknowledging the value of a positive outlook when faced with a short-term crisis, it cautions that a constant striving to maintain high levels of cheerfulness is stressful and potentially unhealthy.

Sex

Sexual enjoyment contributes to people's sense of well-being and sex within a loving relationship may be many people's ideal. However, this is not always easy to achieve—and nor does everyone want an intimate committed relationship. For whatever reason, people without a sexual partner often find that magazines and videos help them express their sexuality, as can sex aids, which are available through the internet, sex shops or mail order catalogues. The Sexware range from The Family Planning Association includes vibrators, vaginas, erection aids, sexual accessories and books. *Guide to Getting It On!* (Joannides, 2001)) is frank and very informative on sexual practices and problems.

Despite numerous public health initiatives, the incidents of sexually transmitted infections (STIs) and unwanted pregnancies in the UK continues to rise. To ensure sexual health it is obviously necessary for people to follow the well-established guidelines.

Guidelines for sexual health and enjoyment

- Don't have sex with any one you don't want to.
- Don't participate in any form of sexual activity you don't want to.
- Use contraception to prevent an unplanned pregnancy.
- Minimize the risk of getting or spreading an STI (sexually transmitted infection) by using a condom. (STIs are usually spread by infected semen, vaginal fluid, or blood. HIV and hepatitis B and C can also be contracted through infected blood, for instance when needles and other drug equipment are shared.)
- Use "extra strong" condoms for anal sex. Whether "extra-strong" or "standard", if a condom displays either a British Kitemark or a European CE mark, it has been tested to the highest standards and, if used properly, will offer the best protection possible. Most importantly, to prevent the condom splitting, use plenty of water-based lubricant, such as KY jelly or liquid—never oil-based products like body lotion, which will damage the condom.

- Protection is also important during oral sex. Use a condom or place a dental dam (a latex square barrier) over a woman's genital area.
- Immediately check out any symptoms that might indicate an STI. Sexual health clinics give free confidential advice and treatment.
- BPAS (British Pregnancy Advisory Service) is a charity offering information, counselling, treatment and a range of services linked with contraception, including vasectomy, sterilization and unwanted pregnancy. (See Useful addresses/resources.)
- Take advantage of free health checks such as cervical smear tests and prostate screening. Examine your body regularly and consult a GP about any changes, like lumps in the breast or under the arms, and swelling in the groin.

The Sexual Health Helpline provides information on HIV, Aids and other sexual health problems. Tel: 0800 567 123 (24 hours, daily).

The Sex and Disability Helpline gives free sexual advice to people who have social, physical, and/or mental health problems. Tel: 0707 499 3527 (11.00 a.m.–7.00 p.m., Mon–Fri). Website: www.outsiders.org.uk.

It is not unusual for people's sexual attitudes, feelings, and preferences to change over time, which may cause sexual or relationship difficulties. Discussing these with a therapist may help. The British Association of Sexual and Relationship Therapy (BASRT) and Relate have details of qualified sexual and relationship therapists.

Contingency plans

People with schizophrenia may find that their symptoms unexpectedly worsen, so a contingency plan seems a sensible idea. This could involve increasing medication, making lifestyle adjustments, drawing more on family or friends for support, or using professional help. A swift response to early signs of illness often lessens the risk of a serious relapse or re-hospitalization.

In addition to such a plan, Mind advises people to set out an advance statement about their medical care—for example, the medication or treatment they would want to refuse.

The charity also wants advance statements to be taken into account by medical professionals and mental health tribunals—and for these statements to be acknowledged in any reforms to England's existing Mental Health Act. At present, people detained in hospital under the 1983 act are unable to refuse treatment, such as ECT. NICE (2002b) are in favour of "advance directives" which respect patients' treatment preferences being developed and documented.

During a period of illness, it may be too difficult for for someone to adequately manage their personal and financial affairs. The Court of Protection is a judicial body responsible for assisting people in such a situation and, if necessary, will decide how their property and financial affairs should be managed. The Public Guardianship Office deals with the administration of the Court of Protection and can give advice and information.

Summary

Improving health and fitness will inevitably require lifestyle changes, such as stress management, eating a balanced diet, taking regular exercise and tackling damaging habits like smoking and alcohol and substance abuse. Good housing and a supportive environment have a positive effect on psychological health. Depression is a common problem, but effective strategies are available. Developing self-acceptance and a positive attitude can help combat prejudice and the ignorance of mental health difficulties that have a demoralizing and damaging effect on people's confidence and recovery. Antistigma campaigns may be effective, but there needs to be a greater determination to confront these issues. This could include action to end irresponsible media coverage of people with a diagnosis of schizophrenia, as part of a government-led antidiscrimination policy.

Useful addresses/resources

Rosemary Conley classes. Tel: 1509 620222; website www.rosemary-conley.co.uk

Slimming World classes. Tel: 02773 521111; postal membership: 0870 330 7755.

Weight Watchers classes and postal course. Tel: 0845 712 3000. Online club: www.weightwatchers.co.uk

The Brain Bio Centre is an outpatient clinical treatment centre specializing in the "optimum nutrition" approach to mental health problems. The clinic is at the Institute for Optimum Nutrition (ION), Avalon House, 72 Mortlake Road, Richmond, Surrey, TW9 2JY. Tel: 0208 332 9600; Website: www.mentalhealthproject.com

Richmond Fellowship provides supported housing with a range of staffing levels, nursing homes for people with mental health problems, community support, services for people living in independent accommodation, and day/resource centres. Head Office/ General Enquiries, 80 Holloway Road, London N7 8JG. Tel: 020 7697 3300; Fax: 020 7697 3301; website: www.richmondfellowship. org.uk

The Richmond Fellowship Scotland, Head Office, 26 Park Circus, Glasgow G3 6AP. Tel: 0141 353 4050; Fax: 0141 353 4060; email: info@trfs.org.uk; website: www.trfs.org.uk

Making Space has residential care homes, supported housing, day centres, befrienders schemes and family support workers who work alongside families and support carers in the north of England. 46, Allen Street, Warrington, Cheshire, WA2 7JB. Tel: 01925571680; Fax: 0192 5231402; website: www.makingspace.co.uk

Rethink Northern Ireland can give information on supported accomodation in the region. Tel: 01232 402323.

Scottish Association for Mental Health, Cumbra House, 15 Carlton Court, Glasgow G5 9JP. Tel: 0141 568 7000.

The Ramblers Association, 2nd Floor, Camelford House, 87–90 Albert Embankment, London SE1 7TW. Tel: 0207 339 8500; email: ramblers@london.ramblers.org.uk; website: www.ramblers.org.uk Concession rates for people with disabilities.

Alcohol Advice Drinkline provides confidential information on treatments. Tel: 800 917 8282 (Tues–Thurs 9.00 a.m.–11.00 p.m. and from Friday 9.00 a.m.–Monday 11.00p.m.). Alcohol Concern's website, www.alcoholconcern.org.uk, also has useful information and lists support groups. AA (Alcoholics Anonymous) groups help people to get and stay sober and should be listed in the telephone directory.

Depression Alliance. Tel: 0207 633 0557; Fax: 0207 633 0559; email: information@depressionalliance.org; website: www.depressionalliance.org. Information on depression is available on the website: www.dipex.org, which also has interviews with people who experience depression and their coping strategies.

Voices Forum Local Groups Information. Tel: 0208 547 9226 (at Rethink); website: www.voicesforum.org.uk

The Press Complaints Commission, 1 Salisbury Square, London, EC4Y 8JB. Helpline: 0845 600 2757; email: complaints@pcc.org.uk. Scottish Helpline: 0131 220 6652; Welsh Helpline: 029 2039 5570; 24-hour Advice Line: 07659 152656 (for emergency use only); website: www.pcc.org.uk

Advertising Standards Authority, Mid City Place, 71 High Holborn, London WC1V 6QT. Tel: 0207 492 2222; Fax: 0207 242 3696. Text-phone (for people who are deaf or hard of hearing): 0207 242 8159. Online complaints form at www.asa.org.uk

Ofcom, Riverside House, 2a Southwark Bridge Road, London SE1 9HA. Tel: 0207 981 3000; Fax: 0207 981 3333. Textphone: 0207 981 3043. Complaints/Advice Line: 0207 981 3040. Website: www.ofcom.org.uk

British Pregnancy Advisory Service (BPAS), 4th Floor, Amec House, Timothy's Bridge Road, Stratford-upon-Avon, Warwickshire, CV37 9BF. Tel: 0870 365 5050 (Mon–Fri 8.00 a.m.–9.00 p.m, Sat 8.30 a.m.–6.00 p.m., Sun 9.30 a.m.–2.30 p.m.), 24-hour Helpline: 0800 247 1122; Actionline to make appointments 0845 730 4030. For Ireland and abroad: 0044 121 450 7700; email: info@bpas.org; website: www.bpas.org

Sexware. Tel: 0870 444 5116; email: sales@fpsales.co.uk website: www.fpsales.co.uk. A free copy of Sexware's self-help booklet, "Enhancing your Sex Life", is available from F. P. Sales, Mail Order Dept., PO Box 883, Oxford OX4 5NT.

British Association for Sexual and Relationship Therapy, PO Box 13686, London, SW20 9ZH. Tel/Fax: 0208 543 2707; email: info@ basrt.org.uk; website: www.basrt.org.uk

Relate, Herbert Gray College, Little Church Street, Rugby CV21 3AP. Tel: 0845 456 1310; website: www.relate.org.uk

The Public Guardianship Office offers advice and information on financial and property issues. Tel: 0845 330 2900 (Mon–Fri, 9.00 a.m.–6.00 p.m.); Fax: 0207 664 7705; email: custserv@guardianship. gov.uk; website: www.guardianship.gov.uk

CHAPTER SIX

Employment—paid and voluntary

Eighty-five per cent of people with a long-term mental illness are unemployed (Mental Health Foundation, 2002) and in the UK they have the highest unemployment rate of any group of people with a disability. A national Healthcare Commission survey (2006) found that only half the people who requested help from their community mental health services in finding a job received it.

Yet work can be a valuable coping mechanism for people, and provide a sense of purpose and value (Mental Health Foundation, 2000b) and returning to work after an absence due to illness may be a confirmation to someone that they have recovered.

In Graham's experience, work also often helps people's recovery.

> I needed a reason to get out of the house and not sit in a corner all day and listen to the constant voices. I needed a reason to move on and work gave me that reason. It was just a minor admin role, but it helped me recover.

Graham coordinates a mental health users' employment service. He believes that the mental health field can be an ideal setting for people to use their personal experience to help others and encourage them to take a positive attitude towards their mental health.

> It may be hard for some people to accept that they have a mental health problem. They prefer to keep it quiet and not be reminded of it. But it's not something you signed a contract for—or anything to be ashamed of.

He has also found that an eagerness to be employed, almost at any cost, sometimes leads individuals to make unrealistic job choices. To help them adopt a considered, self-protective approach, Graham compiled the following guidelines.

Working well guidelines

- Am I ready to commit to regular paid employment? Or do I need more training and/or a longer period of recuperation?
- Is this the right sort of job for me or am I so desperate to get into employment that I'm setting myself up for failure?
- It is standard practice for a care plan to cease when people get a job. What other support networks will I have in place before I start work?
- Not everyone in the mental health field is supportive. Do I know where I can get help should I feel under pressure, or unfairly treated?
- It may be hard, but not disclosing mental health problems perpetuates the myth that it is something to be ashamed of. Instead of being embarrassed, consider how you can use your experience in a positive way to help yourself and, hopefully, others.

Good workplace support has been found to have a protective effect on mental health. It may help people avoid work-related stress, which contributes to the growing incidents of depression and anxiety (Health and Safety Executive, 1988). Yet another reason for individuals to be open about their mental health problem, or any other disability, is that they are then protected under the Disability Discrimination Act.

Disability Discrimination Act (DDA) and employment

Under the DDA the employment selection procedure must not treat someone less favourably on the grounds of disability. This covers three areas:

- *The selection procedure and offering employment*
  This covers the advertisement of a job, the interview, selection procedure, and terms of employment. Employers are expected to consider what skills a job requires, rather than what sort of person might fit the job, as well as how the job and working conditions might reasonably be made to suit someone with a disability. For instance, allowing regular time off for someone to receive supportive counselling or see their psychiatrist.
- *Considering people for promotion, dismissal or redundancy*
  The DDA states that people's chances of promotion, transfer, training, or other benefits should not be less than other workers, or that their requests for these be unfairly refused. Nor, when it comes to dismissal or redundancy, should someone be treated less fairly than other workers.
- *Obligation to make changes*
  The Act also includes an "obligation to make changes". This requires employers to make reasonable adjustments when a physical feature of their premises occupied by the employer or any arrangements made by, or on behalf of the employer, put a person with a disability at a disadvantage. (The lower the cost and inconvenience of the adjustment in relation to the employer's resources and the more practicable the adaptation, the more likely it is to be reasonable.)

The Disability Rights Commission (DRC) has an information helpline. The Rethink website has more information on the DDA. (See "Useful addresses/resources" section at the end of the chapter.)

Learning from psychosis

Jan takes a positive attitude towards her mental health history and her experience of psychosis has formed the basis of the workshops she runs with her business partner, Sybil.

Sybil and I met when we were both psychiatric patients in hospital. Our workshops, "Learning from Psychosis", are individually tailored either for people who are living with mental health problems, or healthcare professionals and organizations. We use visual presentations and discussions to help people appreciate their skills as well as their problems. We also emphasize the importance of clear communication if people are to have their needs and wants met—and get the best from the services and healthcare professionals.

The workshops also give professionals an opportunity to explore what it might be like to experience mental health problems themselves—to be on the receiving end of services—as well as the value of adopting a positive attitude.

We both know that people can learn from their experiences, can recover, and can move on with their lives. We want to instil hope in mental health workers, so that they can get across the message—that a diagnosis of schizophrenia is not the end of the world.

The trainers at the Moving On project, based at Mind in Birmingham, have a similar aim. Their recovery training groups try to match service users with mental health professionals, who often have personal experience of mental health issues, to create greater mutual understanding and, ultimately, more appropriate and inclusive mental health services.

Ways into work

The New Deal for Disabled People (NDDP) is a government initiative to help people with a disability to enter, or re-enter, employment. Depending on their skills and needs, individuals are offered a range of work-related options. These include training, work experience, work trials, help with job applications and interviews, or self-employment. Personal "job brokers" offer support which extends for the first six months of employment. People on the NDDP can continue with other Jobcentre Plus programmes and services, such as Work-based Learning, provided they meet the eligibility criteria.

Worries about being financially worse off in work may have put some people off seeking employment in the past, but with the

NDDP individuals can continue to receive benefits. These include incapacity benefit, severe disablement allowance, a disability premium, in addition to income support, housing benefit or council tax benefit, disability living allowance, unemployability supplement, or national insurance credits for incapacity for work.

However, people must not do more than sixteen hours paid work a week or be receiving jobseeker's allowance. Further information is available from The NDDP Helpline (0800 137 177, textphone 0800 435 550), a person's local Jobcentre Plus and the website: www.jobbrokerssearch.gov.uk.

Getting back into employment

One way back into employment is through work placements. After ten years out of the workplace, six months ago Simon began a voluntary placement with The Sheffield Care Trust, which helps people return to work.

Simon's story—"I'm glad I took the plunge"

The prospect was fairly daunting. But the utter futility, the lack of structure you feel when you've no work spurred me on and got me over my reservations. Besides, it's the total opposite of the commercial environment I'd known before I got ill. The office atmosphere is calm and quiet and not pushy. The work's five hours, two days a week and not that demanding—opening the post, typing, doing mail shots, replacing and ordering stock.

Recently, the trust has offered me a paid job with longer hours. I've to give them my CV so the job will be tailored to fit my skills—not me trying to fit it. I thought: Am I ready for another challenge? And I think I am. I'm looking forward to having more responsibility.

After my first episode of illness, the early intervention service picked me up and I met others who'd had similar experiences of being sectioned. Some people have no expectations but to be permanently on benefits. That was depressing. There are only so many outings you can go on before you begin to think there must be more to life than this.

When I hit the big 40 last year I thought, I've got to start moving. What probably brought it to a head was the news that the government plan to get people on disability benefit back to work. Rather than being pushed into an environment I wasn't comfortable with I decided to make the move myself. My CPN had given me the number of the care trust's voluntary training officer about two years earlier, so I gave him a ring and he got me this job in the chief exec's office.

Even though it's only two days a week it's brought a structure to my life and also it's made me a bit more hopeful about the future, which is something you need. I was gobsmacked to be offered a paid job after six months. The day-to-day experience of working at the trust is that it's too easy, that someone is going to come along and say you've been doing it wrong all along. But that's me being self-critical, I think. One of the line managers in charge of service user involvement seems to be really positive about how I'm doing and I think that's rubbed off on me.

I have the choice of eighteen or twenty-seven hours a week. Either way I'm looking forward to a fuller workload. Depending on the hours, I may combine the job with a college course. I'm going to arrange an interview with work and pensions to see how it'll affect my benefits.

I don't think work's made a difference to other parts of my life. I tend to be a bit up and down. When I'm not working I spend a lot of time in bed. At the moment I tend to have plans in my head, more than I practically fulfil them—or go out and try to accomplish them. But even though it's undemanding, having a job helps me get up in the morning. I get most out of actually being there. If the work's sparse I don't want to knock off early—even when my line manager tells me I can.

The best part has been having to talk to people and then doing it unconsciously. That interpersonal thing is important. I can talk more easily to people now. I went in thinking, how can I communicate with anyone. I've got all this baggage and that puts you on the back foot. But conversations don't work on the basis of where have you been the last ten years? Really, I was just being over-sensitive, a lack of confidence, perhaps—or just the willingness to say hello and get on with it. I'm glad I took the plunge. Even the times when you don't feel like doing it and think, "Oh, no, I can't be bothered today", once you get in there you're glad. You come home and you're glad you've done it.

Marie's story—"Not ready for the scrap heap yet!"

I've always worked and I suppose I feel there's something missing from my life if I don't have a job. So when arthritis meant I had to give up caring for dogs it wasn't long before I was looking for another job. Before that I spent eighteen years with the Civil Service so office work was a realistic option, though after five years away I knew my skills needed polishing up. I decided to apply to Rethink to do voluntary work. I'd become a member soon after I was diagnosed nearly twenty years ago and have been working two days a week in their Belfast office for about a year. I'm also a committee member for Rethink Northern Ireland. This involves attending quarterly meetings. The members include other service users and we all give our input on budget and policy issues.

My aim is to have part-time employment. I'd do full-time, but my parents are elderly and need lots of support. My arthritis can make walking painful and I'm deaf in one ear so I could quite easily sit at home. But I'm only forty-four and not ready for the scrap heap yet!

The Rethink office is small and friendly. I do the post, keep records up to date, photocopying, just run of the mill stuff, but coming back to the workplace makes me feel that even with this illness I can hold it together. I hope that's how employers will see me when I apply for jobs. Yes, I have a mental illness, but I'm just the same as everybody else. I just want to be given a chance.

Of course, I realize that despite the Disability Discrimination Act there is still prejudice, so I'll be looking for jobs with mental health charities or organizations, like Rethink. Work gives me a sense of fulfilment and I feel lucky that I'm able to do it. Some people I know aren't so fortunate. They wouldn't be able to hold down a job because they're on such heavy medication or have other problems, like not being able to concentrate. I still get paranoia—just ask my husband! But my symptoms are mild compared to many others. People with schizophrenia aren't all the same—we're individuals.

Richard's story—"Somehow I persuaded the psychiatrist to let me out for interviews"

Acting was my first job and I was playing a madman when I became ill. Fortunately, we were still in rehearsals so the audience was spared the experience. That was in the 1960s. Between 1960 and 1970 I was locked up nine times and in some very rough old places. But I've always wanted to earn my living and while in hospital I'd go through the job ads and then somehow I persuaded the psychiatrist to let me out for interviews. One job I got in a furniture shop [and] I commuted from the hospital every day for quite a while.

When going for jobs I've always been honest about my diagnosis. At the furniture shop interview I told the boss, "I've been mentally ill, but I'm now recovered and happy to take any test you like." She replied, "Don't worry, we're all barmy here." I stayed for three years until the business closed down.

Even though I've been honest, I think it's a good idea to play down your mental health problems. If you go into too much detail it can be a terrible shock to some people. As you get to know them better you can tell them more—if you want. But in my experience you then come in for some ribbing.

Also, if you're asked specific questions it's best to answer truthfully. Nowadays, everyone knows about mental illness and can talk about it. In the 1960s they weren't just ignorant, they hated any mention of it. So things have improved.

After the furniture shop, I was a computer operator with BT for ten years and left with a pension. But I've never completely given up the stage. Apart from acting in lots of amateur productions, I devised a one-man magic show. I'm officially retired, but enjoy taking it to residential homes and the like. I don't want to stop working completely—at least not yet. For me it's never been just to keep a roof over my head, important though that is. It's about being part of the working world—and having my independence. I've always valued that.

Changes to Incapacity Benefit

At the time of writing, the government has announced that Incapacity Benefit (IB) is to be replaced by a new benefit: Employment and Support Allowance. This is both for people who wish to return to work or undertake training to enable them to find employment, and those individuals who are assessed as too severely incapacitated to work.

It is anticipated that the new benefit will be fully implemented by 2008. The new benefit will only apply to new claimants. However, there are likely to be some changes to IB for those already receiving this benefit.

Permitted work

Permitted work enables people to do up to four hours a week paid work without affecting their benefits. (See Appendix I for more details.) Liz P says that permitted work gave her the confidence to return to full time employment and has been important in her recovery.

Liz's story—"Coping with the job further increased my self-esteem"

Permitted work was a very positive experience and enabled me to change my life. Previously, I'd become very ill and was sacked from my job, but encouraged by my CPN I started voluntary work, which included working for an advocacy project and the Citizens Advice Bureau.

That helped me gain confidence. With my interest in mental health issues, a friend suggested that I consider doing research, but I didn't think anyone would consider me capable. Then I heard of a local community evaluation project, started doing voluntary work with them, and was then offered a job. I was involved in interviewing people about their views on user involvement in mental health services. I really enjoyed it, though it was quite stressful going back into work and having a lot of responsibility and just as the project ended I got ill again. At that point I felt depressed and quite worthless. I'd already been sacked from two jobs and now my attempt to do another job had again ended in illness. I knew that would be on my record and wondered if I'd ever get another job.

Work has always been very important to me, not only to have economic independence, but for the sense of purpose it gives me. Also voluntary work still left me with quite a lot of time on my hands and as I have a problem with alcohol that's when I can start drinking too much.

Then a friend told me that our local Mind branch wanted to pay someone to visit drop-ins and libraries on their behalf and I arranged to do it as permitted work. This meant I could work four hours a week on top of income support and get paid £20. It was a step beyond voluntary work, but not too many hours and when people asked what I did, as often they do, I could say I worked for Mind. I think there is a status attached to paid employment— though I'm not saying that's right—and having a responsible role I felt more valued.

Mind provided regular supervision and getting positive feedback that I was coping with the job further increased my self-esteem and sense of self-worth. I felt I was getting my life in order and began looking to the future with more hope, especially knowing that I could apply for jobs on the basis of a reference from Mind. Because I was representing them I also became more conscious of how I looked, not so much dressing up, but being clean and tidy. If I'd just been at home on my own I knew I'd be less motivated to take care of myself in that way—and possibly be less in control of my drinking.

I think the only negative aspect was that previously I'd been quite socially isolated and felt quite shy and lacking in social skills when I met new people. And I did become anxious about my ability to do the job as well as I thought I should be able to. My CPN suggested I speak to my supervisor at Mind about my concerns, but I didn't want to show any vulnerability. I was worried they'd think I wasn't capable of doing the job.

In retrospect, that wasn't the best decision as I'm sure my supervisor would have provided me with support and encouragement, which so it proved when I saw a job advertised for someone with personal experience of psychosis to develop user-led research. It seemed an ideal job for me and my supervisor couldn't have been more encouraging, even going over the application with me. He explained that permitted work was aimed to help people go on and get further employment.

The research I helped carry out on recovery showed that a key issue is feeling better about yourself and understanding yourself more and that resonates with my experiences. Empowerment was another key theme identified in recovery, and I think experience of mental health problems and mental health services can be very disempowering, so for us service users to look at self-empowerment strategies is essential to our recovery.

What our research also revealed is that there is no one way of recovery. It is a unique journey. Different things will be important to different people and each person has their own ways of progressing their recovery. Our different life experiences affect our sense of self-esteem and our sense of personal power, so we have different ways of rebuilding it.

My recovery is an ongoing and uneven process, but there have been turning points and milestones. Getting permitted work, and then my current user-led research post were definitely milestones for me. Not only is research into recovery from psychosis an area I'm very, very interested in, but there's been no stigma attached to my experience of psychosis. Quite the reverse, I've been accepted and valued.

(Liz Pitt and her research colleague Martina's findings were published in the journal *Mental Health Practice* (April 2006).)

Work and training advice

Rethink (Northern Ireland) and the National Schizophrenia Fellowship (Scotland) provide flexible employment training.

Richmond Fellowship offer career advice, vocational rehabilitation and training, work experience and support into employment.

Mindful Employer is an initiative aimed at increasing awareness of mental health at work. By providing support for businesses in recruiting and retaining staff, it's hoped that more people with mental health issues will be able to gain employment and stay well in the workplace. Website: www.mindfulemployer.net

A Survivor's Guide to Working in Mental Health Services and *A Guide to Surviving Working Life* are two useful publications from Mind. The latter can also be read on the Mind website.

Volunteering

Not every one is able to cope with the demands of paid employment, but, of course, that doesn't necessarily mean they're incapable of working. Most charities would probably grind to a halt were it not for their volunteers, who help run their shops and assist with administrative tasks and community projects. Rarely is experience required to help with gardening, DIY, woodworking, or cooking.

Respondents to Mind's 2001 *Roads to Recovery* survey rated volunteering as one of the most popular ways of staying well, possibly because people can enjoy some of the positive aspects of employment, such as companionship and a sense of achievement, without having to cope with workplace stress.

Learning such skills may be a stepping-stone into paid employment, but even if that's not an aim, volunteering can be fun, or at least a break from a person's usual routine. That's been Alistair's experience.

> I first became involved in volunteering through helping a physically disabled person to use computer software. Since then I've become a community rep with a social inclusion partnership, representing a self-help group for people with mental health problems. Making the initial commitment was a bit scary, but I made it clear that I wouldn't do anything to undermine my mental health and that if I became unwell I'd stop.
>
> I've never been put under pressure, and having to keep a commitment has widened my horizons, enabling me to see beyond myself and my personal problems. I think I've stumbled on a universal law, which is that when you help others, in some strange way you also help yourself. There are several types of economy and the "financial economy" of employment and investment is only one. I am part of the "social economy" and that knowledge has boosted my self esteem.

Alistair's experience that volunteering benefits the volunteer is supported by a survey of others with mental health problems (National Centre for Volunteering, 2003). Specifically, they found it gave structure, direction, and meaning to their life, widened their social networks, improved their vocational and interpersonal skills, and helped them to gain access to employment, although some respondents did not want another paid job because they felt employment had made their mental health worse.

These views were also echoed in a survey on workplace practices (The Mental Health Foundation, 2002). Nearly two thirds of the respondents believed that unrealistic workloads or pressure at work had caused or worsened their mental health. One of the report's recommendations is that mental health awareness training should be part of the school curriculum, so that future employers and colleagues have a better understanding of such problems and will, therefore, be able to look after their own mental well-being.

Voluntary work is advertised in the local press, libraries, and community centres. There is a voluntary work website: www.do-it.org.uk. For the over-50s, at www.experiencecorps.co.uk; or call 0207 921 0565.

Volunteering England offers opportunities throughout the UK. This includes supported volunteering for individuals with any sort of disability. Freephone 0800 028 3304 (9.30 a.m.–5.30 p.m., Mon–Fri).

Summary

Paid employment may improve someone's quality of life and self-esteem and there's probably never been more support and encouragement for people with mental health problems to find work, through voluntary placements, permitted work, or government initiatives. However, despite the Disability Discrimination Act, individuals may experience prejudice in the job market and a lack of ongoing support in the workplace. The mental health field and organizations committed to "mindful", inclusive policies possibly offer greater support and opportunities, but ultimately people need to consider the benefits or otherwise of paid employment and its possible effect on their recovery. For some individuals, volunteering is a more realistic and rewarding option.

Useful addresses/resources

Disability Rights Commission, Freepost, MID 02164, Stratford-upon-Avon CV 37 9BR. Tel: 08457 622 633; Fax: 04457 778 878; Textphone: 0457 622 644. (8.00 a.m.–8.00 p.m., Mon–Fri); website: www.drc-gt.org

Learning from Psychosis Workshops, 156 Odessa Road, Forest Gate, London E7 9DU. Tel: 0208 519 4062; Mobile: 07921 085 162; email through the website: www.learningfrompsychosis.com

Moving On (based at Mind, Birmingham), 17 Graham Street, Hockley, Birmingham B1 3JR. Tel: 0121 608 8001; email: info@mind-birmingham.co.uk; website: www.mindbirmingham.co.uk

Volunteering England (London) Regents Wharf, 8 All Saints Street, London N1 9RL. Volunteering England (Birmingham), New Oxford House, 16 Waterloo Street, Birmingham B2 5UG. Tel: (London & Birmingham) 0845 305 6979; Fax: 0121 633 4043; email: volunteering@volunteeringengland.org. Freephone 0800 028 3304.

CHAPTER SEVEN

Complementary therapies

Complementary therapies are not a substitute for orthodox Western treatments, but may be used to support and complement them. In 1997, a survey *Knowing Our Own Minds* (The Mental Health Foundation) of 401 UK-wide mental health service users reported that, while only a few respondents had experienced alternative or complementary therapies, those who had found that they benefited their mental health. Also, a high proportion of those who had not received such therapies were keen to be given the chance to try them.

A 2002 survey among members of the Schizophrenia Association of Great Britain (SAGB) revealed a similar story, with overwhelming support for a more holistic approach to treatment and for complementary therapies to be used as well as orthodox medicine. In the same year, a survey by Mind, *My Choice*, reported that over half the users of mental health services wanted more complementary therapies. More recently, a survey among readers of *Perceptions* magazine (2005) indicated that they wanted mental health professionals to provide more information on complementary therapies.

There is an increasing use of complementary therapies within the NHS (Adams, 1995) and some clinical trials have been conducted (Hattan, King, & Griffiths, 2002; Hewitt, 1992; Passant, 1990; Stevenson, 1992; Trevelyan, 1996). Complementary therapies are available in some of the five NHS homoeopathic hospitals, but at the time of writing there are no plans to incorporate these therapies fully into the NHS. However, GP surgeries and mental health units often provide some on the NHS, as do aftercare programmes, drop-in and day centres.

Although not an alternative to orthodox medical treatment, complementary therapies may help people manage the side-effects of medication, relieve stress and anxiety and, by treating physical ailments, improve their overall health and sense of well-being. This is confirmed by research evidence. Studies also suggest that the benefits may partly derive from people having the sense that by choosing to use a complementary therapy *they* are in charge of their health—rather than healthcare professionals (Astin, 1998; Downer et al., 1994; Oh, 1994).

Evidence for complementary therapies

Research evidence tends to be published mainly in scientific journals and may be available at Medlineplus www.medlineplus.gov, which is an offshoot of Medline (the world's largest database of medical research papers).

The Cochrane website publishes "plain language" summaries and the full text of their systematic reviews of scientific studies of complementary and orthodox treatments. These reviews are regularly checked and updated as necessary at: www.cochrane.org.

More specifically, the Cochrane Schizophrenia Group reviews research studies of orthodox and complementary treatments with people who have a diagnosis of schizophrenia. These are also available on the Cochrane website.

Reuters Health eLine and Healthwatch websites have healthcare news and features on conventional and complementary medicine. At: www.reutershealth.com and www.healthwatch-uk.org

There are scientifically based reviews of complementary and alternative medicine and treatments at: www.inteliheath.com

Townsend Letter for Doctors & Patients is an American magazine that publishes research and clinical findings on complementary and alternative medicine. Tel: 360.385.6021; Fax: 360.385.0699; email: info@townsendletter.com; website: www.townsendletter.com

Of the dozens of recognized therapies, the following are among the most widely available, have registered practitioners, and, to some degree, can be practised independently of a therapist in a person's own home.

The Alexander Technique

The Technique is named after its originator, a nineteenth century Australian actor, Frederick Mathias Alexander. It is not a therapy, Alexander insisted, but a simple method whereby individuals learn, or more accurately, relearn, to use their body easily, efficiently, and without undue stress or strain, the way they did as young children. Crucial to this is for people to "free" or "release" their necks, since habitual tensing and tightening of the neck interferes with people's natural good "use of the self", as Alexander called it.

In addition to encouraging people to free their necks, Alexander teachers use their hands to guide the person through simple movements and positions, such as sitting, walking, and bending the knees, which are basic to all activity.

Anecdotal evidence indicates that the Alexander Technique (AT) is an effective treatment for a wide range of conditions associated with tension or poor posture, like repetitive strain injury, back, neck, and shoulder pain, as well as stress and anxiety. Though a gentle, non-manipulative treatment, teachers suggest that people check with their GP before taking lessons. These are not recommended during the first three months of pregnancy.

Clinical evidence indicates that a high proportion of people have AT lessons for back and limb pain. A single case study of a woman with lower back pain (Cacciatore, Horak, & Henry, 2005) reported a lessening of pain and improvements in posture. At the time of writing, a national study on the Technique and back pain is being undertaken by Southampton University.

Austin and Ausubel (1992) reported "enhanced ease of breathing" among healthy adults who had AT lessons. A study of people with Parkinson's Disease found a reduction in depression and improved management of their disability (Stallibrass, 1997). These positive effects were reported in a follow-up study (Stallibrass, Sissons, & Chalmers, 2002), in addition to improved self-attitude.

Improved self-attitude is a common anecdotal finding among people who have had lessons. In addition to physical benefits, people often report feeling "lighter" and more confident. This has been Sharon's experience. "I always feel better afterwards. I'm relaxed, confident and as if all the bits of me have been put back together—almost as if I'm walking on air."

Norman wrote to *Voices* (December, 1994) about the benefit he derived from the technique. This is an extract from his letter.

> I am diagnosed as schizophrenic and I suffer from paranoia and have panic attacks when I'm ill . . . I came across a therapy called the Alexander Technique and after a number of lessons, which were very expensive, I found I was coping better, and had some control over the panic attacks if I wished. Even though I was not able to afford an adequate number of lessons, I was able to come off my medication for nearly six months, whereas before I usually only lasted one month. I am unsure of any decent research which may have been done on this technique and am therefore unsure about recommending it solely on my experience, but it worked for me.

A lesson lasts about 30–45 minutes. Teachers charge from around £30, though group lessons of about twelve people at further education institutes cost much less. For a nominal charge, people can become a "body" at a training school. This involves being "worked on" by a number of senior students, under the supervision of a qualified teacher.

STAT (The Society for Teachers of the Alexander Technique) provides information on teachers and schools. *The Alexander Technique* by Glyn Macdonald (Dorling Kindersley) has photographs which give a clear idea of what happens during a lesson. The physical and mental benefits of the Technique are described in *The Alexander Principle* by Wilfred Barlow (Gollancz), who was the first doctor to train as an Alexander teacher.

Lying down

Between lessons AT teachers suggest that their "pupils" lie down for 15–20 minutes once or twice a day, on the floor—not a bed or sofa—away from draughts with three or four slim paperbacks beneath their head. The head should be in line with the shoulders, not tilted back. Nor should the chin be dropping on to the chest. The knees are bent in a semi-supine position and the arms are bent, at right angles to the body, with the fingers touching just below the solar plexus.

The idea of lying down is to enable the spine's vertebrae to "plump up" with spinal fluid, which helps the back to regain its natural length and springiness, while the muscles in the body are in a better position to release tension.

In accordance with Alexander principles, lying down is also an opportunity for the person to think about allowing their neck to be free, so that their head can release naturally away from the neck and for their whole torso to lengthen and widen. This, it is said, further helps the body to release accummulated tension, break bad postural habits, and relearn its inherent good co-ordination.

While there is no scientific evidence, numerous clinical accounts suggest that lying down has a calming and rejuvenating effect on the mind and body and relieves neck, back and limb pain and insomnia.

Aromatherapy

The use of concentrated, "essential" oils from aromatic flowers, plants, trees, and the rinds of fruits, to treat emotional and physical problems pre-dates civilization (Walters, 1998). The sense of smell is strongly linked to the emotions, through the olfactory nerves, and aromatherapists claim that the scent of certain essences can energize, calm, and comfort. Torii and colleagues (1988) found that stimulating oils, such as jasmine, increased the amplitude of brain waves, as when a person is alert and concentrating, but that brain waves slowed when participants were exposed to lavender and other sedating fragrances.

When massaged into the skin in a "carrier oil", like vegetable or almond, essences quickly enter the blood stream and are circulated to all parts of the body. A clinical study with hospital patients reported that compared to ordinary massage, aromatherapy massage produced a marked lessening of pain, wakefulness, and high blood pressure (Hewitt, 1992).

It seems, therefore, that the oils themselves are an important factor in the effectiveness of aromatherapy. A study by Buckle (1993), referred to by Jan Wallcraft in her report for The Mental Health Foundation on complementary therapies *Healing Minds* (1998, p. 59), found that hospital patients who were massaged with a hybrid lavender (*lavandula burnatii*) experienced twice as much relief from anxiety as those who had been massaged with *lavandula angustifolia*, which is generally thought to be more therapeutic, though participants in both groups reported similar positive effects on their mood and coping ability. These positive experiences were confirmed by physiological measurements and Buckle suggested that aromatherapy might be considered as an alternative to the usual anti-anxiety drugs.

This is what happened at the Oxford Nursing Development Unit. A study (Sanderson & Ruddle, 1992) reported that some of the patients found aromatherapy massage with lavender and marjoram an effective alternative to the sedative temazepam.

A single case study (Crinon, Van Wersch, & Van Schaik, 2004) reported increased levels of vitality, happiness, and "peace" for a woman with multiple sclerosis after a course of aromatherapy treatments. These also decreased her feelings of fatigue, depression, and anxiety. Compared to a placebo, lavender oil administered in an aroma stream, was moderately effective in reducing agitated behaviour in patients with severe dementia (Holmes et al., 2002).

A systematic review of six studies of aromatherapy (Cooke & Ernst, 2000), however, concluded that despite having a mild and temporary effect on anxiety, this was probably not strong enough for aromatherapy to be considered as a treatment.

However, many people, like Rita, find aromatherapy helps them to relax.

> Often my husband Ray gives me a massage with lavender oil before I go to bed. It's so calming and soothing and helps me to sleep well. I use oils in the bath, especially lavender, and that's very relaxing too. When I feel low sometimes we'll burn some lavender or rose oil which gives me a lift.

A couple of drops of oil can be inhaled from a paper tissue or vaporized by adding a few drops to a small bowl of boiling water.

It is also claimed that an uplifting, calming, or energizing atmosphere is easily created with oils and an aromatherapy stone or burner. Liz P's experience of these effects was very positive.

I went to an aromatherapy relaxation class and that was very beneficial. We did exercises and the therapist had a machine which blew out the aromatherapy oils. At the end of it I felt transformed— relaxed and uplifted. It amazed me. I wouldn't have thought it possible to feel so different without taking a drug or alcohol. I've since moved, but I might make the journey back because the class was so good.

Traditional mood improvers

- Ylang ylang, from the flowers of the "perfume trees" of the Far East, is said to lift the spirits. Recommended as a tonic for the nervous system. Add four drops to a warm bath.
- Clary sage is another antidepressant with a history of medicinal use. Its euphoric effects are apparently best experienced in a massage or by vaporization.
- Jasmine has a heady aroma that encourages a sense of optimism.
- Clary sage and juniper, as well as juniper and basil, are recommended to allay feelings of paranoia and fear, though not as an alternative to antipsychotics.

The effect of being pampered may also contribute to the effect of aromatherapy. Clive wishes he could afford more regular sessions.

Of all the alternative remedies I've tried, I get the most benefit from aromatherapy. The massage is great because the drugs give me shoulder and neck tension. The smell of the oils really adds something. My aromatherapist is very nice. I trust her and that's important if you're going to be able to relax and get the most out of it. Afterwards I'm totally calm and a bit detached, but in a nice way. I try to hold on to that feeling for as long as I can. Knowing that I can feel like that makes me optimistic about the future.

Good quality oils, sold in dark glass bottles, to help protect them from deterioration, are widely available. Tisserand Aromatherapy also sells vaporizers and aromatherapy books and has a telephone advice clinic. The Aromatherapy Consortium and the International Federation of Aromatherapists can give details of aromatherapists and training schools. Aromatherapy treatments cost from around £35 upwards, depending on session length. *Aromatherapy: An Illustrated Guide* by Clare Walters (Element) is a well-presented and practical introduction to the therapy.

Bach flowers remedies

These are liquid remedies derived from the flowers of plants and trees and take their name from Dr Edward Bach (1886–1936), who devised this method of treatment. He believed that illness is caused by disharmony between the mind and body and the symptoms are a physical indicator of these negative emotional states. His research led him to conclude that some thirty-eight wild flowers contained properties able to remedy feelings such as bitterness, resentment, anxiety, and depression.

Chemical analysis of the remedies shows that benefits are likely to be due to a placebo effect. Bach's belief, however, was that though not a cure, the remedies could effect a balance in the mind, body, and spirit, because they had the power to elevate people's "vibrations". Carol is not sure whether she is convinced by Bach's theory, but she often uses the remedies.

> I have a bottle of Rescue Remedy in my bag and take a swig when I feel stressed. I've used lots of the others—vine, particularly, when I'm absolutely shattered. Mustard for depression and holly for my jealousy, which I get a lot. Holly mixed with willow is good because it treats the bitterness that goes with my jealousy.

There are numerous anecdotes about successful treatment with Bach flowers and some clinical findings (De Vries, 1985). Though scientific evidence is very limited, the department of Health Psychology at Plymouth University is currently researching the effects of flower essences.

Existing research appears to be confined to studies of anxiety. A review (2005) of fifteen such trials by Natural Standard concluded that many of the studies were poorly designed and the reported benefits were similar to those of a placebo.

Bach Flowers, however, seem to have no negative side-effects, except, perhaps, for someone with a plant or flower allergy, and can be taken safely in combination with medication. They do contain a small amount of alcohol as a preservative, and therefore are not suitable for people with an alcohol problem, or those taking medication for this, such as Antabuse.

Choosing a remedy

The following remedies are recommended. Several can be used in combination.

Deep despair—Sweet Chestnut
Overwhelmed by responsibility—Elm
Post-traumatic stress—Star of Bethlehem
Poor self-image and shame—Crab Apple
Guilt complex—Pine
Oversensitivity—Walnut
Unwanted thoughts and worrry—White Chestnut
Panic or fright—Rock Rose
Fear of losing control—Cherry Plum
Fear of the unknown—Aspen
Sudden depression—Mustard

The remedies are available from chemists and health food stores, or direct from The Bach Centre, which can also supply a list of qualified practitioners. Sven Sommer's *The Little Book of Bach Flower Remedies* (Vermillion) is a comprehensive introduction to their use.

Crystal healing

Crystals are pieces of rock composed of crystallized minerals. The ancient Egyptians used crystals in beauty treatments and for healing. Rose quartz, for instance, was thought to soften and smooth the skin, as well as absorb feelings of anguish and anxiety. Although there appears to be no scientific support for the idea, some people today also believe that crystals can have a positive effect on the emotions.

Nicholas began using crystals after reading about them in a spiritualist magazine over twenty years ago. He finds them especially good for relaxation.

> I don't always sleep well at night, but just resting with a rose, or snowy white crystal in my hand is enough for me to slip into a deep state of relaxation, even to drop off to sleep on occasions. I may use crystals while listening to a meditation tape. I'll imagine myself in a beautiful garden and I can feel the crystal getting warm in my hand and the energy travelling up my arm and into my body. It can be very calming and relaxing, and sometimes energizing at the same time.

The rose crystal is one of the most widely used by crystal healers, who may ask the person to hold one, or any number of other crystals, during the course of a session. Sometimes these are placed on, or around the person's body. Healers also 'dowse' with crystals, which, they claim, enables them to divine the client's true needs. Although many healers pride themselves on working from intuition, some have formal training.

The International Association of Crystal Healing Therapists gives details of qualified practitioners. Crystals are widely available from health food and specialist shops. Mysteries in London have a mail order service and aim to meet specific requests. Simon Lilly's *Illustrated Elements of Crystal Healing* (2002) is a beautifully illustrated guide.

Homoeopathy

Theoretically, homoeopathy is not complementary, but an alternative, to conventional medicine, though in practice it is often used in conjunction with orthodox treatments. It was developed by Samuel Hahnemann (1755–1843), a German chemist, who was strongly opposed to the bleeding and purging practices of his day. Through experimentation Hahnemann came up with his "like cures like" principle: a substance that produces symptoms in a healthy person can cure these symptoms when they appear as a sign of illness.

Hahnemann also claimed that the smaller the dose the greater its effectiveness. Homoeopathic medicines are derived from animal, mineral, or vegetable sources, but as the extracts are so diluted they are undetectable to the taste. Homoeopathy believes that it is quality rather than quantity that stimulates the body to heal itself and Hahnemann's theories are credited with forming the basis of current vaccination and allergy treatments. For instance, a minute amount of the polio virus stimulates the body to create the antibodies which give immunity to the disease.

A major review of studies of homoeopathy (Linde & Melchart, 1998) reported that though individualized homoeopathy had an effect over a placebo, no firm conclusions could be drawn since many of the research studies were poorly designed.

However, a systematic research review of over 100 studies (Kleijnen, Knipschild, & ter Riet, 1991), indicated positive results in eight out of ten scientific trials on its use for mental or psychological problems. Although the reviewers found that most trials did not meet rigorous scientific standards, they stated that overall the evidence for homoeopathy was mainly positive.

A Mental Health Foundation report *Complementary Therapies in Mental Health* (1999) observed that clinical evidence indicates that homoeopathy might be a helpful treatment for depression, panic attacks, anxiety, phobias, neurosis, obsessive thoughts, and schizophrenia.

For instance, in *Healing Minds* (1998, p. 40), Jan Wallcraft refers to a clinical case study by Reichenberg-Ullman and Ullman (1990), which reported the successful treatment of a patient with schizophrenia. Also in *Healing Minds* (*ibid.*, p. 39) Wallcraft refers to an interview with a homoeopath who claimed success in treating people with psychotic symptoms.

Nor is there a shortage of anecdotal and clinical evidence for homoeopathy's effectiveness with persistent, but relatively minor ailments, such as skin rashes, or fungal infections—and, unlike some herbal treatments, homoeopathic remedies do not interfere with prescribed medication.

The UK has five NHS homoeopathic hospitals and dozens of homoeopathic clinics, though the majority of these are private. Some GPs provide homoeopathic treatment either privately or within the NHS. GPs can refer people for outpatient treatment at a homoeopathic hospital. The British Homoeopathic Association provides a practitioners' directory.

Laughter

Galen, the Greek physician, who lived in the 2nd century AD, believed that people who laughed were less likely to become seriously ill than melancholic individuals. Laughter certainly lightens people's mood, and research suggests that it reduces the stress of traumatic situations (Gavrilovic et al., 2003), the perception of pain (Weisenberg, Raz, & Hener, 1998), increases tolerance to pain (Weisenberg, Tepper, & Schwarzwald, 1995), and aids recovery from heart surgery (Tan, Tan, Berk, Lukman, & Lukman, 1997).

Laughter also appears to strengthen the body's imune system, thus helping it to fight disease (Berk, Felten, Tan, Bittman, & Westengard, 2001). A study by Bennett, Zeller, Rosenberg, and McCann (2003) reported that participants who found a comedy film sufficiently funny to laugh out loud had significantly healthier immune systems afterwards than those who watched a tourism film.

The late American journalist Norman Cousins was probably one of the first people to try laughter therapy. In the 1960s, Cousins developed severe *ankylosing spondylitis*, a painful spinal condition, and had to give up his job. Having read about the effects of positive emotions on body chemistry, when hospital care and painkillers didn't improve his condition he moved into a hotel room—at a third of the cost—and began watching Marx Brothers and Candid Camera films.

In his own account, *Anatomy of an Illness as Perceived by the Patient* (1979), Cousins records that ten minutes' belly laughter gave him two hours of pain relief. He credited laughter—and vitamin C—for his recovering sufficiently to eventually return to full-time work.

Obviously it is not too difficult for someone to increase their daily laughter quota, with radio or television comedy programmes, funny films, and books. This was the approach used by Jon Williams, a regular contributor to *Voices* magazine. Below is an extract from his last article, published in the Summer, 2006 edition, shortly after his death.

The uses of humour and other coping strategies

> I used to hear a lot of derogatory voices—between sixteen and twenty on a bad day. But what I learnt was that humour was help-ful. Whenever my concentration was okay, I would read joke books and humorous stories. I'd listen to comedy on the radio and watch it on television—and I started to to make up some very bad jokes. What I found was that if I put a smile on somebody's face it would make me feel better. The negative voices always take advantage of when I am vulnerable. So the less vulnerable I am the easier my life is. For me there is nothing much better than being on a natural high laughing with other people. When I am with happy people and the whole place is alive with good spirit, I know the voices will not come. To be honest, I know this really annoys the critical voices.

There is more about Jon's use of humour in his pamphlet *Life*, avail-able from The Hearing Voices Network.

Even if someone finds that little amuses them, there are clubs where people can learn to laugh. First established in the USA by Dr Madan Kataria, there are now 5000 international Laughter Yoga Clubs. The idea is that by using gentle yoga breathing and simple laughter exercises, anyone can laugh in a group for 15–20 minutes, without needing to have a great sense of humour, a store of jokes, or a comedy routine. Membership is free, and though, at the time of writing, there are only three UK clubs, it is expected that more will follow. The website: www.laughteryoga.org has further infor-mation.

Massage

A good massage combines rhythm, pressure, continuity, and focused contact. It should resemble a melodious piece of music, with one stroke flowing into the next (Maxwell-Hudson, 2006).

There are different forms of massage. Reiki, for instance, is a comparatively gentle method, directed at "balancing body energy", whereas Swedish massage is more vigorous, associated with the treatment of sports injuries and to relieve tension and fatigue.

Considerable anecdotal evidence indicates that massage makes people feel better. Research with hospital patients has reported that

massage eases tension and promotes a sense of calmness and relaxation (Holmes, 1986; Turton, 1989). There is also clinical evidence
that massage can improve mental health, by reducing anxiety,
stress, and depression (Field et al., 1996).

Hilliard (1995), referred to in the Mental Health Foundation
report *Complementary Therapies in Mental Health*, also cites clinical
evidence that massage can reduce stress in people with mental ill
health, including schizophrenia, although in his opinion, massage
is not necessarily beneficial for all people who have serious mental
health problems.

Studies of the stress-reducing effect of massage summarized by
Cochran-Fritz (1993) attribute the benefits to dissipating the stress
hormones linked to the body's "fight or flight" mechanism. He
concluded that therapeutic massage might be used in combination
with drug treatments for stress, or, in the case of mild symptoms, to
replace them.

Guidelines

It is not unusual to feel twinges as tense muscles start to relax and
unknot, but at no time should someone find the massage painful.
Anyone with chronic muscular problems, phlebitis, thrombosis,
varicose veins, acute back pain, fever, or any lumps or swellings
should check with their GP before having a massage. Obviously,
fractures, bruises, and skin infections should not be massaged, nor
should women have a massage during the first three months of
pregnancy.

After being given a course of massages at a local complementary health centre, Liz P was keen to have them regularly.

> They did make me feel more relaxed. Also I'm very conscious of
> gaining a lot of weight on my medication. With the massage I felt
> a lot better about my body and in my body and that was very posi-
> tive and made me feel stronger about myself. But after ten
> massages that was the end of it, which I think was a shame because
> if you could have massage regularly it could be very helpful—well,
> certainly for me.

Standards and qualifications vary and people may advertise
massage as a cover for sexual services. In telephone directories

genuine practitioners are usually listed under therapists or aromatherapy. Massage schools will often refer someone to local graduates and there is the chance of a low cost massage with trainees, whereas professionals usually charge between £45 and £60 for a 1–1½ hour session. The British Massage Therapy Council (BMTC) can advise on therapists and training schools.

Learning to massage

Though most practitioners have completed a training course, the techniques are not difficult to learn from a book. One of the best is Clare Maxwell-Hudson's *Massage: The Ultimate Illustrated Guide* (1999). As a body is essential for practice it is an idea to find someone who would also like to learn.

Massaging others might sound like hard work, but a good massage need not take longer than fifteen minutes and, its practitioners claim, giving a massage can be as beneficial as receiving one. That's possibly because a good massage requires the masseur or masseuse to be relaxed and focused so that the energy flows between the giver and receiver.

Self massage

Massaging a tense neck or shoulders is almost automatic and regular head and foot massage may prevent the build-up of painful tension and ease stress. If the massage is to be followed by a bath or shower it may be worth using sesame oil, a traditional remedy for stress.

- Sit comfortably on a chair. Place the fingertips on the top of the head and breathe slowly for a few moments.
- With the fingertips gently massage the entire head for a couple of minutes.
- With the tips of the two index fingers massage the bone behind the rim of each ear in upward circular movements for a minute or so.
- Use the fingertips and upward circular movements to massage the entire lower half of the head—not the neck—for a minute or so. Gradually, continue the action upwards, to the crown of the head and downwards towards the temples for a further minute or two.

- Take another minute to gently massage each ear in turn with the thumb and tips of the index fingers. End by gently stroking the ear lobes.
- Using the pads of the fingers, gently massage the entire face with light upward circular strokes. Massage the back of the neck in the same way.
- Cover the face with both hands—or a damp, warm face flannel—resting them there for a minute or so.

The entire massage need not take longer than ten minutes.

Foot massage

In many parts of the world a daily foot massage is seen as essential for good health, with family members taking turns to massage each other's feet. A study of twenty-three "essentially healthy" people who received thirty minutes of Reiki touch foot massage, reported significantly reduced levels of stress and anxiety (Wardell & Engbretson, 2001), while twenty-five patients who received foot massage following cardiac surgery were significantly calmer than the control group or patients who received guided relaxation (Hattan, King, & Griffiths, 2002).

Feet do not need to be bare, but using body lotion or hand cream may make it more enjoyable. Massage each foot in turn, from ankle to toe, occasionally circling the ankle and gently stretch each toe. Even five minutes for each foot is sufficient to induce feelings of calm and relaxation.

Nature

Watching birds peck nuts from a garden feeder, sitting in the park on a sunny day, or simply gazing up at the stars at night can improve a person's health and well-being. Based on dozens of studies, Pretty, Griffin, Sellens, and Pretty (2003) found that contact with nature prevents illness and improves people's overall health, particularly if someone has been sick or mentally distressed.

While researching her book, *Madness in its Place: Narratives of Severalls Hospital, 1913–1997* (1998), the historian Diana Gittins discovered that many patients attributed improvements in their mental health partly to having access to spacious grounds and natural beauty, rather than to psychiatric treatment.

The health of many inmates of the Victorian-built asylums also benefited from being involved in the growing, harvesting, and preparing of their own food. By the twentieth century many were self-sufficient communities, with farm animals and workshops that were virtually run by the patients. There are numerous clinical accounts of when, in the 1960s, this "exploitation" ceased and the patients lives changed, some of them became severely distressed, their symptoms worsened, and some never recovered.

Many of these hospitals and their grounds have been converted into private housing. In the haste to effect care in the community, the policy makers may have missed an opportunity to establish a network of therapeutic communities in which people might have benefited from meaningful employment, companionship, and the healing power of nature.

Gardening

On a smaller scale, gardeners often mention the positive effects of spending time in close contact with nature, as well as seeing an end product from their efforts. A study of "horticulture therapy" (O'Reilly & Handforth, 1955) reported marked improvements in the symptoms and interactive behaviour of the participants of a psychiatric hospital gardening group—most of whom had a diagnosis of schizophrenia and were not being treated with antipsychotics.

Gardening can help people cope with mental health problems, provide a sense of purpose, enable them to meet new friends, and improve self-esteem and confidence, according to a report, *Strategies for Living* (The Mental Health Foundation, 2003). Communal gardening, in particular, has been found to maintain older people's health and mental well-being as it allows new friendships to flourish and provides "spaces" for people to discuss issues of common concern (Gatrell, 2004).

Similar positive experiences were reported by participants with mental ill health in a horticulture study (Sempik, Aldridge, & Becker, 2005). They especially valued eating and marketing their produce, extending their social network, making new and significant friendships, and the opportunities for self-reflection, relaxation, and restoration. In addition, the participants felt that they had gained in self-confidence and independence.

Timothy belongs to a gardening group.

> It's amazing, but once I start I forget my worries and become totally involved—planting bulbs and seeds, digging, weeding, pruning, mowing, raking leaves. It's hard work at times, makes you sweat sometimes. Every week, there's always something to do, even in bad weather, though I don't mind that. If it's very cold or wet we'll work in the greenhouse or maybe sort pots in the shed. But I'd rather be outside. The air's different in the garden. It feels fresher, makes you feel more at ease with yourself—we all say that.

Meditation

Meditation has links to Hindu philosophy and plays a central role in some other religions, particularly Buddhism. Religious centres hold group meditations that can last for an hour or more. But meditation is essentially a non-religious technique and setting aside 15–20 minutes twice a day, preferably morning and evening, or even just once a day, is sufficient to help quieten and relax the mind and body, and, over time, meditation seems to reduce the accumulated stress that commonly contributes to health problems. Cassette tapes with guided meditations can be relaxing and encourage sleep. Another option is to choose a simple meditation exercise like the one below.

- Choose a time and place when you're unlikely to be interrupted or disturbed by noise. Sit upright, but not stiffly, in a comfortable chair, close your eyes and relax. (Do not lie down unless you are ill in bed.)
- Begin to mentally repeat your mantra. A simple two-syllable "word", such as lah-lee is sufficient.
- Repeat the mantra mentally, not out loud, whenever it comes to mind. Inevitably your thoughts will wander, but it is not necessary to try to control them, as in some forms of meditation. But each time you remember the mantra, repeat it mentally.

- Continue to meditate for 15–20 minutes. (With practice, it is easy to judge when the time has elapsed, but until then it is not advised to set an alarm.)

New meditators are encouraged not to worry whether they are doing it "right", and to accept that any unexpected feelings, say of irritability, restlessness, or dropping off to sleep, are part of the "unwinding" process. Anecdotal evidence suggests that it is worth giving meditation at least a few weeks' trial. However, should unwanted feelings persist, it is recommended to meditate only three or four times a week, building up to more frequent sessions if wished.

One of the best known forms of meditation is TM (transcendental meditation), which was introduced to the West by the Maharishi Mahesh Yogi in the 1960s. Research with Vietnam veterans experiencing post traumatic stress disorder reported that TM reduced their levels of depression, anxiety, insomnia, alcohol consumption, and emotional numbness (Brooks & Scarano, 1985). A research review by Sharma (1996b) quotes several studies which link practising TM with improved mental health.

TM is not difficult to learn. The Maharishi course is not available in mainland Britain at the time of writing, but an alternative is The Transcendental Meditation Independent (UK) Association, founded by two TM teachers who were trained by the Maharishi. The association operates a sliding scale for fees, based on income.

Robert finds doing TM once a day helpful.

I have meditated for ten years nearly every day. It keeps me calm and stops me losing my temper with people. It gives me a peaceful feeling and a break from the stress I experience on a day-to-day basis because of my illness. I'd recommend others give meditation a try.

Prayer

Praying for someone to get better, or absent, intercessory, or distant healing, as it is also known, has been practised since time immemorial. It is not thought necessary to be a believer to benefit—or even for individuals to know that they are being prayed for.

Anecdotal evidence suggests that prayer can be healing, but exactly how is a mystery. The spiritualist Harry Edwards (1893–1976), co-founder of the National Federation of Spiritual Healers, was convinced that prayer could transmit healing energy, and groups of federation members regularly pray for people who request this form of healing, for themselves or others. Of course, it is not necessary for someone to belong to an organization in order to pray.

Healing does not necessarily mean a cure. But, it is claimed, the person prayed for often develops a more positive outlook and so feels better able to cope with their symptoms, which may lessen in intensity and frequency. A study (Walach, Reuter, Wiesendanger, & Werthmuller, 2000) reported an improved quality of life among chronically ill patients given distant healing, compared to those who were not.

A systematic review of studies of intercessory prayer (Roberts, Ahmed, & Hall, 2000) reported that there were too few completed trials to justify a conclusion of its possible value. They stated that if prayer is beneficial it may be beyond the power of any scientific enquiry to either prove or disprove. At the time of writing, the Cochrane Schizophrenia Group is undertaking a systematic review of intercessory prayer and expect the findings to be published in 2007.

Reflexology

Reflexologists view the soles of the feet as a map of the entire body and the reflex points on the feet and hands as corresponding to every muscle, nerve, organ, gland, and bone. Pressure applied to the bare feet, and sometimes the hands, is said to break up congestion and help the blood and the chi—the body's vital energy as it is known in Oriental medicine—to flow more freely. This, reflexologists claim, rebalances the body by stimulating under-active areas and calming over-active ones and can improve concentration and encourage a positive mental outlook.

Though people usually find reflexology relaxing and enjoyable, there is scant scientific evidence to support its claims to improve mental and physical health. However, a small study was carried out by the Asssociation of Reflexologists (1994) with patients in a psychiatric assessment ward. This reported a significant reduction in anxiety among those receiving reflexology, compared to those who had either been talked to or had received no treatment.

A foot reflexology study (Dong, 1996) with thirty-four people who had neurasthenia (anxiety, tiredness, and listlessness) reported a ninety-eight per cent effectiveness rate, but, since the research methods were not described, it is not possible to assess how rigorous they were.

The benefits of reflexology may result from being touched in a caring way, the so-called therapeutic touch, as reported in a study with cancer patients (Sims, 1986), or to the pressure from the reflexologist's thumbs and forefingers releasing endorphins, which may promote increased energy and a sense of well-being.

However, unpleasant feelings may also be experienced, including tiredness, dizziness, nausea—even the recurrence of an old health problem, such as a skin condition. These are considered to be signs of healing, but, obviously, if any persist a doctor should be consulted. Reflexology is unsuitable for anyone with diabetes, thrombosis-type problems of the lower limbs, or acute infections that could be worsened by increasing the circulation.

Sessions last between thirty and sixty minutes and usually cost between £35 and £60. The Association of Reflexologists can provide further information. *The Reflexology Handbook: A Complete Guide* by Laura Norman, Thomas Cowan and Thomas Conran (1989) is a good introduction to one of the most popular complementary therapies.

Shiatsu, or finger pressure

Shiatsu means finger pressure in Japanese, but in addition to the fingers practitioners may use their thumbs, hands, knee, elbow, or the soles of their feet, to apply pressure along the "meridians" and "acupoints" on the head, face, and body.

Like reflexology, shiatsu, also called acupressure, aims to rebalance chi, to maintain and improve health. It claims to be especially helpful for stress-related ailments, such as sleeping problems, anxiety, depression, and pain relief (Agarwal et al., 2005; Tsay, Cho, & Chen, 2004; Yip & Tse, 2004.

A session lasts 1–1½ hours and can cost anything from £35 upwards, though with a student at a training school it may be much less. The Shiatsu Society can give details of schools and registered practitioners.

Shiatsu training tends to be lengthy, but several techniques are easily learnt. For example, squeezing the web of skin hard between the thumb and forefinger is said to relieve pain, including headaches and period pains. There are other self-help strategies in *Shiatsu: The Complete Guide* (1999), an illustrated manual on theory and practice by Chris Jarmey and Gabriel Mojay.

Spiritual/psychic healing

Spiritual, or psychic, healers may give distant healing, but they are more likely to work face-to-face. This can involve touch, or be directed towards the person's aura, an area invisible to the majority of people that is said to surround the body. The colours and quality of the aura apparently indicate the presence of physical, mental, or emotional illness. By moving their hands around someone's body space, healers attempt to cleanse and heal the aura, and thereby the whole person. This may give rise to not unpleasant feelings of heat or cold.

Some churches have special healing services or meetings, for which there is generally no charge, but healers who advertise expect to be paid for their services. The National Federation of Spiritual Healers provides information on groups and absent healing, as does The College of Psychic Studies in London, which holds free healing sessions.

A large number of studies into various forms of healing have been carried out, mostly with hospital patients. In a systematic review, Astin, Harkness, and Ernst (2000) stated that much of the research failed to meet rigorous scientific standards. Even so, of the twenty-three studies reviewed that used prayer, visualization, laying on of hands, and non-contact therapeutic touch, fifty-seven per cent reported significant positive benefits.

These included faster healing rates, less use of medication and treatment support, less post-operative pain and anxiety, improved mood, and, in a group of people with AIDS, less new AIDS-related illness, severity of illness, doctors' visits and hospitalization. The other studies showed no treatment effect and one study, which might have been methodologically flawed, showed a negative effect (Miller, 1982).

No one with a diagnosis of schizophrenia participated in any of these studies, but people with chronic depression, anxiety, and stress made up more than half of the participants in a study of healing by Brown (1995) at a GP surgery, discussed in *Healing Minds* (1998, p. 50). Brown reported that healing resulted in significant and long-lasting improvements in people's emotional and social functioning. Of course, these improvements may have been coincidental, or because the healer gave them time and attention.

Another study of healing at a GP practice found that some of the chronically ill patients reported improvements in their health. However, soon after the healers joined the practice, the doctors, in addition to the usual medical treatment, began to give more time and attention to these patients (Jonas & Crawford, 2003).

Jacob has had regular healing for several years. He finds it helps him cope better with nervousness and anxiety.

I need to be on a lot of medication to control my voices, which makes me quite nervous and anxious. I was a bit reluctant to go to healing, but a woman friend persuaded me to give it a try. There's a circle of about ten healers. They're all nice and I like the atmosphere. While you wait you might have a chat with someone and you can have a cup of tea or coffee.

A healer touches your head and back. Or just cleanses your aura. Once or twice I've felt quite warm in some areas. But no miracles! Although I think I'm less nervy than when I started and I intend to continue going.

Spirituality

Though not usually regarded as a therapy, many people find religious practice is emotionally supportive, as David explains.

Spiritual life means everything to me. I'm Jewish and attend a syna-
gogue now and again. The rabbi, Colin, has become a good friend.
He visits me and we talk about spiritual concerns. After the disaster of mental illness, I have emerged to find meaning in my life
through spirituality. I find comfort and meaning in the psalms and
recite them in Hebrew. There are days when it's very difficult to get
through the business of living. Then I'll recite a Hebrew blessing
which, translated, begins: Blessed art though O lord, king of the
universe, who gives strength to the weary and faint-hearted. That
particular blessing gives me the spiritual strength to keep going.

Carole also finds that spirituality gives a structure and meaning
to her life.

I'm not an orthodox Roman Catholic, but I do believe there's a
power to which we return and I find that Catholic spirituality
works for me. I practise what's known as contemplative prayer. It's
about emptying your mind, letting thoughts go rather than hang-
ing on to them, which gives your mind a rest so that you find a
place of peace within yourself. That's very healing and I do it every
day for twenty to thirty minutes. It is spiritual too because I feel
closer to my parents and all the friends who've passed on and to
the power of God—the ultimate life force.

Although traditionally associated with practising a particular
religion, spirituality may, of course, encompass whatever belief or
take any form a person chooses. For Molly, it is connected with her
love of classical music.

Some classical music, especially music composed for the piano, is
so poignant and soothing. The only way I can describe it is that it's
like balm to my soul. It's healing and comforting and somehow lifts
me up and out of myself both at the same time.

A review of five studies with people who used spirituality as a
"coping strategy" showed that it may enhance self-empowerment
and lead people to find meaning and a purpose in their illness
(Baldacchino & Draper, 2001).

Mind's *Guide to Spiritual Practices* explores spirituality in relation
to mental well-being and has ideas on how people can discover and

express their individual spirituality. It can be bought or read free on the Mind website.

Traditional Chinese medicine

Traditional Chinese medicine (TCM) dates back over 5000 years, but present-day practitioners aim to combine ancient practices with the knowledge gained from modern scientific research (Xuan Ke, 2006). TCM claims that in contrast to western orthodox medicine, it treats the whole body and the individual person, not specific areas or diseases.

In the UK, acupuncture and herbal treatments are relatively well-known and increasingly popular, but TCM comprises five therapies, of which a doctor of TCM may prescribe one or more.

Acupuncture involves inserting very fine sterilized needles into the body's energy channels, known as meridians, to effect an energy circuit that is said to stimulate healing responses and restore the system's natural balance.

TCM uses acupuncture—often in addition to antipsychotic drugs—to treat mental health problems, including schizophrenia. On the basis of a limited number of clinical trials, a systematic review (Rathbone & Xia, 2005) found that a small number of studies did favour acupuncture when combined with antipsychotics, compared to the use of antipsychotics alone. However, the reviewers concluded that better designed and more comprehensive studies were needed to determine acupuncture's effects on the symptoms associated with schizophrenia.

There are over 8000 herbs and many thousands of prescriptions in TCM. Herbs are taken in teas, pills or powders, and sometimes creams. Herbal treatment is said to be effective for many common chronic conditions, including headaches and migraine, arthritis, skin problems, such as psoriasis, as well as asthma, hay-fever, allergies, and chronic fatigue or emotional problems.

A systematic review of TCM (Rathbone et al., 2005) reported that only one of of seven randomized controlled trials evaluated TCM for schizophrenia. The others evaluated Chinese herbs taken in combination with antipsychotics or antipsychotic drugs alone. The combination treatment seemed better tolerated by the participants, who were also significantly less constipated. The researchers concluded that, when taken with antipsychotics, herbal medicines might be beneficial.

Tuina is Chinese therapeutic massage, which uses finger pressure, stretching, and leverage to stimulate the energy channels and acupuncture points. Tuina massage is often used in conjunction with acupuncture for musculo-skeletal problems, like lower back pain, frozen shoulder, and slipped discs. It is also claimed to improve other problems, particularly of the digestion and insomnia.

Qigong combines meditation, breathing, and physical exercises to increase feelings of health and activate the body's "internal energy system". Taijiquan and Gongfu, the traditional Chinese martial arts, may also be recommended to promote dexterity, strength, and well-being.

Training in TCM is lengthy, but it is possible to learn the basics of the different therapies relatively quickly. Local newspapers and telephone directories have advertisements for TCM. But the practitioners are not necessarily qualified or licensed, like members of The British Acupuncture Council, The British Medical Acupuncture Society, or The Register of Traditional Chinese Herbal Medicine.

A session of acupuncture or herbal treatment can cost from about £40 to £60. Some teaching establishments give concessions with student practitioners. For example, the Asante Academy of Chinese Medicine in London is a teaching and research centre that offers a free consultation with senior trainees and charges a nominal fee per session thereafter.

Although TCM herbal remedies may not interfere with antipsychotic medication, it is obviously important that a practitioner knows what prescribed or non-prescribed drugs someone may be using. Also, the individual's GP or psychiatrist should be kept informed of any complementary or alternative remedies which are being taken.

Yoga

Possibly the most popular of all complementary therapies, yoga was first practised in India at least 6000 years ago. The word derives from the ancient Sanskrit for yoke, and is based on the Hindu philosophy that mind, body, and spirit are one—yoked together. According to the yoga sutras, or texts, a person should practise the postures, breathing techniques, relaxation, and meditation exercises. But the beauty of yoga is that simply practising the postures can promote relaxation and reduce stress. In the survey *Knowing Our Own Minds*, eighty-five per cent of the people who had tried yoga, exercise, or movement therapy had found it helpful.

Yoga is suitable for all ages and fitness levels, though it is sensible for people to check with their GP beforehand. Naturally, not everyone takes to yoga, but people who practise even the basic sitting, standing, and lying down positions for 10–15 minutes a day often report increased awareness and focus, feelings of calmness, confidence, and inner tranquillity. This has been Martin's experience.

> I'm definitely not as tense as before I took up yoga. I found it more relaxing than actual relaxation therapy! Learning to breathe properly was calming and helped me feel "together". I liked the unhurried pace. Taking time to breathe and change positions was good too.

> You can learn yoga positions from a book, but if you go to a class there's the instructor talking you through the positions and showing you the correct way to do them. That is very helpful.

Research evidence indicates that yoga is an effective treatment for a wide range of physical problems. It's been shown to improve handgrip, dexterity, strength, and pain levels in people with rheumatoid arthritis and osteoarthritis of the hands (Dash & Telles, 2001). People with carpal tunnel syndrome who practised yoga reported similar improvements, compared to those who had the usual wrist splints treatment (Garfinkel et al., 1998).

One study found that yoga improved the quantity and quality of cancer patients' sleep and reduced their use of sleep medication (Cohen et al., 2004). Vedanthan and colleagues (1998) reported that people with asthma who practised yoga tended to use their inhalers less and experienced a significant increase in positive attitude and relaxation.

A systematic review (Ramaratnam & Sridharan, 2002) concluded that a lack of well-designed studies made it impossible to draw any reliable conclusions on the possible benefit of yoga for people with epilepsy.

Yoga may improve mental health, according to a study with twenty-eight people, aged 18–29 with mild depression (Woolery, Myers, Sternlieb, & Zeltzer, 2004). Participants who attended a weekly class for five weeks, during which they performed postures designed to alleviate depression, reported significant decreases in symptoms of depression and anxiety. Following the yoga class they also experienced decreased levels of negativity and tiredness.

Of the numerous books on yoga, two in the Yoga for Living series, *Boost Energy* by Peter Falloon-Goodhew (2002) and *Relieve Stress* by Ruth Gilmore (2002), have easy-to-follow instructions and inspiring photographs, making them excellent for both beginners and more advanced students.

Even though it is possible to pick up the basics from a book or video, as Martin points out, a qualified teacher can help someone learn the positions correctly and safely. The British Wheel of Yoga has information on classes.

Choosing a complementary therapist

Some complementary therapies are more regulated than others and obviously it is sensible to check a practitioner's qualifications with the organizations involved in their training and registration and/or umbrella organizations, such as the Institute of Complementary Medicine.

Before booking an appointment it is also a good idea to consider—or ask the therapist—the following questions:

- Do I know the purpose of the therapy, what it is capable of treating and if there are any studies which support the claims?
- When and where was the therapist trained?
- How long was the course(s) s/he took?
- Was the course full or part-time?
- What certificates/diplomas was s/he awarded?
- Is s/he a member of the professional organization?
- Does s/he hold any other qualifications?
- How long has s/he been in practice?

- Does s/he have professional indemnity insurance? (Against injury resulting from the therapy.)
- Does s/he have public liability insurance? (Cover in case I have an accident while on the premises.)

Summary

Complementary therapies might help people with a diagnosis of schizophrenia to manage their symptoms and the side-effects of medication, and reduce stress, anxiety, and depression. By alleviating physical problems they might also improve people's general health and quality of life. Some of the benefits may relate to the therapies being treatments individuals choose for themselves and believe will be helpful. However, their availability within the NHS is patchy at best, particularly for some of the most popular "touch" therapies, and regular treatment with private practitioners is likely to be beyond the means of most people.

Useful addresses/resources

The Institute for Complementary Medicine (ICM) provides information and administers the British Register of Complementary Practitioners (BRCP), which is a register of professional, competent practitioners all of whom have been assessed individually. Contact the ICM at PO Box 194, London SE16 7QZ. Tel: 0207 237 5165; Fax: 0207 237 5175; email: info@i-c-m.org.uk; website: www.i-c-m.org.uk

The Society of Teachers of the Alexander Technique, 1st Floor, Linton House, 39–51 Highgate Road, London NW5 1RS. Tel: 020 7284 3338; Fax: 020 7482 5435; email: office@stat.org.uk; website www:stat.org.uk

Aromatherapy Consortium, PO Box 6522, Desborough, Kettering, Northants, NN14 2YX. Tel/Fax: 0870 7743477; email: info@aromatherapy-regulation.org.uk; Mon–Fri 10.00 a.m.–2.00 p.m.; website: www.aromatherapy-regulation.org.uk

International Federation of Aromatherapists, email: office@ifaroma.org; website: www.ifaroma.org

Tisserand Aromatherapy Products Ltd, Newtown Road, Hove, Sussex, BN3 7BA. Tel: 01273 325666. Full-time telephone clinic answers queries. Email: info@tisserand.com; website: www. tisserand.com

Bach Flowers, The Bach Centre, Mount Vernon, Bakers Lane, Sotwell, Oxfordshire, OX10 OPZ. Tel: 01491 834678; e-mail: mail@ bachcentre.com; website: www.bachcentre.com

International Association of Crystal Healing Therapists, IACHT, PO Box 344, Manchester M60 2EZ. Tel: 01200 426061; Fax: 01200 444776; email: info@iacht.co.uk; website: www.iacht.co.uk

Mysteries, 9 Monmouth Street, Covent Garden, London WC2H 9DA. Tel: 0207 240 3688; website: www.mysteries.co.uk

The British Homeopathic Association, Hahnemann House, 29 Park Street West, Luton LU1 3BE. Tel: 0870 444 3950; Fax: 0870 444 3960; email: info@trusthomeopathy.org; website: www.trusthomeopathy. org

Clare Maxwell-Hudson School of Massage, Lower Ground Floor, 20 Enford Street, London W1H 1DG. Tel: 0207 724 7198; email: admin@ cmhmassage.co.uk; website: www.cmhmassage.co.uk

British Massage Therapy Council, 17 Rymers Lane, Cowley, Oxford OX4 3JU. Tel: 01865 774123; website: www.bmtc.co.uk

Transcendental Meditation, 24 Linhope Street, London NW1 6HT. Tel: 0207 402 3451; website: www.tm.org

Transcendental Meditation Independent (UK), website: www.tm-meditation.co.uk. Free information pack for the North of England: 0191 2132179; email: chris@tm-meditation.co.uk. For the South: 01843 841 010; ; email: colin@tm-meditation.co.uk

Association of Reflexologists, 5 Fore Street, Taunton, Somerset TA1 1HX. Tel: 0870 5673320; email: info@aor.org.uk; website: www.aor. org.uk

Irish Reflexology Institute, Fitzwilliam Business Centre, Singleton House, Laurance Street, Drogheda, County Louth, Ireland. Tel: 041 980 6904; Website: www.reflexology.ie

The Shiatsu Society, Eastlands Court, St Peters Road, Rugby CV21 3QP. Tel: 0845 130 4560; Fax: 01788 555052; website: www.shiatsu. org

National Federation of Spiritual Healers, Old Manor Farm Studio, Church Street, Sunbury-on-Thames, Middlesex, TW16 6RG. Tel: 01932 783164; Fax: 01932 779648; website: www.nfsh.org.uk

The College of Psychic Studies, 16 Queensberry Place, London SW7 2EB. Tel: 0207 589 3292; website: www.collegeofpsychicstudies. co.uk

Asante Academy of Chinese Medicine, Clerkenwell Building, Archway Campus, 2–10 Highgate Hill, London N19 5LW. Tel: 0207 272 6888; Fax: 0207 272 1998; email: info@asante-academy.com; website: www.asante-academy.com

The British Wheel of Yoga, 25 Jermyn Street, Sleaford, Lincs, NG34 7RU. Tel: 01529 306 851; Fax: 01529 303 233; email: office@bwy. org.uk; website: www.bwy.org.uk

The British Acupuncture Council, 63 Jeddo Road, London W12 9HQ. Tel: 020 8735 0400; Fax: 020 8735 0404; email: info@acupuncture. org.uk

The British Medical Acupuncture Society (BMAS), BMAS House, 3 Winnington Court, Northwich, Cheshire CW8 1AQ. Tel: 01606 786782; Fax: 01606 786783; email: admin@medical-acupuncture. org.uk

The Register of Chinese Herbal Medicine, Office 5, 1 Exeter Street, Norwich NR2 4QB. Tel: 01603 623994; Fax: 01603 667557; email: herbmed@rchm.co.uk

CHAPTER EIGHT

Counselling and psychotherapy

Access to "talking treatments" frequently tops the list of priorities of people with mental health problems (Rankin, 2005). But it seems that sometimes GPs or psychiatrists are reluctant to refer someone for counselling or therapy. This may reflect the shortage of counsellors working in the NHS. It is not unusual to wait six months, or even longer for an appointment. (Though if someone's care plan includes counselling, Rethink believes it can be worth writing to the hospital trust, which may be able to speed up the process.) Alternatively, the apparent reluctance may reflect concern that the patient sees counselling as an alternative to medication, or possibly as a "cure". Some health professionals also consider counselling inappropriate, or even dangerous, for people with schizophrenia.

Considerable research indicates that psychodynamic "insight" therapies, especially psychoanalytical therapy, which comprises intensive (two to three times a week) deep psychological exploration, can be experienced as traumatic and worsens people's symptoms. This was the finding of a review of the negative effects of psychotherapy (Drake & Sederer, 1986). The researchers also reported that people having these therapies with experienced practitioners were more likely to leave therapy, needed longer periods of hospitalization, and subsequently functioned less well.

However, a survey by the Healthcare Commission (2006) of over 19,000 people using community mental health services reported that fifty-two per cent of those who had received counselling definitely found it helpful, and research dating back to the 1950s indicates that psychotherapy might augment and support drug treatments (Bishbee, 1983), particularly in reducing hallucinations and delusions (Beck, 1952; Shapiro & Ravenette, 1959). Since then, many studies have shown that therapies that are supportive and non-judgemental, teach social skills, or strategies for managing symptoms, may benefit individuals.

A review of the research data published in the medical journal *Schizophrenia Bulletin* reported that not only do people find these therapies helpful, but that the benefits are significant and long-lasting (Mojtabai, Nicholson, & Carpenter, 1998).

Counselling and psychotherapy—is there a difference?

The words psychotherapy and counselling tend to be used interchangeably—including by many practitioners themselves, and there are similarities between the two. Most forms of therapy and counselling involve talking about problems to a person who is not a friend or a family member.

However, it has been claimed that therapy tends to view a person's difficulties in a holistic manner—the ways in which their problems are part of their life experiences and how they relate to events and other people. Resolving their problems in a therapeutic way, therefore, may take months—even several years with some approaches. By contrast, counselling is said to be briefer and focused on a specific problem, such as bereavement or a relationship difficulty. This definition is far from being shared by all practitioners; in fact, there seems to be no absolute distinction between counselling and therapy and, after resolving one problem with someone who calls themselves either a counsellor or a therapist, the person may choose to continue to explore other issues on a longer term basis.

Among the dozens of different kinds of counselling and psychotherapy, cognitive–behavioural therapy (CBT) is probably the most researched, with numerous studies testifying to its effectiveness.

Cognitive–behavioural therapy (CBT)

Devised by the psychiatrist Aaron Beck (1921–), CBT is based on the theory that virtually all emotional problems can be traced to unhelpful beliefs or illogical thinking (cognitions). An often quoted example is of the man who sees an aquaintance across the street and smiles and waves, but the woman fails to acknowledge him. The man might choose to think that he must have done something to upset her—or that for no good reason he has been snubbed. The first explanation might lead to his feeling puzzled and the second to his being annoyed. But if the man chooses to think that her behaviour was not about him, but because she was preoccupied with a problem, he would be less likely to blame himself or feel hurt by the behaviour.

Practitioners emphasize that CBT is not about ignoring reality. The aquaintance might have snubbed him! But therapists encourage people to relinquish automatic, fixed ideas about people and situations and substitute more positive, helpful interpretations. Traditionally, CBT has been used to treat depression, compulsions, and obsessions, but in recent years some people have found that it helps them manage hallucinations and delusions and to feel more positive about themselves.

The success of CBT in this respect may be, partly, because as several studies show, people who experience persecutory delusions are significantly more likely to make unrealistic and negative assumptions about themselves and the cause of external events (Bentall, 2000; 2001; Bentall, Kinderman, & Bowen-Jones, 1999; Bentall, Corcoran, Howard, Blackwood, & Kinderman, 2001).

It seems that these misattributions give rise to specific brain activity that can be detected with brain imaging techniques. It is also suggested that difficulties with memory and attention, as well as individual and interpersonal problems, stem from these misattributions.

CBT sessions are usually one-to-one, but sometimes combined with group sessions. They last between thirty and sixty minutes

and involve learning specific ways of coping with symptoms, prob-
lem-solving, and relapse prevention strategies. It has been reported
that some people discontinue CBT thinking that it will not be effective, or might make their symptoms worse (Tarrier, Yusupoff,
McCarthy, Kinney, & Wittkowski, 1998). However, while CBT is not
effective for everyone, there is no research evidence to suggest that
it worsens symptoms.

Moreover, it seems that between twelve and twenty sessions can
significantly reduce hallucinations, delusions, and some negative
symptoms, such as social withdrawal. CBT also seems to render
any remaining delusions much less distressing, to the point where
they are not troublesome.

The effectiveness of CBT, however, depends partly on someone's willingness to give up, or at least modify, a delusional belief.
For example, CBT might not be appropriate for someone in the grip
of psychosis, though it has been successful with acutely ill patients
(Drury, Birchwood, Cochrane, & Macmillan, 1996a,b) and these
benefits can be significant and enduring (Drury, Birchwood, &
Cochrane, 2000).

Nor is CBT particularly recommended for delusions that do not
cause individuals distress or put them at risk of harm, such as a
mistaken belief that they are related to royalty, though it might be
different if the person believed that royal connections entitled him
or her to preferential treatment and he or she was distressed at not
receiving it. In this case the aim of CBT would be partial modifica-
tion. Without challenging the belief directly, a therapist might
encourage the person to accept that not everyone knows, or is willing to believe, that he or she is related to royalty, and therefore
expecting special treatment is unrealistic.

Although generally CBT is used to treat positive symptoms like
hallucinations and delusions, one study (Tarrier et al., 2001)
reported that a reduction in positive symptoms was associated with
a reduction in depression. In addition, there was a significant lessening of negative symptoms (See Chapter One) in comparison to
participants who received "routine care".

Such improvements are also enduring (Garety et al., 1997;
Kuipers et al., 1997; Kuipers et al., 1998; Tarrier et al., 1999). A
follow-up study (Tarrier et al., 2004) with over 225 severely ill
people experiencing first or second episodes reported that CBT had

beneficial effects on psychotic symptoms at eighteen months and, compared to supportive counselling, auditory hallucinations responded better to CBT. However, CBT did not significantly reduce incidents of relapse. Noting that family therapy (see below) has been shown to reduce relapse, the study's authors recommended a combination of this and CBT for people with "early schizophenia".

Despite CBT's effectiveness, "booster" sessions may be needed to maximize the benefits. While a review of research findings (Rector & Beck, 2001) concluded that despite producing large improvements in positive and negative symptoms "refinements" are needed to help those individuals who gain only minimal benefit.

This may involve extending CBT beyond the usual 8–12 sessions. For example, a trial with people experiencing acute psychosis (Drury, Birchwood, Cochrane, & Macmillan, 1996a) reported that cognitive therapy lessened their positive symptoms and increased their insight. However, the researchers noted that these improvements required about twenty weeks of CBT.

For the study by Tarrier and colleagues (2004) mentioned above, participants received eight hours of CBT, whereas the researchers had proposed 15–20 hours and concluded that this might have made the treatment even more effective.

As well as a greater number of initial sessions, people might benefit from ongoing CBT. Shuresh says that regular CBT helps him manage his voices and delusions more effectively while reducing his medication.

> CBT has meant that I can challege my persecutory voices or not listen to them at all. I used to think that I was the devil or Mahatma Ghandi. I got nervous when I went to the shops and thought everyone was speaking about me. My therapist told me to question this idea and say to myself: "What makes you think you're so important that everyone is interested in you?" Then to substitute a more helpful thought. So now if I think everyone is talking about me I tell myself that I'm just an ordinary person, getting on with my own life and doing the best I can—and that works.

> Since I started having CBT three years ago—along with counselling—the hallucinations and delusions have bothered me much less and my psychiatrist has reduced my Depixol by sixty per cent.

I used to be on 50 mg a week, walking around like a zombie. Now it's 20 mg and I find it easier to study, though the Parkinson-like tremors are still a problem a couple of days after the injection.

I'm studying psychology and I really hope I can use less medication in future. That will take time. In my experience, the 12 weeks of CBT offered on the NHS is not long enough for a single (5 mg) reduction. I've had to cope with substantial withdrawal symptoms, such as an increase in hearing voices, paranoia and delusional ideas. CBT has been an excellent replacement for the higher level of medication. As a disabled student, my therapy's paid for by my education authority. But, of course, not everyone's so fortunate in that respect.

However, as with any therapy, CBT does not suit everyone. This may be because people do not hit it off with their therapist, as in Sheila's case.

I was willing to give CBT a try, but I couldn't get on with the therapist. She didn't come across as someone I could relate to. When you're having a one-to-one you need to be on the same wavelength and we never were. It's hard to pinpoint exactly what it was. Perhaps the timing was wrong. It was just after I lost my dad and I was getting over that. But I never felt that she listened to me so after a couple of sessions I told her I wouldn't be continuing.

Supportive counselling

This covers a variety of approaches. For example, person-centred, transpersonal, gestalt or transactional analysis are some of the most widely practised. But supportive counselling is as much about style as theory. Essentially, the person feels listened to, respected, and valued. Supportive counselling sees a trusting, collaborative relationship between counsellor and client—the therapeutic alliance, as it is known—as essential to effective therapy. This idea has been consistently confirmed by clinical and research evidence (Martin, Garske, & Davis, 2000).

Supportive counselling may help someone through a difficult period, to cope with ongoing difficulties, or to resolve negative experiences and emotions. These may date back many years, even to childhood. But unlike some "insight" therapies, such as psycho-analysis, supportive counselling does not view exploration of a person's past as an essential part of therapy, although past issues may surface during the course of the sessions.

It is said that, like true love, the course of counselling rarely runs completely smoothly, and there may be times during or after sessions when people experience a range of negative emotions—sometimes directed towards the counsellor. But it is thought to be the sign of a good therapeutic relationship if people feel able to discuss and "work through" these feelings with their therapist. Despite experiencing such emotions at times, overall Nicholas found counselling very useful.

> Don't keep your problems to yourself. Bottling them up only makes them worse. Find someone you can trust and talk to them. Counselling can be difficult. I went for about a year and I talked about my emotional, sexual and family problems. I got rid of the guilt and the sense of inferiority I'd had for so long. I felt worse at first, but it did help. By the end I was much more self-confident. It was strange because I wasn't aware of getting better. Only afterwards I knew it had worked because there were positive feelings where they'd been only negative ones before.

Studies show that supportive counselling can be as effective as CBT in the treatment of negative symptoms (Tarrier et al., 1999) and in lessening delusions (Tarrier et al., 2001; Tarrier et al., 2004) and that these effects are long-lasting. Increased self-esteem and sociability are other reported benefits of this form of counselling (Davidson, Stayner, & Haglund, 1998).

However, as mentioned, its effectiveness depends partly on the individual and the counsellor being able to establish a good therapeutic relationship. Otherwise, as William found, the experience can be totally counter-productive.

> My social worker suggested counselling otherwise I don't think I'd have tried it. I found the sessions very difficult and after a year couldn't take it anymore and dropped out. I wanted to talk about my sexual feelings, but the counsellor always changed the subject and I would feel even more closed in and upset than before.

A study by Frank and Gunderson (1990) examined the effect of the therapeutic alliance with 143 people diagnosed with schizophrenia and undergoing therapy. This showed that those who formed good alliances with their therapists within the first six months of treatment were significantly more likely to remain in therapy, use prescribed medication—and achieve better outcomes after two years. This included using less medication than participants who did not have a good alliance with their therapist.

Personal circumstances also affect the effectiveness of therapy. A three-year study with 151 people with a diagnosis of schizophrenia or schizoaffective disorder (Hogarty et al., 1997a) found that personal therapy helped prevent psychosis and relapse among those who lived with their family. But among participants living independently of their family, therapy increased the rate of relapse. The researchers concluded that personal therapy might best be delayed until people's symptoms and living conditions were stable.

Psychoanalysis

Possibly the first and best known talking therapy is psychoanalysis—the creation of the nineteenth century psychologist Sigmund Freud (1856–1939). Freud believed that mental health problems largely result from disturbances in people's psychological and sexual development and the inevitable conflict between their unconscious wishes and drives and society's rules and expectations.

Freud came to realize that psychoanalysis was not the cure for schizophrenia he originally believed and, as mentioned, research suggests that this sort of "insight" therapy is not effective (Heinrichs & Carpenter, 1981; Mueser & Berenbaum, 1990) since it can be more than people can cope with. However, David, who saw his first analyst for about ten years, believes psychoanalysis was invaluable in his recovery, after being diagnosed with schizophrenia at the age of nineteen.

David's story—"The analyst didn't treat what I said as abnormal. I could trust him"

I've never come across anyone with my diagnosis who has had psychoanalysis. I wouldn't have been able to afford it, but my father believed in me and my parents made sacrifices to pay for it privately after the NHS psychiatrist told my father that nothing could be done to help me, but that medication would keep me stable. I found psychoanalysis a revelation. The whole atmosphere was so unlike a hospital. There were no medicines, white coats, syringes or other medical paraphernalia. I lay on a comfortable couch, in a quiet, book-lined room. The analyst didn't treat what I said as abnormal. I could trust him.

Psychoanalysis is the opposite of alienation—it's being listened to and understood. Over a period of ten years I went two or three times a week. Psychoanalysis brought me into the real world—out of my deluded fantasy world. It enabled me to face my predicament and fulfil myself in appropriate ways, such as through painting, drawing and writing poetry.

Later, after finishing with analysis, I joined a group, which I also found helpful. It's a pity you're never told about therapy. There are a lot of low-cost therapies, but I've never seen any information about them in a day centre. It's something the medical people tend to ignore.

David found the respectful, supportive relationship with his analyst was an important element in his recovery (Kanwal, 1997). While this relationship is important to the success of therapy, research indicates that the therapist's skill and the client's motivation are equally important factors, irrespective of the therapeutic approach. However, there is no scientific evidence that psychoanalysis, or any other form of psychotherapy, is a "cure" for schizophrenia.

Analytical/psychodynamic therapies

Some followers and contemporaries of Freud, among them his daughter, Anna, and the psychologists Carl Jung and Melanie Klein, developed their own analytical approaches. Like psychoanalysis, these can be very lengthy. Jan had analytical psychotherapy two to three times a week for a period of ten years.

I was seeing a therapist when I got psychotic, but she couldn't handle it. I'd heard that the Arbours Organisation in London were happy to work with people with psychosis, which many therapists aren't willing, or able to do. Arbours helped me understand the roots of my psychosis and gain insight into my relationships and their effect on me. It was hellish at times and not cheap, but on more than one occasion it helped me avoid relapse and being hospitalised.

I also learned a lot about myself. I still have symptoms, but I'm able to step back and make changes that are right for me. Some people see psychosis in wholly negative terms, but you can develop from those experiences.

People can refer themselves to The Arbours Organisation and to the Philadelphia Association, whose therapists are also trained to work with people with a diagnosis of schizophrenia.

A systematic review of psychotherapy (Malmberg & Fenton, 2001) did not identify any scientific trials of psychodynamic therapy. However, the reviewers suggested that such approaches may be more acceptable to people than a "cognitive reality-adaptive therapy", such as CBT. Moreover, a study that compared psychodynamic, CBT, and person-centred approaches, practised in UK NHS settings (Stiles, Barkham, Twigg, Mellor-Clark, & Cooper, 2006), reported that the therapies tended to have equivalent outcomes.

Family therapy (FT)

The idea of therapy for the family of people with schizophrenia began in the 1960s, when hospital clinicians observed that patients' symptoms fluctuated according to the level of tension between them and their parents. It has since been found that in families where there is high expressed emotion (EE) in the form of arguments, criticism, hostility, and over-protectiveness, higher rates of relapse occur (Leff, Kuipers, Berkowitz, Eberlein-Vries, & Sturgeon, 1982; Rund, 1994), but that the person improves when family members relate more harmoniously to each other and show lower EE (Butzlaff & Hooley, 1998). This has led to the idea that the "family system" should become the focus of treatment, rather than the designated sick person.

This is not to say that families cause schizophrenia. But this "systems" approach regards the family as a whole and emphasizes factors such as relationships and communication patterns—rather than the traits or symptoms of the individuals—which may affect the mental and emotional health of one or more family members.

Family therapy involves a therapist, or more often a pair of therapists, working with the immediate or extended family, helping them to understand their relative's problems and to adjust appropriately. This includes treating the person as normally as possible and not labelling his or her every expression of emotion, such as irritation, impatience, or even anger, as "schizophrenic" and indicative of illness or relapse.

Families are also encouraged not to be over-protective or treat the person as if he or she were incapable of being cooperative, taking decisions for themselves, or behaving in a socially acceptable way. Adopting a more flexible family system with calmer, less conflictual ways of resolving difficulties, is the hoped-for outcome.

FT is associated with fewer relapses and re-hospitalizations, improved social skills, and a decrease in parental levels of expressed emotion from high to low or lower (Barrowclough & Tarrier, 1987; Falloon et al., 1982; Falloon et al., 1985). A long-term study by Hogarty and colleagues (1997b) found that following FT people with schizophrenia coped better with family life, while a systematic review of studies of "group psycho-education" with families (Pekkala & Merinder, 2002) concluded that this variant of family therapy also benefitted people with schizophrenia.

Undoubtedly, many people and their families find FT effective, but research suggests that there might be additional benefits if the person has individual therapy as well. Data from a study on relapse rates over an eight-year period suggests that a combination of individual and family/carer therapy might be the best way for people to maintain the benefits they have derived from previous therapy and to avoid relapse (Tarrier, Barrowclough, Porceddu, & Fitzpatrick, 1994; Tarrier, Yusupoff, McCarthy, Kinney, & Wittkowski, 1998; Tarrier et al., 1999).

Family therapists work in hospital clinics and are often attached to GP surgeries. Anyone in the family can request therapy, though not all members may be willing or able to attend regular sessions. At The Institute of Family Therapy in London, families can have preparatory sessions before their relative leaves hospital.

Group therapy

People often derive support from the knowledge that others have problems similar to their own. By listening to other members of a group, individuals may gain understanding and insight into their own difficulties and learn from the success of others. This is the philosophy behind group therapy and self-help groups. However, someone might also feel "attacked" if the group therapist or others make what feels like unkind or unjustified comments. Nor is it unusual for a person in a group to have difficulty trying to think of something to say. Robert recalls:

> I wanted to talk to a counsellor individually, but I was asked to join a group as that was all there was available. I felt very nervous at the prospect. I attended three sessions and it was a terrible strain. I had no idea what to say and couldn't think of anything anyway. I knew I didn't want to reveal personal details about myself or talk about my problems in front of complete strangers. But I felt pressure on me to do so.

The skill of the facilitator(s) and the number and behaviour of other group members obviously affects each person's experience. But, most importantly, people need to feel that it is the right type of therapy for them at that time. If not, then obviously it's better that they do not continue.

However, some people, like Gillian, find group therapy helpful.

> The feedback from the rest of the group is the best thing. Before joining I was quite critical of myself for not coping better. I suppose I blamed myself for having got schizophrenia. I also thought that I was weak and couldn't manage as well as other people. Yet often in the group when I talk about how I've dealt with situations the comments are positive, even complimentary. I feel people are on my side. That's helped me feel better about myself.

As Gillian found, the support of other group members can boost self-esteem. Group therapy also allows people to develop and practise social skills, though this is specifically the focus of social skills training.

Social skills training (SST)

This is not so much a therapy as a set of techniques that offer people practical information and teach strategies for becoming more socially adaptable, confident, and assertive. The intention is to improve someone's chances of forming new friendships, gaining employment, if that is an aim, or simply their quality of life. SST programmes usually cover assertiveness techniques, written and verbal communication, body language and role-playing.

A review of psychosocial therapies (Bustillo, Lauriello, Horan, & Keith, 2001) found that SST improved the social skills of people with a diagnosis of schizophrenia, while a systematic review reported that, compared to standard care, SST significantly reduced relapse rates over the two years of treatment (Pilling et al., 2002).

Some NHS clinical psychologists give individual SST, but most often someone is encouraged to enrol on a specially-tailored course run by colleges of further education or at a day centre. A person's care coordinator can help with an application.

Therapy practice guidelines

There are several evidence-based practice guidelines for psycho-social treatments that might interest people considering therapy. These include social skills training (Heinssen, Liberman, & Kopelo-wicz, 2000); cognitive/cognitive–behavioural therapy (Beck & Rector, 1998; Garety, Fowler, & Kuipers, 2000; Granholm, McQuaid, McClure, Pedrelli, & Jeste, 2002; McQuaid et al., 2000) and family therapy (Dixon, Adams, & Lucksted, 2000).

Non-talking therapies

A number of therapies involve some form of creative activity, such as dance, play, and drama. Probably the most widely avail-able within the NHS are music and art. As with any form of ther-apy, they won't appeal to everyone, though even people who consider themselves unmusical or not "artistic" may find them beneficial.

Art therapy

Ancient records indicate that art therapy was offered to mentally-ill patients as long ago as 2630 BC, during the reign of the Egyptian king Djoser (Puri, Brown, McKee, & Treasaden, 2005). It was originally introduced into the old asylums as a way of keeping patients occupied. It soon became clear, however, that their artwork was often an expression of deep feelings and conflicts and a means of releasing and better managing disturbing thoughts and emotions.

Usually, each person works as part of a small group, which is supervised by an art therapist who, through observations, helps people to gain a clearer understanding of their artwork and thereby of themselves. Art therapy may be particulary helpful for someone who is unable or reluctant to express themselves verbally.

A systematic review of art therapy for schizophrenia that assessed all the studies (Ruddy & Milnes, 2005) found only two that met rigorous scientific criteria. So, despite references to positive mental changes, interpersonal relationships, and social networking, the authors stated that no conclusions could be drawn.

There is no shortage of anecdotal evidence for the benefits of art therapy, however. One of the best known is by Mary Barnes (1923–2001). The book she co-authored with her therapist, Joseph Berke, *Two Accounts of a Journey Through Madness* (Barnes & Berke, 1991), describes how she painted her way through psychosis, as she put it. Linda Hart, whose *Phone At Nine Just to Say You're Alive* (1997 edition) was Mind's 1996 Book of the Year, also finds painting therapeutic.

> I think being creative is putting outside the things that are inside and thus making them more manageable. You can take a walk round them and view them from a different perspective and maybe make friends with them, or at least keep them at arm's length, say, in a drawer. I think everyone is capable of some form of creativity, but it's squashed inside them. They just need releasing. You don't necessarily need to work with an art therapist. There is a saying which goes: "If you can walk, then you can dance. If you can talk, then you can sing." I would add: "If you can hold a pencil, then you can draw." For me, it's an amalgamation of risk-taking, playing and pushing the "frame" or boundaries which gives me an escape from the material, physical and psychological world.

Some of Linda's artwork can be seen and purchased through the Mind website.

Cathleen enjoys group sessions at a local day centre.

> At school they said I couldn't draw and I failed my "O" level art. But it doesn't matter in the group. I pick up a crayon I fancy and just let it go all over the paper as it pleases. Then I do the same with another one. Somehow I end up with a picture. But none of us are [sic] forced to do conventional pretty pictures, thank goodness because I couldn't. Sarah [the art therapist] comes round and may ask a question. We talk for a bit about the picture and I like that. It's all therapeutic—painting, Sarah, being with other people.

Day hospitals and drop-in centres run art classes. The British Association of Art Therapists (BAAT) provides details of art groups or individual art therapy.

The Other Side Gallery (TOSG), based in north London, provides a website for artists, aged eighteen or over who live in the area and have experienced mental health difficulties, among other problems. TOSG also offers mentoring, volunteering and education facilities and holds exhibitions. The website: www.theothersidegallery. org has further information.

Music therapy

We are all innately musical—from the rhythm of our heartbeat, to the melodies and harmonies of our speech, sighing, laughing, and crying. Just as music can capture and create many different moods it can also create a harmonious, integrated state of mind and body—that is the theory behind music therapy. Encouraged by their community psychiatric nurse, Gita and Darren joined a music therapy group. Darren went for five sessions, but didn't feel he gained much from the experience.

> It was supposed to be about expressing yourself, but it wasn't easy with the percussion instruments they gave you. If you want to express yourself you need some skill at a musical instrument. I can imagine that playing the drums loudly could help you get out your frustrations. With a violin you can express sadness and joy, not with a drum, though. But then the approach was all about making

music, perhaps if it had been about listening I might have got more out of it. I know if I'm feeling down I can get something from listening to a favourite song or piece of music.

Gita, on the other hand, continued going to the group for over a year.

> I'd play the rainmaker (a long tube filled with beads). When you turned it there was the sound of the sea. That was very soothing. I liked going, but people would sometimes bang instruments very aggressively, which disturbed some of us. Then the therapist would play on a drum to redirect the sound back to the person and they might calm down a bit.

Drumming can be therapeutic, it seems. A study of weekly sessions of West African Dagbama drumming for clients at two mental health centres in Kansas City reported that its "highly participatory and easily accessible nature" produced a sense of compentency, strengthened group identity, and through concerts and performances gave the partipants an opportunity to contribute to society (Longhofer & Floersch, 1993).

While music making with others can be beneficial, music therapy is often provided on an individual basis. Working one-to-one enables the therapist to improvise the music to meet a person's specific needs. At the Nordoff-Robbins Centre in north London, the therapists often use a piano, though they, or the clients, might play other instruments, as well as singing or "voicing" sounds. It is not necessary for the person to have any formal musical ability or training, and the centre accepts self-referrals.

In addition to clinical and anecdotal evidence, some studies show that music therapy can be effective in relieving feelings of stress, anxiety, and depression. A systematic review (Gold, Heldal, Dahle, & Wigram, 2005) found that, compared to receiving standard care alone, people who also did music therapy experienced improvements in their mental state and social functioning. These benefits, however, were related to the number of sessions that people attended, which varied between seven and seventy-eight, over periods of one to three months.

Similar improvements were reported in a one-month study with people in hospital. Those who listened to music and sang popular songs became more interested in outside events and social interactions. They also experienced fewer negative symptoms (Tang, Yao, & Zheng, 1994). Jo enjoyed attending one such group.

> The last time I was in hospital one of the nurses set up a music group, which I thought was a great idea. We'd just listen to different pieces of music, some were classical music that people had brought along and that was really nice. Using music that way can be really good. Before I go to sleep I may put on some music, like Gregorian chants, which are lovely. Just listening to some soothing music with a spiritual nature I find nice. I use music to lift my mood as well. If I'm feeling a bit sluggish and have things to do I'll put on something from the charts that's energetic and will get me going.

The Association of Professional Music Therapists (APMT) and The British Association of Music Therapists (BAMT) provide information on individual and group music therapy.

Writing

Even if someone has never kept a diary, writing down thoughts, feelings, and experiences can be a safe, creative, and pleasurable form of expression—rather than have them constantly whirl around inside their head.

Richard's articles have been published in several national newspapers and magazines. He wholeheartedly recommends writing as a form of therapy.

> Write about your experiences! Write down your symptoms, your madness—everything! I have found it very helpful. It enables you to stand outside yourself and see the whole picture, which can only be good for you. Writing probably prevented me from being re-hospitalized on more than one occasion. It's also interesting to read again as a record of what you've been through and survived.

Sheila agrees. She has kept a journal for many years.

> It gets things out of my head. It may be only a few words some days, but it helps. When I was in hospital, I expressed my rage and torments. After my mum died, I began recording small, new

achievements: taking over the tenancy of the house, dealing with medical professionals—I hadn't been very good at that while Mum was alive—opening a bank account for the first time. They've been steps which have improved the quality of my life. Recording this sort of event still brings me pleasure and also helps me to continue to move on.

Sheila's partner, Philip, also finds writing therapeutic. "It's a therapy in itself, even if no one else reads it, it's still helpful. You crystallize your thoughts on the page and you feel freer afterwards."

Perceptions, the magazine of The National Voices Forum (NVF) publishes readers' poems, cartoons, short stories, personal accounts, and viewpoints. The NVF also runs an annual poetry competition.

There's little research into "writing therapy", but *The Writing Cure: How Expressive Writing Promotes Health and Wellbeing*, edited by S. J. Lepore & J. M. Smyth (2002) and *Writing Cures: An introductory Handbook of Writing in Counselling and Psychotherapy* (Bolton, Howlett, Lago, & Wright, 2004), are two interesting books on the subject. Anyone who lacks the inspiration to put pen to paper might also consider *The Self-Esteem Journal* by Alison Waines (2004) which is a step-by-step guide to self-discovery through writing.

Private therapy

The demand for counselling currently outstrips the number of counselling and clinical psychologists working in the NHS and a long wait for an appointment is not unusual. Private counselling is an option, of course, but can be expensive, with a 50–60 minute session costing from around £35 upwards. London, and other large city practitioners, generally charge most, though some may offer concessions for people who are unemployed or on low incomes.

Many psychotherapy training establishments, voluntary organizations and charities, such as Mind, offer low or no-cost therapy, mainly with trainee counsellors or psychotherapists. In common with qualified counsellors, the trainees will be of different ages, backgrounds and ethnicity, but the majority of therapists tend to be white, middle-aged, middle class women.

Individuals who would prefer to talk to a therapist who is the same sex as themselves or from their own ethnic group or sexual orientation, need to make this clear at the outset. Pink Therapy has a register of therapists experienced in working with gay, lesbian, bisexual and transgender clients.

Qualifications

Currently, anyone can call themselves a counsellor or therapist, but most British counsellors and therapists who practise privately belong to a recognized organization, The British Association for Counselling and Psychotherapy (BACP), for example. Their directory lists members' fee scale, qualifications, experience, specializations with specific problems, and their accreditation status.

Psychotherapy training usually takes three to four years and to gain accreditation therapists also need to provide evidence of a substantial number of hours of professional practice. The UK Council of Psychotherapy (UKCP) represents almost eighty psychotherapy organizations and provides details of accredited therapists. The British Psychological Society can provide details of counselling psychologists working in the NHS and in private practice. The British Association for Behavioural and Cognitive Psychotherapists (BABCP) has details of accredited members on their website and will also send enquirers a printed list.

Choosing a therapist

Counselling is a financial and emotional commitment and best not entered into lightly. Some practitioners suggest an initial assessment session so that they and the client get an idea of whether they will be able to to work together, but no one need feel obliged to sign up for a series of sessions on the basis of one appointment. Someone may be lucky first time, but finding the right therapist could take longer. The Department of Health free booklet, *Choosing Talking Therapies?*, is a useful introduction to counselling and psychotherapy.

No matter how well-qualified or experienced the counsellor or therapist may be, it is important that people also heed their instinct as to whether they feel sufficiently comfortable with the person to talk to them freely.

Reputable therapy and counselling organizations expect their members to follow a code of ethics and good practice. This involves maintaining client confidentiality, being reliable, respectful, and not exploiting clients emotionally or financially. But relationships between clients and counsellors do sometimes go wrong. It might be a "personality clash" or a case of financial, emotional, or sexual abuse. Incidents of abuse can be reported to the practitioner's professional organization. POPAN (Prevention of Professional Abuse Network) offers support for those who feel that they have been abused by a therapist.

Self-help/support groups

Countless people find that joining a self-help or support group is the first step towards overcoming their problems. Research shows that groups for people with psychological difficulties are not harmful and have a largely positive effect, sometimes equivalent to the benefit of established therapies (Hodgson & Miller, 1982). Support and encouragement, a reduction in guilt through finding others with similar problems, and hope are some of the reported benefits. In addition, there is a chance for the "helped" to become helpers, which may be just as, or more, beneficial.

A report on self-help groups for individuals who experience mental distress (The Mental Health Foundation and Rethink, 2004) refers to research by Hatzidimitriadou (2002), which found that the empowering effect of attending a group may help members cope better with difficult or stressful experiences.

A review of studies of peer support among people with severe mental health problems (Davidson et al., 1999) indicates that self-help groups may also help people extend their social networks, enhance their quality of life, and improve their symptoms. This is borne out by the experiences of members of a self-help group for South Asian women in Bradford that promotes a holistic approach to mental health and well-being.

Hamdard (meaning "companion" or "someone who gives support")

> Gaining my confidence back again. That's been the best thing.
> And just getting out again. And socialising with people.
> And I really, really enjoy coming here.
> And I enjoy going anywhere now. I could do anything now.

> What's important is the fact that it's a friendly environment and
> it's safe and it's confidential and I've got like strong bonds with
> the women now. And I feel like I belong somewhere because the
> group's helped me and I know it's helping other women as well
> because they've . . . told me . . .

> It's brilliant, it's good, it boosts me up and I would like to see all
> the women out there who haven't got any confidence in them-
> selves build themselves up by coming along.
>
> > (From: *Hamdard: A Collection of Poems and Stories*
> > (Sharing Voices Bradford))

Research into recovery (Pitt & Kilbride, 2006) highlighted the
need for more self-help groups, particularly in relation to psychosis,
to provide opportunities for people to share their experiences and
coping strategies. The authors recommend that in the first instance
these groups be facilitated by mental healthcare professionals.

The Hearing Voices Network (HVN)

This is a network of groups for people who are, or have been,
disturbed by voices, or other sorts of hallucinations. The first group
was set up in Holland in 1998 by a psychiatrist, Marius Romme,
who had been exploring with his patients ways of controlling
voices without medication.

A systematic review of distraction techniques for those who hear
voices (Crawford-Walker, King, & Chan, 2005) reported that, despite
there being only a few unsatisfactory studies, the techniques could
prove more acceptable than other more intrusive treatments.

HVN is now a worldwide network. At meetings, members have
the choice whether or not to share their experiences with others.
There are discussions on coping strategies and training workshops,

often facilitated by others who hear voices and so have a good understanding of the problems. In line with the HVN mission statement, the groups aim to provide the support that can enable people to change from being "patients" to living the life that's right for them. There's also an online support group.

When there has not been a group in their area, some voice hearers have set up their own by advertising on the *Voices* magazine notice board: info@hearing-voices.org. *Starting and Supporting Hearing Voices Groups,* by Julie Downs, is available from the HVN head office. They can also recommend other useful publications. Their helpline is an opportunity to talk in confidence about any aspect of hearing voices.

HVN tips for voice hearers

- Voices which nobody else can hear may be misinterpretations of other sounds or, more usually, your own thoughts sounding aloud. For example, as in a dream when you "hear" people speaking.
- Voices may not sound like your own voice. They may be memories of someone else's, voices you don't recognize, and of a different sex to your own.
- Voices cannot make you do anything. Thinking that may make you feel worse initially. But because the voices are from your own mind it is up to you whether you act on what they say. Tell yourself and them that however distressing they might be—they CAN'T hurt you or force you to do anything you don't want to do.
- Directing your time and attention to other activities can lessen the effect of voices. So, perhaps, switch on the radio, listen to music, talk to a friend, go for a walk, read a newspaper or make yourself a drink.
- Just relax—in a warm bath, with a relaxation tape (battery operated)—or whatever unwinding strategy works best for you.
- Keep a voices diary. Discovering whether there's a pattern to why and when the voices start can help you devise better ways of dealing with them.

- If they begin to bully or give you orders, explain that you are in control of your own life and won't take orders from them!
- Consider discussing with your doctor or psychiatrist what medication might help you better cope with the voices.

    (*Reprinted with permission of the Hearing Voices Network*)

Feedback from members suggest that the groups play a vital role in helping them to cope with voices and not to feel so alone with their problems. Attending a group also inspired Rachel to set up her website, www.madnotbad.co.uk.

The idea was born out of my own experiences of mental distress and those I'd met through my psychiatric "career". I'd reached a point where I realized that I had gained more from the support and empathy from fellow survivors than I had from most of my official treatment. The site was launched the same week as my best friend killed herself. Susan, a fellow member of Leicester Hearing Voices group, was a strong supporter of the project —which is one reason I kept on with it at what was a really difficult time.

The site is for those affected by mental ill health/distress to share their experiences, opinions and creative talents. There's also a support and discussion forum. The aim is to combat the isolation, stigma and misconceptions that tend to surround mental illness and promote the idea that being "mad" doesn't make you bad. It's also a place where anyone wanting to know more about mental health can learn from people with first-hand experience, instead of solely relying on textbook accounts and their own imagination.

Summary

Counselling and psychotherapy may help people resolve problems and emotional issues. Social skills training often improves confidence and interpersonal communication. Cognitive–behavioural therapy, supportive counselling, and family therapy can be effective in reducing depression, positive and negative symptoms, and rendering any remaining symptoms less troublesome, though with all approaches success depends on the person's motivation, the skill of the therapist, and a good therapeutic alliance.

Talking therapies do not suit everyone and, in some instances, therapies which enable people to express their imagination and creativity, such as art, music, and writing, may be more beneficial and increase their social network.

Self-support groups can be similarly rewarding. The opportunities for friendship can reduce feelings of loneliness and isolation and, through supporting others, encourage feelings of self-worth and empowerment.

Acknowledgement

I wish to thank Professor Dave Mearns for his helpful comments on this chapter.

Useful addresses/resources

British Association for Behavioural and Cognitive Psychotherapists, PO Box 9, The Globe Centre, St James Square, Accrington, Lancashire BB5 0XB. Tel: 01254 875277 (Mon–Fri, 9.00 a.m.–5.00 p.m.); website: www.babcp.org.uk

The Arbours Association, 6 Church Lane London N8 7BU. Tel: 0208 340 7646; email: info@arboursassociation.org; website: www. arboursassociation.org. In addition to the psychotherapy service, there is also a crisis centre that provides intensive residential and non-residential care for those in acute emotional distress and three therapeutic communities for those whose emotional and social problems require low level support. The long-term aim is for people to overcome their difficulties and live independently.

The Philadelphia Association, 4 Marty's Yard, 17 Hampstead High Street, London NW3 1QW. Tel: 020 7794 2652; email: office@ philadelphia-association.co.uk. Offers psychotherapy (low-cost for unemployed), and has three therapeutic community houses in London.

Institute of Family Therapy (London), 24–32 Stephenson Way, London NW1 2HX. Tel: 0207 391 9150; website: www. instituteoffamilytherapy.org.uk. Registered charity fees on sliding scale according to income.

The British Association of Art Therapists (BAAT), 24–27 White Lion Street, London N1 9PD. Tel: 020 7686; Fax: 020 7837 7945; email: info@baat.org

The Other Side Gallery, c/o The Resource Centre, 76–80 Isledon Road, London N7 7LB. Tel: 07981453293; email: admin@ theothersidegallery.org; website: www.theothersidegallery.org

The Nordoff–Robbins Centre, 2 Lissenden Gardens London NW5 1PP. Tel: 0207267 4496; Fax: 0207 267 4369; email: admin@nordoff-robbins.org.uk; website www.nordoff-robbins.org.uk. Fees are on a sliding scale. No one is turned away for lack of funds.

NRMT in Scotland, Room 1 Community Buildings, 8 Academy Lane, Loanhead, Midlothian EH20 9RP. Tel: 0131 440 4822; Fax: 0131 448 2423; email: chris@nrscot.fsnet.co.uk

Association of Professional Music Therapists (APMT). Booklet: "How can music therapy help adults with mental health problems?" from Louise Karena, 61 Church Hill Road, East Barnet, Herts, EN4 8SY. Tel/Fax: 0208 440 4153; e-mail: APMToffice@ aol.com; website www.apmt.org

The British Society for Music Therapy (BSMT), 61 Church Hill Road, East Barnet, Hertfordshire, EN4 8SY. Tel: 0208 441 6226; Fax: 0208 441 4118. Useful books and videos are detailed on the website: www.bsmt.org

Pink Therapy, 1 Harley Street, London WC1G 9QD. Tel: 020 7291 4480; Fax: 0207 7739 5542; email: info@pinktherapy.com; website: www.pinktherapy.com

British Association for Counselling & Psychotherapy (BACP), BACP House, 15 St John's Business Park, Lutterworth, Leicestershire LE17 4HB. Send sae for a list of practitioners in your area. Tel: 0870 443 5252; Fax: 0870 443 5160; email bacp@bacp.co.uk; www.bacp.co.uk. (All calls charged at BT National Rate.)

UK Council for Psychotherapy, (UKCP), 2nd Floor, Edward House, 2 Wakley Street, London EC1V 7LT. Tel: 020 7014 9955; email: info@psychotherapy.org.uk; UKCP website: www.psychotherapy.org.uk

British Psychological Society (BPS), St Andrews House, 48 Princess Road East, Leicester LE1 7DR. Tel: 0116 254 9568; website: www. bps.org.uk

Choosing Talking Therapies, DoH Publications, PO Box 777, London SE1 6XH. Fax: 01623 724524; email: doh@prolog.uk.com; website: www.doh.gov.uk/download pdf file.

POPAN Community Health Sciences, St Georges, University of London SW17 0RE. Email: pcel@squl.ac.uk; website: www. POPAN.org.uk

Hearing Voices Network (HVN) recommended publications for voice-hearers include: *Accepting Voices* by Marius Romme & Sondra Escher (Mind). The HVN publications *Coping with Voices and Visions and Starting and Supporting Hearing Voices Groups* are available from HVN, 79 Lever Street, Manchester M1 1FL. Enquiries and information: Tel: 0845 122 8641; (Mon–Fri, 10.00 a.m.–4.00 p.m.); email: info@hearing-voices.org Hearing voices confidential helpline: 0845 122 8642 (Mon–Fri, 10.00 a.m.–4.00 p.m.). To join the HVN online support group, email: voice-hearers-subscribe @yahoogroups.com; website: www.hearing-voices.org.uk

Scottish Hearing Voices Network, The Haven, 216–220 Hilltown, Dundee DD3 7AU. Tel: 01382 223023. Details of networks around the country are also on the website: www.hearingvoicesnetwork.com

Hearing Voices Network Cymru, c/o West Wales Action for Mental Health, Brighton Chambers, 124 Main Street, Pembroke, Pembrokeshire, SA71 4HN. Tel: 01646 692535 (Mon–Fri, 9.00 a.m.–5.00 a.m. and out-of-hours answerphone).

National Voices Forum/Rethink, 28 Castle St., Kingston on Thames KT1 1SS. Email: voiceforum@rethink.org; Perceptions email: perceptions@rethink.org; website: www.voicesforum.org.uk

Hamdard, Sharing Voices (Bradford), 99 Manningham Lane, Bradford BD1 3BN. Tel: 01274 731166; email: www.sharingvoices. org.uk

The Disability Rights Commission (DRC) Freepost MID02164, Stratford upon Avon CV37 9BR. Tel: 08457 622 633 (8.00 a.m.–8.00 p.m., Mon–Fri); Textphone 08457 622 644; website: www.drc-gb.org

Conclusion

I n 1994, the researchers Harding and Zahniser reviewed two decades of scientific studies into what they described as the "seven psychiatric myths" about people diagnosed with schizophrenia and reported it was not true that:

- Families cause schizophrenia;
- All people with schizophrenia are the same;
- Rehabilitation can be provided only after stabilisation of symptoms;
- Psychotherapy is useless for people with schizophrenia;
- People must be on medication all their lives;
- People with schizophrenia hold only low level jobs;
- Once a person with schizophrenia always a person with schizophrenia.

Schizophrenia has been described as the most debilitating mental illness and, unfortunately for some individuals, the symptoms worsen over time. But this is not inevitable, or even the "norm". While some myths about schizophrenia persist, outcome studies and personal accounts, including from the contributors to this book, indicate that many people's symptoms improve, they continue to recover, and are able to move on with their lives. In Linda's words:

> It has the potential to be a lot better than some illnesses, apart from the stigma. You can come through it and some people can get well, although most people can't be cured and you might always have some symptoms. But it is possible to live a fulfilling life, so long as you're not drugged up to the eyeballs.
>
> I can see there are enormous benefits too. It's all experience and however horrendous it is at the time you learn from it. I didn't think that at the beginning, but looking back I have seen another dimension and lived with terror, depression and joy and all those experiences make me what I am—it's given me a lot of knowledge and extraordinary resources to deal with whatever life throws at me.

State benefits

B ritain's social security system has been described as the best in the world, but it can seem complicated when someone wants to find out their entitlements. Benefits may be means tested, others depend on the amount of National Insurance (NI) contributions made. At the time of writing, the following benefits are available, but as the entitlement rules and benefits will change, in order not to miss out it is important to check the eligibility criteria.

Statutory Sick Pay (SSP)

This is a taxable payment made to employees by their employers for up to twenty-eight weeks in any period of sickness which lasts four or more days. SSP does not depend on NI contributions. A person can be employed either full- or part-time, but he or she must earn at least the lower earnings limit, currently £84 a week. Unemployed and self-employed people are not eligible for SSP, but may be able to claim incapacity benefit instead.

Incapacity Benefit (IB)

Previously known as Sickness Benefit and Invalidity Benefit, IB is for people who cannot work because of illness or disability and who have not reached retirement age (sixty for women and sixty-five for men). Usually it is related to NI contributions and requires regular medical certificates (sick notes) from a doctor that state that the person is still unable to work. But this does not apply if the person was incapable of work before age twenty, or, in some cases, twenty-five, and they claim in time. In that case the person claims "IB in youth". For people aged sixty or over, IB has been replaced by pension credit.

IB is not affected by savings or most kinds of income other than occupational and personal pensions. Individuals can claim if they cannot get statutory sick pay (SSP) because, for instance, they are not employed or are self-employed, or their SSP has run out. Young people aged sixteen or over can claim "non-contributory" or "no-contribution" IB.

In 2006 the government announced that Incapacity Benefit was to be replaced by a new benefit: Employment and Support Allowance. This is both for people who wish to return to work or undertake training to enable them to find employment and those individuals who are assessed as too severely incapacitated to work. It is anticipated that the new benefit will be fully implemented by 2008. At the time of writing, the new benefit will only apply to new claimants. However, there are likely to be some changes to IB for those already receiving this benefit.

Income Support (IS)

Anyone who is sixteen or over and has no income is eligible for IS. It is also paid to people whose income is below a certain level and varies according to circumstances. For instance, it may be paid to top up low earnings if a person works part-time, or receives other benefits. IS is means-tested or income related, but is not dependent on the person having paid NI contributions. IS can help towards mortgage interest payments and certain other housing costs. People who get IS may also get housing benefit and council tax benefit and they will not need to go through a separate means test.

Anyone who gets IS may also be entitled to other help, such as housing grants, help from the social fund, free prescriptions, dental and chiropody treatment and school meals, and help with transport fares to hospital.

Disability Living Allowance (DLA)

Disability Living Allowance (DLA) is a weekly payment to adults and children because of illness or disability. It is tax free, not means-tested, and it is not necessary to have paid any NI contributions. It is paid on top of any other income someone may have. It is payable whether or not the person is in work and no matter how much he or she earns. It is almost always paid in full and in addition to other benefits like IS or IB. If a person gets DLA it sometimes triggers other benefits, like an increase in IS or Invalid Care Allowance for a friend or relative. There is no lower age limit for DLA and it can be paid indefinitely. But to establish their entitlement people must make a successful claim no later than the day before their sixty-fifth birthday. (A claim can be started with a call to the Benefit Enquiry Line (BEL) freephone 0800 88 2200. If successful, the allowance will be backpaid to the day of the call.) Otherwise the person can claim AA instead. (See below.)

DLA is made up of two components each with different rates.

Care Components are paid if someone needs help with personal care, attention, or supervision from another person. This is paid at three rates: highest, middle, or lowest. Someone receiving DLA at the middle or highest rate care component will also be eligible for the range of benefits available to people receiving the lowest rate. Among these are a disability premium payment, a Christmas bonus, and a home-energy efficiency scheme grant.

Mobility Components are paid if a person cannot go out alone or needs someone to help them get around in unfamiliar places. The mobility problem must be due to physical or mental disability This is paid at a higher or lower rate. At the lower rate people may be able to walk, but cannot make use of the ability unless acccompanied by someone. An example would be if they become anxious on their own due to mental health problems. As with the Care Component, if a person receives the higher rate he or she will also be eligible for the range of benefits available to people receiving the lower rate.

Severe Disablement Allowance (SDA)

This was abolished in 2001. Anyone who would have qualified for SDA, for example if they were 80% disabled, are now eligible to claim IB, but will only qualify for this if they have paid sufficient contributions. Those now on SDA will continue to receive the benefit as long as they continue to be incapable of work and satisfy the SDA conditions.

Attendance Allowance (AA)

This is a tax-free benefit for people aged sixty-five and over who are physically or mentally disabled and need help with personal care or supervision to remain safe. It is not means-tested, not related to NI contributions, and not usually affected by savings or income. Individuals do not actually have to be getting any help, it is the help they qualify for, not the help they get, which counts. A person can get AA even if he or she does not have a carer and lives alone.

Constant Attendance Allowance (CAA)

This is paid when a person's disablement assessment totals ninety-five per cent or more and because of this they need a lot of personal care and attention or supervision as a result of an industrial accident or disease. It is paid at four different weekly rates. Regulations specify the level of care needed for each rate to be payable. CAA overlaps with AA and the DLA care component. Should someone qualify for both he or she will be paid the higher amount. When claiming, the person can choose to have a medical or complete a self-assessment claim pack.

Carer's Allowance (CA)

A person is eligible if he or she is aged sixteen to sixty-five and regularly spends at least thirty-five hours a week caring for a person who receives either DLA care component at the middle or highest rate, or AA at either rate, or CAA allowance paid with a war pension, industrial disablement pension, workmen's compensation, or equivalent benefit. A carer does not have to be related to, or live with, the disabled person. People can claim CA even if they have never worked, but they must not be in full-time education, which is defined as attending a course for twenty-one hours or more a week.

If individuals are aged sixty-five or over and were entitled to CA on 12 October 2002, they can continue to get CA, even if they stop caring for thirty-five hours a week, or if the DLA or AA of the person they look after stops. Or if the carer starts full-time work, though carers must continue to meet other CA rules.

Support for carers

Anyone who looks after someone who is ill or disabled, or is a person who could not manage without their care, may be able to get help from the local council or the NHS. The person does not need to be an "official" carer to qualify for help. The local council's Social Services Department can give information on what is available. GP practices, district nurses or health visitors can help someone contact the council. There is also information for carers on the websites: www.direct.gov.uk, www.carersonline.org.uk, and www.carers.org.

HB6, A Practical Guide for Disabled People or Carers, is for anyone who has a disability or who looks after a disabled relative or friend. It has information about rights, benefits, holidays, housing, leisure activities, and the services provided by central and local government and voluntary organizations, such as the Royal Association for Disability and Rehabilitation (RADAR) and Age Concern. Available free through the Department of Health Publications Orderline: 08701 555 455 Mon–Fri 8.00 a.m.–6.00 p.m. Or write to the Department of Health, PO Box 777, London SE1 6XH.

Work and benefits

Permitted work (PW)

Formerly "therapeutic work", PW enables people to try some paid work while they are getting IB, SDA, NI credits, or IS because of illness or disability. It is no longer necessary for a doctor to agree that the work will help someone's medical condition, as was the case with therapeutic work, but the person is required to inform the office that deals with their benefit before starting work and to fill in an application form.

Individuals can work and earn up to £20 a week at any time for as long as they are on benefit. The £20 limit means that entitlement to IS, housing benefit (HB) or council tax benefit (CTB) should not be affected. DLA and AA are payable whether or not someone is working.

Supported permitted work (SPW)

Someone can do work which is supervised by a person employed by a public or local authority or voluntary organization which gives/arranges work for people with disabilities, for example, in the community or a sheltered workshop. The support must be ongoing and regular. Work can also be part of a treatment programme, done under medical supervision, for example, as an inpatient or outpatient in a hospital or similar setting.

Because of the national minimum wage no one will be able to work more than sixteen hours a week, since individuals cannot earn more than £81.00 after allowable deductions. It is advised that people notify the Department of Work and Pensions (DWP) to check if the work is deemed SPW. Earnings from SPW may affect a person's entitlement to other benefits.

Permitted work higher limit (PWHL)

A person can work for up to sixteen hours a week. He or she can earn no more than £81.00 week, after any allowable deductions. Individuals can normally work for up to a maximum of fifty-two weeks in any year, but they must notify the DWP within six weeks of starting work.

Working Tax Credit (WTC)

Individuals are entitled if:

- they are at least sixteen and either they or their partner are working for sixteen or more hours a week and are responsible for a child who normally lives with them;
- they have a physical or mental disability that disadvantages them in getting a job and they were previously receiving some form of disability benefit;
- They or their partner are twenty-five or over and work at least thirty hours a week;
- They and their partner are fifty or over and qualify for the 50 plus element, which is subject to certain conditions. For instance, either they or their partner must work at least sixteen hours a week.

WTC disability element

A person needs to be working at least sixteen hours a week and have a physical or mental disability which puts them at a disadvantage in getting a job, and meet one of several other conditions. But people are eligible if at any time in the last twenty-six weeks before their claim for WTC they, or their partner, if they have one, were getting higher rate short-term IB, or long-term IB or SDA.

Social Fund

This makes extra payments to people on certain benefits to meet expenses that they have difficulty meeting out of their regular income. It is divided into two parts, Regulated and Discretionary.

Regulated social fund provides Sure Start maternity grants, funeral, cold weather, and winter fuel payments. Individuals who satisfy the regulations are entitled to a payment and can appeal against decisions to a tribunal. The Disability Benefits Helpline can advise. (See below.) The claim form, SF100, is available from local Job Centres Plus or antenatal clinics.

Discretionary social fund provides grants and loans to meet a variety of other needs. For instance, someone might apply for a Crisis Loan to meet an immediate financial crisis. Although payments are discretionary and budget-limited, people can apply for a review if their application is refused.

Pension Credit

This is a means-tested benefit. People aged sixty and over may be entitled to this credit even if they have a partner who is younger. It has two parts. If a person has an income below a certain level the difference will be made up by Guaranteed Credit, to help with personal care, acting as a carer, or having certain housing costs, for example, mortgage interest payments.

Savings Credit can be paid if the person or their partner is sixty-five or over. Entitlement is not affected by someone receiving Attendance Allowance, Disability Living Allowance, Housing Benefit, or Council Tax Benefit. For further information call freephone 0800 99 1234.

Complaints procedure

If a mistake has been made, an individual should receive an explanation and an apology. Each DWP agency has its own complaints procedure, but the following points may help resolve the problem.

- Complain as soon as it is clear that something has gone wrong.
- Ask the office who has been dealing with the matter for their complaints leaflet and charter.
- Contact the person who dealt with the matter. (It is a good idea for someone to try to remember or jot down the name of staff they deal with for possible future reference.)
- If the complaint is not resolved, the manager at the office dealing with the claim is the person to contact. If this does not result in a satisfactory response, it might help to contact the district manager for that office or the area's chief executive.
- If the complaint remains unresolved for some time it can be useful for the person to involve their MP, who can help if someone would like the Ombudsman to investigate. There's information on their website: www.bioa.org.uk.

How not to miss out

If someone is confused or worried about an entitlement or has lost or been denied a state benefit to which he or she thinks they are entitled, the local Citizens Advice Bureau or branch of Mind can give advice (see the local telephone book), as well as The Benefit Enquiry Line (BEL) Tel: 0800 882200 (Mon–Fri 8.30 a.m.–6.30 p.m. and Sat 9.00 a.m.–1.00 p.m.), branches of CAB (The Citizen's Advice Bureau), or Dial UK (Disability Information and Advice Line) Tel: 01302 310123. The Benefits and Work website www.benefitsand-work.co.uk has information on the benefits available to people with disabilities and their carers.

(The benefits and entitlements quoted tend to rise yearly in line with inflation.The figures quoted are correct at the time of publication.)

Local Authority benefits

Most local authorities give travel concessions to people with severe mental health problems who are receiving DLA or other benefits. The council's One Stop Shop, Customer Benefit Service, or the Citizens Advice Bureau can give advice.

Housing Benefit (HB)

For people who need help to pay their rent, HB is tax-free and not dependent on NI contributions. It does not cover some service charges, fuel costs, meals, or mortgage interest payments.

Council Tax Benefit (CTB)

This is for people on a low income who have difficulty in paying their council tax. It has similar rules to Housing Benefit.

Useful addresses/resources

The Disability Rights Handbook: A Guide to Benefits and Services for All Disabled People, Their Families, Carers and Advisers is published annually in May, price £19 and £13.50 for people on benefits. For more information, or to order a copy, contact Disability Alliance, Universal House, 88–94 Wentworth Street, London E1 7SA. Tel:

0207 247 8776; email: office.da@dial.pipex.com; website: www.
disabilityalliance.org. *Your Voice*, the magazine for members of
Rethink, has regular features on benefits and services for people
with mental illness and their carers.

Legal rights and the Mental Health Acts

Historically, people with mental health problems have been neglected and unfairly punished and imprisoned. Under current legislation, people who are severely mentally ill can be hospitalized against their will, but individuals still have rights, which by law have to be respected. Currently, proposals to introduce a new English Mental Health Act have been dropped, though it is anticipated that the government will seek to revise the existing legislation. In the meantime, the Mental Health Act (England) 1983 covers the admission, treatment, and rights of people with a mental disorder living in England, Wales, and Northern Ireland. A Code of Practice also provides guidance on the use of the Act and good practice. Scotland has its own act, The Mental Health (Care and Treatment) (Scotland) Act 2003.

The Mental Health Act (England) 1983

Voluntary and involuntary admission

Someone who voluntarily admits him or herself is described as an "informal" patient. A person who is admitted without his or her consent is known as a "formal" patient and is often referred to as being detained or "sectioned", the latter term being used because they are admitted under a particular section of the Mental Health Act.

Grounds for compulsory admission

A person is admitted or detained on the grounds that he or she has a mental disorder and that it is in the interests of his or her health, personal safety, or the safety of others.

Either a person's nearest relative or an approved social worker (ASW) can apply for the compulsory admission of a person with a mental disorder if they consider this to be appropriate. A court can also apply for the compulsory admission of an offender convicted of a criminal offence, or of a person already in prison. An informal patient who is already in hospital can be detained by a doctor or nurse qualified to work with mentally ill people.

How long does a Section last?

Sections 2, 3 and 4 of the Mental Health Act govern the length and reason for admitting someone to hospital.

Section 2—admission for assessment and any necessary treatment

Section 2 lasts up to twenty-eight days. Two doctors must give a recommendation, and people should be informed in writing under which section of the Act they are being detained, what this means, and be given information about their right to a Mental Health Review Tribunal, which will review the detention (see below). The hospital must also inform the person's nearest relative of the situation and their own rights under the Act.

Section 3—admission for treatment

This allows for someone to be admitted for treatment for up to six months. This period can be renewed for a further six months, then for one year at a time. As soon as is practicable after admission, the hospital must inform the person which section of the Act he or she is being detained under, what this means, and give information about their right to a Mental Health Review Tribunal (MHRT).

Section 4—admission for assessment in an emergency

In the case of an emergency, someone can be detained for up to seventy-two hours or up to six hours hours if detained by a first level nurse. The person must be assessed within seventy-two hours and if the doctor carrying out the assessment believes the person should remain in hospital for treatment, he or she can be detained for up to twenty-eight days, though this requires a second medical recommendation. Again, the person must be informed in writing under which section of the Act he or she is being detained and what this means.

Section 5—compulsory detention of an informal patient

A person already in hospital voluntarily can be compulsorily sectioned by the doctor treating him or her, or by a senior level nurse qualified in work with mentally ill people, if they believe the individual should be detained. The doctor must make a recommendation and the person should be detained under sections 2 or 3 within seventy-two hours if detained by a doctor and six hours if detained by a nurse.

Sections 7–10—guardianship

The nearest relative or an approved social worker (ASW) can apply for a person over sixteen to be received into the guardianship of a local social services department, or an individual approved by the local social services in the area where the person lives.

Sections 35–38

These allow the transfer of an individual to hospital from prison for a medical report, for treatment, and an interim hospital order. These last from twenty-eight days to a maximum of twelve weeks.

Other sections of the Act also allow the courts to authorize admission to hospital. Section 135, the right of access order, for instance, allows a magistrate to issue a warrant to search for and remove from their home someone who it is believed is suffering from a mental disorder and, as a consequence, is at risk of being ill-treated, or neglecting or endangering themselves. The person can be kept in hospital for up to seventy-two hours, pending an application for a section.

Section 41—detention ordered by the court

This allows a Crown Court, which has imposed a Hospital Order under Section 37, up to six months, and renewable, to impose a Restriction Order without specifying a time limit if it is considered necessary for protecting the public from serious harm. In this case, one of the two doctors who made the recommendation must give spoken evidence to support the order.

Discharge

Someone who is detained under Sections 2 and 3 can be discharged on the recommendation of a Responsible Medical Officer (RMO), a decision by hospital managers, an application by the person's nearest relative, or a Mental Health Review Tribunal.

Consent to treatment

Someone's consent to treatment for mental health problems is not always required. Treatment includes medication, nursing and behaviour therapy, seclusion, and restraint. However, the Code of Practice states that any proposed treatment must be discussed with both the individual and their nearest relative. Individuals who admit themselves voluntarily must give consent to any examination and treatment and can make a complaint if this condition is not followed. People admitted under Section 4 must also give their consent before being given any medical treatment for their mental distress.

Other formal patients can be examined and given medical treatment for their mental distress during the first three months of admission without consent—though it is regarded as good practice to obtain this consent—except with treatments considered to be irreversible or potentially hazardous, such as ECT (electro-convulsive therapy). Under Section 57, these treatments require both consent and a certificate by a second opinion appointed doctor (SOAD). At the end of the three months, continued treatment can be given with or without the person's consent, subject to the approval of an SOAD.

Rights to information

Care managers, who are usually doctors, are duty-bound to:

- provide written and oral information to the person who is detained;
- ensure that the person understands which section of the Act he or she is being detained under, and the implications of that provision;
- inform the person of their rights to a Mental Health Review Tribunal;
- inform the person of the implications of the sections of the Act concerned with discharge, compulsory treatment, the existence of the Code of Practice and the Mental Health Commission;
- ensure that the person's nearest relative receives a copy of any written information given to the individual, unless he or she raises an objection.

Mental Health Commission (MHC)

This was set up to ensure that patients are cared for properly while in hospital. If someone has a complaint he or she can write to the MHC while they are in hospital or after they have left. (See Further information at the end of this Appendix.)

Medical Health Review Tribunal (MHRT)

The MHRT is an independent body responsible for hearing appeals against a patient's detention. The tribunal panel comprises at least a lawyer; who acts as the chairperson, a doctor, and a lay member. The patient and a social worker must be present at the hearing. The patient can have legal representation at an MHRT. All patients who appeal to a MHRT have a right to legal representation through Legal Aid. The Law Society publishes a list of solicitors who are approved for MHRT representation. (See Further information.)

The tribunal has the powers to:

- discharge the patient from hospital;
- recommend leave of absence;
- recommend supervised discharge;
- decide on a delayed or conditional discharge, or transfer to another hospital;
- reconvene if their recommendation is not complied with.

Patients must automatically be referred to an MHRT if they:

- are detained under Section 3, patients who have not been to an MHRT within the last six months;
- have their detention renewed, and have not appealed to an MHRT in the last three years if aged sixteen years or over, or the last one year, if aged less than sixteen years.

The Secretary of State can refer any patient to an MHRT at any time.

- The appeals of patients who want to appeal to a MHRT are governed by time guidelines.
- Patients under Section 2 must do so within fourteen days of the start of their detention. The hearing must be heard within seven days.
- If between making the appeal and the hearing a patient under Section 2 is transferred to a Section 3, the MHRT will still hear the original appeal and it will not affect the patient's right to appeal under Section 3.

- Patients detained under Section 3 may appeal to an MHRT once in a six month period.
- Patients under Section 37 can only apply to an MHRT after the first six months. Thereafter their rights of appeal are the same as for Section 3 patients.

Prior to the MHRT hearing

- written reports on medical, nursing, and social circumstances must be provided to the MHRT members, the patient, and the patient's solicitor;
- the medical member of the MHRT will examine the patient before the hearing and may make copies of notes. The patient's solicitor may request an independent psychiatric report. Any information that could be harmful to the patient's health or safety, or to the health and safety of others if it is disclosed to the patient, is required to be submitted in a separate confidential report. Confidential reports should include the reasons why the information should be withheld from the patient;
- a patient's solicitor will see all the reports written for the MHRT, but does not have automatic rights to the patient's records. The MHRT has the legal right to obtain any information it thinks necessary and to call witnesses.

Withdrawing an appeal to an MHRT

Appeals can only be withdrawn in writing and should be backed by the patient's solicitor. The MHRT will then decide whether to accept the withdrawal.

How long should it take to get an MHRT?

For patients detained under Section 2, an MHRT should be heard within seven days. Hearings for patients detained under other sections should be arranged within eight weeks of the request being received at the Tribunal office. Written reports should be submitted to the Tribunal within three weeks of a request for the written report.

However, there are often much longer delays. On 23 April 2002, a High Court judge in the UK ruled that lengthy delays in getting a tribunal hearing are a breach of human rights (Article 5, 4 of the European Convention on Human Rights). Following this ruling, many detained patients who do not get a speedy tribunal hearing could claim compensation.

*What is the procedure if a suspect or offender no longer
needs treatment?*

If an MHRT finds that a patient detained under Sections 47/49 or
48/49 no longer needs hospital treatment the patient becomes liable
to return to prison (Section 47) or to court to stand trial (Section 48).
If the MHRT feels that the patient should be conditionally or
absolutely discharged under the Mental Health Act, it is obliged
to refer the case to the Home Secretary, who must then make the
decision.

Complaints procedure

If someone has a complaint while in hospital he or she can speak to
the doctor, nurse, or social worker. If the person is not satisfied with
the answer, it is recommended that they write to the hospital
mangers. He or she can also write to the Mental Health Commission. (See Further information.)

Rethink can give further information on the MHRT, the Mental
Health Act, and an individual's rights under the European Convention of Human Rights. (See References.)

After discharge from hospital

Under Section 117, the District Health Authority and the Social
Services Department have a legal duty to provide after care for people who have been detained under Sections 3, 37–41 and 47–49. The
Responsible Medical Officer must hold a multi-disciplinary discussion to hear the views of the person and his or her carers. These are
taken into account in devising a care plan for the person's continuing health and social needs. Once agreed, the care plan, whether
Standard or Enhanced, is written down and a care coordinator
appointed.

Sometimes people believe that their care plan is merely a way of
ensuring they continue to take medication, and this will almost
inevitably be part of their care plan. But ultimately, the care
programme approach is meant to provide the treatment and
support that can help someone to stay well and live independently.

However, if people object to their plan a first step would be to express such concerns to their care coordinator, or contact their psychiatrist. If people still have concerns they could contact an advocacy project for advice.

Mental Health Law: A Practical Guide (Hodder Arnold) provides clear and comprehensive information on mental health law in a easy-to-read format.

The Mental Health (Care and Treatment) (Scotland) Act 2003

The Act affects people in Scotland with mental health problems. This term is used to include people with personality disorders and learning disabilites. The main points are summarized in a series of booklets for service users and their carers. These are:

- *The New Mental Health Act: An Easy Read Guide* (see below).
- *A Guide to Emergency and Short-term Cover.*
- *A Guide to Compulsory Treatment Orders.*
- *The Role of the Mental Welfare Commission.*
- *A Guide for People Involved in Criminal Justice Proceedings.*
- *A Guide to Independent Advocacy.*
- *A Guide to the Roles and Duties of NHS Boards and Local Authorities.*

The booklets are available free from Blackwells Bookshop in Edinburgh, or can be read/downloaded from the Scottish Executive website: www.scotland.gov.uk.

The New Mental Health Act—An Easy Read Guide

What the new law means to you

The new law sets out the rules for when you can be sent to hospital or kept in hospital even when you do not want to be there. The new law also sets out the rules for when you can be made to have medical treatment.

Medical treatment

This means pills, medicine, counselling or anything else that will help you to get better when you are ill.

These rules apply to you if:

- You have learning disabilities or a mental health problem.
- Medical treatment can make you better.
- You might hurt yourself or someone else if you did not have medical treatment.
- You cannot make decisions about medical treatment on your own.
- There is no other way to help you.

The new rules apply to Councils and Health Boards as well

- Councils and Health Boards must try to make sure that you understand what is happening to you.
- Health Boards will have to set up special services for children and young people.
- Local councils will have to provide more services in the community.
- The council willl have to do an assessment of your needs. They will have to do it quickly.

Assessment

This is when someone like a social worker fills in a form about the help you need.

Your rights

- You have the right to have a named person
- You have the right to get help from an independent advocate
- You have the right to make an advance statement
- You have the right to go to a Mental Health Tribunal

Advance statement

An advance statement is your statement about how you would like to be treated or not treated if you are ill. It is for the people who are looking after you to read. You can only make an advance statement when you are well enough to say what you want. The statement must be:

— in writing
— signed and dated by you
— witnessed.

Named person

A named person is someone who will support you. They can be a relative, a carer or someone else you choose.

Advocate

An independent advocate is someone who will speak up for you. They will tell people what you want to happen.

Mental Health Tribunal

A doctor can say you need to go into hospital or need to have medical treatment. If you disagree they will have to ask a special panel for permission to treat you. The panel is called the Mental Health Tribunal

The Mental Welfare Commission

> The commission checks that the new law is working for you. They visit people in hospitals and other places. They will look into things if they think there is a problem with how you are being treated. (*Reprinted with permission from the Scottish Executive*)

In contrast to the previous act, the new one is based on a set of guiding principles. As a general rule, anyone who takes any action under the Act has to take account of the principles. There are ten principles:

1. Non-discrimination—People with mental disorder should, wherever possible, retain the same rights and entitlements as those with other health needs.
2. Equality—All powers under the Act should be exercised without any direct or indirect discrimination on the grounds of

physical disability, age, gender, sexual orientation, language, religion or national or ethnic or social origin.

3. Respect for diversity—Service users should receive care, treatment and support in a manner that accords respect for their individual qualities, abilities and diverse backgrounds and properly takes into account their age, gender, sexual orientation, ethnic group and social, cultural and religious background.

4. Reciprocity—Where society imposes an obligation on an individual to comply with a programme of treatment of care, it should impose a parallel obligation on the health and social care authorities to provide safe and appropriate services, including ongoing care following discharge from compulsion.

5. Informal care—Wherever possible, care, treatment and support should be provided to people with mental disorder without the use of compulsory powers.

6. Participation—Service users should be fully involved, so far as they are able to be, in all aspects of their assessemnt, care, treatment and support. Their past and present wishes should be taken into account. They should be provided with all the information and support necessary to enable them to participate fully. Information should be provided in a way which makes it most likely to be understood.

7. Respect for carers—those who provide care to service users on an informal basis should receive respect for their role and experience, receive appropriate information and advice, and have their views and needs taken into account.

8. Least restrictive alternative—Service users should be provided with any necessary care, treatment and support both in the least invasive manner and in the least restrictive manner and environment compatible with the delivery of safe and effective care, taking account where appropriate of the safety of others.

9. Benefit—Any intervention under the Act should be likely to produce for the service users a benefit that cannot reasonably be achieved other than by the intervention.

10. Child welfare—The welfare of a child with mental disorder should be paramount in any interventions imposed on the child under the Act.

(Reprinted with permission from the Scottish Executive)

Further information

Rethink Advice Service, 0208 974 6814 Mon–Fri, 10.00 a.m.–3.00 p.m.; email: advice@nsf.org.uk

The Mental Health Act Commission, Maid Marian House, 56, Hounds Gate, Nottingham NG1 6BG. Tel: 0115 943 7100; Fax: 0115 943 7101; email: chief.executive@mhac.org.uk

The Law Society, Tel: 020 7242 1222; email: info.service@lawsociety. org.uk.To search for a list of solicitors by location, name, and specialization, websites: www.solicitors-online.com; www.lawsociety. org.uk

The Mental Welfare Commission, K Floor, Argyle House, 3 Lady Lawson Street, Edinburgh EH3 9SH. Tel: 0131 222 6111 or service user and carer freephone 0800 389 6809; website: www.mwcscot. org.uk

Mental Health Law Team, Scottish Executive Health Department, St Andrew's House, Edinburgh EH1 3DG. Tel: 0131 244 2591; email: mentalhealthlaw@scotland.gsi.gov.uk; website: www.scotland. gov.uk/health/mental-health

Blackwell's Bookshop, 53 South Bridge, Edinburgh EH1 1YS. Tel: 0131 622 8283 or 0131 622 8258; Fax: 0131 557 8149; email: business.edinburgh@blackwell.co.uk

REFERENCES

Adams, M. (1995). With complements. *Health Service Journal*, 23: 1 June.

Agarwal, A., Ranjan, R., Dhiraaj, S., Lakra,. A., Kumar, M., & Singh, U. (2005). Acupressure for prevention of pre-operative anxiety: a prospective, randomized, placebo controlled study. *Anaesthesia*, 60(10): 978–981.

Aleman, A., Kahn, R. S., & Selten, J. P. (2003). Sex differences in the risk of schizophrenia: Evidence from meta-analysis. *Archives of General Psychiatry*, 60: 565–571.

Allen, K., Blascovich, J., & Mendes, W. B. (2002). Cardiovascular reactivity and the presence of pets, friends, and spouses: the truth about cats and dogs. *Psychosomatic Medicine*, 64: 727–739.

Allen, K., Shykoff, B. E., & Izzo, Jnr., J. I. (2001). Pet ownership, but not ACE inhibitor therapy, blunts home blood pressure responses to mental stress. *Hypertension*, 38(4): 815–820.

Allott, P. (2005). Personal communication.

Allott P., Loganathan, L., & Fulford, K. W. M. (2002). Discovering hope for recovery from a British perspective: a review of a selection of recovery literature, implications for practice and system change. *Canandian Journal of Community Mental Health*, 21(2, special issue) International Innovations in Community Mental Health: 13–34.

American Psychiatric Association (1977). Practice guidelines for the treatment of patients with schizophrenia. *The American Journal of Psychiatry, 154*(Suppl.)1: 1–63).

American Psychiatric Association (1994). *Diagnostic and Statistical Manual of Mental Disorders (4th edn.).* Washington, DC: American Psychiatric Association.

Andresen, R., Oades, L., & Caputi, P. (2003). The experience of recovery from schizophrenia: towards an empirically validated stage model. *Australian and New Zealand Journal of Psychiatry, 37*(5): 586–594.

Angrist, B., Lee, H. K., & Gershon, S. (1974). The antagonism of amphetamine-induced symptomalogy by a neuroleptic. *The American Journal of Psychiatry, 131*: 817–819.

Ashton, A. K., Hammer, R., & Rosen, R. C. (1997). Serotonin reuptake inhibitor-induced sexual dysfunction and its treatment: a large scale retrospective study of 596 psychiatric outpatients. *Journal of Sex and Marital Therapy, 23*: 165–175.

Astin, J. A. (1998). Why patients use alternative medicine: results of a national study. *JAMA, 279*: 1548–1553.

Astin, J. A., Harkness, E., & Ernst, E. (2000). The Efficacy of 'Distant Healing': A systematic review of randomized trials. *Annals of Internal Medicine, 132* (11): 903–910.

Austin, J. H., & Ausubel, P. (1992). Enhanced respiratory muscular function in normal adults after lessons in proprioceptive musculosketal education without exercises. *Chest, 102*(2): 486–490.

Awad, A. G., & Hogan, T. P. (1994). Subjective response to neuroleptics and the quality of life: implications for treatment outcome. *Acta Psychiatrica Scandinavica, 89*(Suppl. 380): 27–32.

Babyak, M., Blumenthal, J. A., Herman, S., Khatri, P., Doraiswamy, M., Moore, K., Craighead, W. E., Baldewicz, T.T., & Krishnan, K. R. (2000). Exercise treatment for major depression: maintenance of therapeutic benefit at 10 months. *Psychosomatic Medicine, 62*(5): 633–638.

Baldacchino, D., & Draper, P. (2001). Spiritual coping strategies: a review of the nursing research literature. *Journal of Advanced Nursing, 34*(6): 833–841.

Baldessarini, R., & Viguera. A. (1995). Neuroleptic withdrawal in schizophrenic patients. *Archives of General Psychiatry, 52*: 189–192.

Baldessarini, R. J., Cohen, B. M., & Teicher, M. H. (1988). Significance of neuroleptic dose and plasma level in the pharmacological treatment of psychoses. *Archives of General Psychiatry, 45*: 79–91.

Ball, P., Coons, V. B., & Buchanan, R. W. (2001). A program for treating olanzapine-related weight gain. *Psychiatric Services, 52*: 967–969.

Barak, Y., Savorai, O., Mavashev, S., & Beni, A. (2001). Animal-assisted therapy for elderly schizophrenic patients: a one-year controlled trial. *American Journal Geriatric Psychiatry, 9*(4): 439–442.

Barlow, W. (1991). *The Alexander Principle.* London: Gollancz.

Barnes, M., & Berke, J. (1991). *Two Accounts of a Journey Through Madness.* New York: Other Press.

Barrowclough, C., & Tarrier, N. (1987). A behavioural family intervention with a schizophrenic patient: a study. *Behavioural Psychotherapy, 15*(3): 252–271.

Beaubrun, G., & Gray, G. E. (2000). A review of herbal medicines for psychiatric disorders. *Psychiatric Services, 51*: 1130–1134.

Bebbington, P. E., Bhugra, D., Brugha, T., Singleton, N., Farrell, M., Jenkins, R., Lewis. G., & Meltzer, H. (2004). Psychosis, victimisation and childhood disadvantage. *The British Journal of Psychiatry, 185*: 220–226.

Bebbington, P., & Kuipers, L. (1994). The predictive utility of expressed emotion in schizophrenia: an aggregate analysis. *Psychological Medicine, 24*: 707–718.

Beck, A. T. (1952) Successful outpatient psychotherapy of a chronic schizophrenic with delusion based on borrowed guilt. *Psychiatry, 15*: 305–312.

Beck, A. T., & Rector, N. A. (1998). Cognitive therapy for schizophrenia patients. *Harvard Mental Health Letter, 15*: 4–6.

Bennett, E. J., Tennant, C. C., Piesse, C., Badcock, C. A., & Kellow, J. E. (1998). Level of chronic life stress predicts clinical outcome in irritable bowel syndrome. *Gut, 43*: 256–261.

Bennett, M. P., Zeller, J. M., Rosenberg, L., & McCann, J. (2003). The effect of mirthful laughter on stress and natural killer cell activity. *Alternative Therapies in Health and Medicine, 9*(2): 38–45.

Bentall, R. P. (2003). *Madness Explained: Psychosis and Human Nature.* London: Penguin.

Bentall, R. P. (1994). Cognitive biases and abnormal beliefs: towards a model of persecutory delusions. In: A. S. David & J. Cutting (Eds.), *The Neuropsychology of Schizophrenia* (pp. 337–360). London: Lawrence Erlbaum.

Bentall, R. P. (2000). Hypnotic and psychotic hallucinations: rich data capable of multiple interpretations. *Contemporary Hypnosis, 17*(1): 21–25.

Bentall, R. P. (2001). Social cognition and delusional beliefs. In: P. W. Corrigan & D. L. Penn (Eds.), *Social Cognition and Schizophrenia* (pp. 123–148). Washington, DC: American Psychological Association.

Bentall, R. P., & Kinderman, P. (1998). Psychological processes and delusional beliefs: implications for the treatment of paranoid states. In: T. Wykes, N. Tarrier, & S. Lewis (Eds.), *Outcome and Innovation in Psychological Treatment of Schizophrenia* (pp. 119–144). Chichester: Wiley.

Bentall, R. P., Kinderman, P., & Bowen-Jones, K. (1999). Response latencies for the causal explanations of depressed, paranoid and normal individuals: availability of self-representations. *Cognitive Neuropsychiatry*, 4(2): 107–118.

Bentall, R. P., Corcoran, R., Howard, R., Blackwood, N., & Kinderman, P. (2001). Persecutory delusions: a review and theoretical integration. *Clinical Psychology Review*, 21(8): 1143–1192.

Bentall, R., Jackson, H., & Pilgrim, D. (1988). Abandoning the concept of schizophrenia: some implications of validity arguments for psychological research into psychotic phenomena. *British Journal of Clinical Psychology*, 27: 303–324.

Bergemann, N., Ehrig, C., Diebold, K., Mundt, C., & von Einsiedel, R. (1999). Asymptomatic pancreatitis associated with Clozapine. *Pharmacopsychiatry*, 32: 78–80.

Berk, L. S., Felten, D. L., Tan, S. A., Bittman, B. B., & Westengard, J. (2001). Modulation of neuroimmune parameters during the eustress of humor-associated mirthful laughter. *Alternative Therapies*, 7(2): 62–76.

Bhugra, D., Leff, J., Mallett, R., Der, G., Corridan, B., & Rudge, S. (1997). Incidence and outcome of schizophrenia in Whites, African-Caribbeans and Asians in London. *Psychological Medicine*, 27: 791–798.

Bhugra, E. (2000). Migration and schizophrenia. *Acta Psychiatrica Scandinavica*, 102(Suppl. 407): 68–73(6).

Bishbee, C. C. (1983). Psychosocial approaches to treatment of schizophrenia. *Journal of Orthomolecular Psychiatry*, 12(3): 208–221.

Blumenthal, J. A., Babyak, M. A., Moore, K. A., Craighead, W. E., Herman, S., Khatri, P., Waugh, R., Napolitano, M. A., Forman, L. M., Appelbaum, M., Doraiswamy, P. M. & Krishnan, K. R. (1999). Effects of exercise training on older patients with major depression. *Archives of Internal Medicine*, 159(19): 2349–2356.

Bobes, J., & Garcia-Portilla, M. P., Rejas, J. Hern Ndez, G., Garcia-Garcia, M., Rico-Villademoros, F., & Porras, A. (2003). Frequency of sexual dysfunction and other reproductive side-effects in patients with schizophrenia treated with Risperidone, Olanzapine, Quetiapine or Haloperidol: the results of the EIRE study. *Journal of Sex and Marital Therapy, 30*: 124–147.

Bockoven, J. S., & Solomon, H. C. (1975). Comparison of two five-year follow-up studies: 1948 to 1952 and 1967 to 1972. *The American Journal of Psychiatry, 29*(2): 125–147.

Bolton, G., Howlett, S., Lago, C., & Wright, J. K. (Eds.) (2004). *Writing Cures: An Introductory Handbook of Writing in Counselling and Psychotherapy.* London: Brunner/Routledge.

Bore, G. M. (1998). Acute neuropathy after exposure to sun in a patient treated with St John's Wort. *The Lancet, 352*: 1121–1122.

Boydell, J., van Os, J., McKenzie, K., Allardyce, J., Goel, R., McCreadie, R. G., & Murray, R. M. (2001). Incidence of schizophrenia in ethnic minorities in London: ecological study into interactions with environment. *British Medical Journal, 323*: 1336–1338.

Boyle, M. (1993). *Schizophrenia: A Scientific Delusion?* London: Routledge.

Bradbury, T. N., & Miller, G. A. (1985). Season of birth in schizophrenia: a review of evidence, methodology and etiology. *Psychological Bulletin, 98*: 569–594.

Breier, A., & Strauss, J. (1983). Self-control in psychotic disorders. *Archives of General Psychiatry, 40*: 1141–1145.

Breier, A., & Strauss, J. S. (1984). The role of social relationships in the recovery from psychotic disorders. *The American Journal of Psychiatry, 141*: 949–955.

Brooks, J. S., & Scarano, T. (1985). Transcendental meditation in the treatment of post-Vietnam adjustment. *Journal of Counseling and Development, 64*: 212–215.

Brown, A. S., Begg, M. D., Gravenstein, S., Schaefer, C. A., Wyatt, R. J., Bresnahan, M., Babulas, V. P., & Susser, E. S. (2004). Serologic evidence of prenatal influenza in the etiology of schizophrenia. *Archives of General Psychiatry, 61*(8): 774–780.

Brown, C. K. (1995). Spiritual healing in a general practice: using a quality-of-life questionnaire to measure outcome. *Complementary Therapies in Medicine, 3*: 230–233.

Brown, G. W., & Birley, J. L. T. (1968). Crises and life changes and the onset of schizophrenia. *US Journal of Health and Social Behaviour, 9*: 203–214.

Brown, K. M., Morrice, P. C., & Duthie, G. G. (1998). Erythrocyte membrane fatty acid composition of smokers and non-smokers: the effects of vitamin E supplementation. *European Journal of Clinical Nutrition, 52*: 145–150.

Brown, M. A., Ridgway, P., Anthony, W. A., & Rogers, E. S. (1991). Comparison of outcomes for clients seeking and assigned to supported housing services. *Hospital and Community Psychiatry, 42*: 1150–1153.

Bryden, K. E., & Kopala, L. C. (1999). Body Mass Index increase of 58% associated with Olanzapine. *The American Journal of Psychiatry, 156*: 1835–1836.

Buckle, J. (1993). Does it matter which lavender essential oil is used? *Nursing Times, 89*(20): 32–35.

Burek, S., Toprac, M., & Olsen, M. (1996). Third-year outcomes of supported housing in Texas: measuring the long-term effects of system change. Presentation at the Sixth Annual National Conference on State Mental Health Agency Services Research and Program Evaluation. Arlington, VA.

Buscaino, G. A. (1978). The amino-hepato-entero-toxic theory of schizophrenia: an historical evaluation. In: W. A. Hemmings & G. J. Hemmings (Eds.), *The Biological Basis of Schizophrenia* (pp. 45–54). Lancaster: MTP.

Bustillo, J. R., Lauriello, J., Horan, W. P., & Keith, S. J. (2001). The psychosocial treatment of schizophrenia: an update. *The American Journal of Psychiatry, 158*(2): 163–175.

Butzlaff, R. L., & Hooley, J. M. (1998). Expressed emotion and psychiatric relapse: a meta-analysis. *Archives of General Psychiatry, 55*: 547–552.

Byerly, M. J., Lescouflair, E., Weber, M. T., Bugno, R. M., Fisher, R., Carmody, T., Varghese, F., & Rush, A. J. (2004). An open-label trial of Quetiapine for antipsychotic-induced sexual dysfunction. *Journal of Sex and Marital Therapy, 30*: 325–332.

Cacciatore, T. W., Horak, F. B., & Henry, S. M. (2005). Improvement in automatic postural coordination following Alexander Technique lessons in low back pain. *Physical Therapy, 85*(6): 91–116.

Cannon, M., Jones, P. B., & Murray, R. M. (2002). Obstetric complications and schizophrenia: historical and meta-analytic review. *The American Journal of Psychiatry, 159*: 1080–1092.

Cantwell, R. (2003). Substance use and schizophrenia: effects on symptoms, social functioning and service use. *The British Journal of Psychiatry, 182*(4): 324–329.

Carney, M. W., Chary, T. K., Laundy, M., Bottiglieri, T., Chanarin, I., Reynolds, E. H., & Toone, B. (1990). Red cell folate concentrations in psychiatric patients. *Journal of Affective Disorders, 3*: 207–213.

Carpenter, W. T. Jnr., Buchanan, R. W., Kirkpatrick, B., & Breier, A. F. (1999). Diazepam treatment of early signs of exacerbation in schizophrenia. *The American Journal of Psychiatry, 156*(2): 299–303.

Carpenter, W. T., Hanlon, T. E., Heinrichs, D. W., Summerfelt, A. T., Kirkpatrick, B., Levine, J., & Buchanan, R. W. (1990). Continuous versus targeted medication in schizophrenic outpatients: outcome results. *The American Journal of Psychiatry, 147*: 1138–1148.

Cartwright, M., Wardle, J., Steggles, N., Simon, A. E., Croker, H., & Jarvis, M. J. (2003). Stress and dietary practices in adolescents. *Health Psychology, 22*: 362–369.

Casey, D. E., Carson, W. H., Saha, A. R., Liebeskind, A., Ali, M. W., Jody, D., & Ingenito, G. G. (2003). Switching patients to Aripiprazole from other antipsychotic agents: a multicenter randomized study. *Psychopharmacology, 166*(4): 391–399.

Casson, J. (2004). *Drama, Psychotherapy and Psychosis. Dramatherapy and Psychodrama with People Who Hear Voices.* Hove: Brunner-Routledge.

Chadwick, P. (1997). *Schizophrenia: The Positive Perspective.* Hove: Brunner-Routledge.

Chilvers, R., Macdonald, G. M., & Hayes, A. A. (2002). Supported housing for people with severe mental disorders. *The Cochrane Database of Systematic Reviews, 4.* Article No. CD000453.DOI:10.1002/14651858.CD000453.

Chouinard, G., & Jones, B. D. (1980). Neuroleptic-induced supersensitivity psychosis: clinical and pharmacologic characteristics. *The American Journal of Psychiatry, 137*: 16–21.

Chouinard, G., Jones, B. D., & Annable, L. (1978). Neuroleptic-induced supersensitiivity psychosis. *The American Journal of Psychiatry, 135*: 1409–1410.

Christensen, O., & Christensen. E. (1988). Fat consumption and schizophrenia. *Acta Psychiatrica Scandinavica, 78*: 587–591.

Ciompi, L., Dauwalder, H. P., Maier, C., Aebi, E., Trutsch, K., Kupper, Z., & Rutishauser, C. H. (1992). The pilot project Soteria Berne. *British Journal of Psychiatry, 161*(Suppl. 18): 145–153.

Clementz, G., & Dailey, J. W. (1988). Psychotropic effects of caffeine. *American Family Physician, 37*: 167–172.

Cochran-Fritz, S. (1993). Physiological effects of therapeutic massage on the nervous system. *International Journal of Alternative and Complementary Medicine, September*: 21–25.

Cohen, L., Warneke, C., Fouladi, R. T., Rodriguez, M. A., & Chaoul-Reich, A. (2004). Psychological adjustment and sleep quality in a randomized trial of the effects of a Tibetan yoga intervention in patients with lymphoma. *Cancer, 100*(10): 2253–2260.

Connolly, M., & Kelly, C. (2005). Lifestyle and physical health in schizophrenia. *Advances in Psychiatric Treatment, 11*: 125–132.

Cooke, B., & Ernst, E. (2000). Aromatherapy: a systematic review. *The British Journal of General Practice, 50* (455): 493–496.

Cott, J., & Hibbeln, J. R. (2001). Lack of seasonal mood change in Icelanders. [Letter to the Editor]. *The American Journal of Psychiatry, 15*(2): 328.

Cousins, N. (1979). *Anatomy of an Illness as Perceived by the Patient.* New York: Norton.

Crawford-Walker, C. J., King, A., & Chan, S. (2005). Distraction techniques for schizophrenia. *The Cochrane Database of Systematic Reviews, 1.* Article No. CD004717. DOI: 10.1002/14651858. CD004717.

Crepaz-Keay, D. (1999). Drugs. In: C. Newnes, G. Holmes, & C. Dunn (Eds.), *This is Madness Too: Critical Perspectives on Mental Health Services.* Ross on Wye: PCCS Books.

Crinon, S., Van Wersch, A., Van Schaik, P. (2004). The effectiveness of aromatherapy for enhancing the quality of life of people with multiple sclerosis. Presentation at the British Psychological Society Annual Conference, 8–10 September, Edinburgh.

Crow, T. J., MacMillan, J. F., Johnstone, E. C. (1986). The Northwick Park Study of first episodes of schizophrenia II. A randomised controlled trial of prophlactic neuroleptic treatment. *The British Journal of Psychiatry, 148*: 120–127.

Csernansky, J. G., & Schuchart, E. K. (2002). Relapse and rehospitalization rates in patients with schizophrenia: effects of second-generation antipsychotics. *CNS Drug, 16*(7): 473–484.

Cullberg, J. (1999). Integrating psychosocial therapy and low dose medical treatment in a total material of first episode psychotic patients compared to treatment as usual: a three-year follow-up. *Medical Archives, 53*: 167–170.

Cullberg, J. (2002). One-year outcome in first episode psychosis patients in the Swedish Parachute Project. *Acta Psychiatrica Scandinavica, 106*: 276–285.

Dash, M., & Telles, S. (2001). Improvements in handgrip strength in normal volunteers and rheumatoid arthritis patients following yoga training. *Indian Journal of Physiology and Pharmacology, 45*(3): 355–360.

David, A. S., & Prince, M. (2005). Psychosis following head injury: a critical review. *Journal of Neurology, Neurosurgery & Psychiatry*, 76(Suppl 1): i53–i60.

Davidson, L., Chinman, M., Kloos, B., Weingarten, R., Stayner, D., & Kraemer Tebes, J. (1999). Peer support among individuals with severe mental illness: a review of the evidence. *Clinical Psychology: Science and Practice*, 6(2): 165–187.

Davidson, T., Stayner, D., & Haglund, K. E. (1998). Phenomenological perspectives on the social functioning of people with schizophrenia. In: K. Mueser & N. Tarrier (Eds.), *Handbook of Social Functioning in Schizophrenia* (pp. 97–120). Needham Heights, MA: Allyn & Baker.

Davies, S., Thornicroft, G., Leese, M., Higgingbotham, A., & Phelan, M. (1996). Ethnic differences in risk of compulsory psychiatric admission among representative cases of psychosis in London. *The British Medical Journal*, 312: 533–537.

Davis, J. M., & Chen, N. (2004). Dose Response and Dose Equivalence of Antipsychotics. *Journal of Clinical Psychopharmacology*, 24(2): 192–208.

Davison, G. C., & Neale, J. M. (1990). *Abnormal Psychology* (5th edn.). New York: John Wiley & Sons.

De Vries, J. (1985). *Stress and Nervous Disorders*. Edinburgh: Mainstream.

Deegan, P. E. (1988). Recovery: The lived experience of rehabilitation. *Psychosocial Rehabilitation Journal*, 11: 11–19.

Department of Health (DoH) (1999). *National Service Framework for Mental Health*. London: DoH.

Department of Health (2004). *At Least Five a Week: Evidence on the Impact of Physical Activity and its Relationship to Health*. London: DoH.

Dickerson, F. (1998). Strategies that foster empowerment. *Cognitive and Behavioural Practice*, 5: 255–275.

Dickerson, F. B., Sommerville, J., Origoni, A. E., Ringel, N. B., & Parente, F. (2002). Experiences of stigma among outpatients with schizophrenia. *Schizophrenia Bulletin*, 28(1): 143–155.

Dixon, L., Adams, C., & Lucksted, A. (2000). Update on family psycho-education for schizophrenia. *Schizophrenia Bulletin*, 26(1): 5–20.

Dixon, L., Krauss, N., Myers, P., & Lehman, A. (1994). Clinical and treatment correlates of access to Section 8 certificates for homeless mentally ill persons. *Hospital and Community Psychiatry*, 44: 1196–1200.

Dohan, F. C. (1978). Schizophrenia: are some food-derived polypeptides pathogenic? Coeliac disease as a model. In: W. A. Hemmings

& G. Hemmings (Eds.), *The Biological Basis of Schizophrenia* (pp. 167–178). Lancaster: MTP.

Dohan, F. C., & Grasberger, J. C. (1973). Relapsed schizophrenics: earlier discharge from the hospital after cereal-free, milk-free diet. *The American Journal of Psychiatry, 130*: 685–686.

Dong, K. (1996). Foot reflexology in the treatment of neurasthenia. Paper presented to the 1996 Beijing International Reflexology Conference. Beijing.

Downer, S. M., Cody, M. M., McClusky, P., Wilson, P. D., Arnott, S. J., Lister, T. A., & Slevin, M. L. (1994). Pursuit and practice of complementary therapies by cancer patients receiving conventional treatment. *British Medical Journal, 309*: 86–89.

Drake, R. E., & Sederer, L. I. (1986). In patient psychosocial treatment of chronic schizophrenia: negative effects and current guidelines. *Hospital and Community Psychiatry, 37*(9): 897–901.

Drake, R. E., Osher, F., & Wallach, M. (1989). Alcohol use and abuse in schizophrenia. A prospective community study. *The Journal of Nervous and Mental Disease, 177*: 408–414.

Drury, V., Birchwood, M., & Cochrane, R. (2000). Cognitive therapy and recovery from acute psychosis: a controlled trial. 3. Five-year follow-up. *The British Journal of Psychiatry, 177*: 8–14.

Drury, V., Birchwood, M., Cochrane, R., & Macmillan, F. (1996a). Cognitive therapy and recovery from acute psychosis: a controlled trial. I. Impact on psychotic symptoms. *The British Journal of Psychiatry, 169*: 593–601.

Drury, V., Birchwood, M., Cochrane, R., & Macmillan, F. (1996b). Cognitive therapy and recovery from acute psychosis: a controlled trial. II. Impact on recovery time. *The British Journal of Psychiatry, 169*: 602–607.

Duke, P. J., Pantelis, C., McPhillips, M. A., & Barnes, T. R. E. (2001). Comorbid non-alcohol substance misuse among people with schizophrenia: epidemiological study in central London. *The British Journal of Psychiatry, 179*: 509–513.

Eaton, W., Mortensen, P. B., Agerbo, E., Byrne, M., Mors, O., & Ewald, H. (2004). Coeliac disease and schizophrenia: population based case control study with linkage of Danish national registers. *The British Medical Journal, 328*: 438–439.

Eberhardt, M. V., Lee, C. Y., & Liu, R. H. (2000). Antioxidant activity of fresh apples. *Nature, 405*(6789): 903–904.

Edward, R., & Lyon, M. (1999). A review of the effects of nicotine and schizophrenia antipsychotic medication. *Psychiatric Services, 50*: 1346–1350.

Emsley, R., Myburgh, C., Oosthuizen, P., & van Rensburgh, S. J. (2002). Randomised, placebo-controlled study of ethyl-eicosapentaenoic acid as supplemental treatment in schizophrenia. *The American Journal of Psychiatry, 159*(9): 1596–1598.

Epstein, L. J., Morgan, R. D., & Reynolds, L. (1962). An approach to the effect of ataraxic drugs on hospital release rates. *The American Journal of Psychiatry, 119*: 36–47.

Ernst, E., Rand, J. I., Barnes, J., & Stevinson, C. (1998). Complementary therapies for depression. *Archives of General Psychiatry, 55*: 1026–1032.

Fadden, G., Bebbington, P., Kuipers, L. (1987). The burden of care: the impact of functional psychiatric illness on the patient's family. *The British Journal of Psychiatry, 150*: 285–292.

Falloon, I., Watt, D. C., & Shepherd, M. (1978). A comparative controlled trial of pimozide and fluphenazine decanoate in the continuation therapy of schizophrenia. *Psychological Medicine, 8*: 59–70.

Falloon, I. R. H. (2006). Antipsychotic drugs: when and how to withdraw them? *Psychotherapy and Psychosomatics, 75*: 133–138.

Falloon, I. R. H., Boyd, J. L., McGill, C. W., Razani, J., Moss, H. B., & Gilderman, A. M. (1982). Family management in the prevention of exacerbation of schizophrenia: A controlled study. *New England Journal of Medicine, 306*: 1437–1440.

Falloon, I. R. H., Boyd, J. L., McGill, C. W., Williamson, M., Razani, J., Moss, H. B., Gilderman, A. M., & Simpson, G. M. (1985). Family management in the prevention of morbidity of schizophrenia. *Archives of General Psychiatry, 42*: 887–896.

Falloon-Goodhew, P. (2002). *Yoga for Living: Boost Energy.* London: Dorling Kindersley.

Farrell, M., Boys, A., Bebbington, P., Brugha, T., Coid, J., Jenkins, R., Lewis, G., Meltzer, H., Marsden, J., Singleton, N., & Taylor, C. (2002). Psychosis and drug dependence: results from a national survey of prisoners. *The British Journal of Psychiatry, 181*: 393–398.

Faulkner, A., & Layzell, S. (2000). *Strategies for Living: A Report of User-led Research into People's Strategies for Living with Mental Distress.* London: The Mental Health Foundation.

Fenton, W. S., Dickerson, F., Boronow, J., Hibbeln, J. R., & Knable, M. A. (2001). A placebo-controlled trial of Omega-3 fatty acid (ethyl eicosapentaenoic acid) supplementation for residual symptoms and cognitive impairment in schizophrenia. *The American Journal of Psychiatry, 158*: 2071–2074.

Field, T., Morrow, C., Valdeon, C., Larson, S., Kuhn, C., & Schanberg, S. (1993). Massage reduces anxiety in child and adolescent psychiatric patients. *International Journal of Alternative & Complementary Medicine*, July: 22–27.

Field, T., Ironson, G., Scafidi, F., Nawrocki, T., Goncalves, A., Burman, I., Pickes, J., Fox, N., Schanberg, S., & Kuhn, C. (1996). Massage therapy reduces anxiety and enhances EEG pattern of alertness and math computations. *International Journal of Neuroscience*, 86(3–4): 197–205.

Fisher, S., & Greenberg, R. P. (Eds.) (1997). *From Placebo to Panacea: Putting Psychiatric Drugs to the Test*. New York: Wiley.

Frank, A. F., & Gunderson, J. G. (1990). The role of the therapeutic alliance in the treatment of schizophrenia: relationship to course and outcome. *Archives of General Psychiatry*, 47: 228–237.

Frese, F. J., the 3rd (1998). Advocacy, Recovery and the challenges of consumerism for schizophrenia. *Psychiatric Clinics of North America*, 21: 233–249.

Frith, C., & Johnstone, E. (2003). Schizophrenia: a very short introduction. Oxford: Oxford University Press.

Gardner, D. M., Baldessarini, R. J., & Waraich, P. (2005). Modern antipsychotic drugs: a critical overview. *Canadian Medical Association Journal*, 172(13). doi:10.1503/cmaj.1041064.

Garety, P. A., Fowler, D., Kuipers, E. (2000). Cognitive-behaviour therapy for medication resistant symptoms. *Schizophrenia Bulletin*, 26(1): 73–86.

Garety, P., Fowler, D., Kuipers, E., Freeman, D., Dunn, G., Bebbington, P., Hadley C., & Jones, S. (1997). London-East Anglia randomised controlled trial of cognitive-behavioural therapy for psychosis II: predictors of outcome. *The British Journal of Psychiatry*, 171: 420–426.

Garfinkel, M. S., Singhal, A., Katz, W. A., Allan, D. A., Reshetar, R., & Schumacher, H. R. (1998). Yoga-based intervention for carpal tunnel syndrome. *The Journal of the American Medical Association*, 280: 1601–1603.

Gaster, B., & Holroyd, J. (2000). St John's Wort for depression: a systematic review. *Archives of Internal Medicine*, 160(2): 152–156.

Gatrell, A. C. (2004). Cultivating health: a study of health and mental well-being amongst old people in northern England, (RCHA241). *The Research Findings Register*. Summary no 1193, at: http://www.ReFeR.nhs.uk

Gavrilovic, J., Lecic-Tosevski, D., Dimic, S., Pejovic-Milovancevic, M., Knezevic, G., & Priebe, S. (2003). Coping strategies in civilians during air attacks. *Social Psychiatry and Psychiatric Epidemiology, 38*: 128–133.

Geddes, J., Freemantle, N., Harrison, P., & Bebbington, P. (2000). Atypical antipsychotics in the treatment of schizophrenia: systematic overview and meta-regression analysis. *The British Medical Journal, 321*: 1371–1376.

Gilbert, P. L., Harris, M. J., McAdams, L. A., Jeste, D. V. (1995). Neuroleptic withdrawal in schizophrenic patients. A review of the literature. *Archives of General Psychiatry, 52*: 173–188.

Gilmore, R. (2002). *Yoga for Living: Relieve Stress.* London: Dorling Kindersley.

Gitlin, M. J., (1995). Effects of depression and antidepressants on sexual functioning. *Bulletin of the Menninger Clinic, 59*(2): 232–248.

Gittins, D. (1998). *Madness in its Place. Narrativesx of Severalls Hospital, 1913–1997.* London: Routledge.

Glen, A. I., Glen, E. M., Horrobin, D. F., Vaddadi, K. S., Spellman, M., Morse-Fisher, N., Ellis, K., & Skinner, F. S. (1994). A red cell membrane abnormality in a subgroup of schizophrenic patients: evidence for two diseases. *Schizophrenia Research, 12*: 53–61.

Godfrey, P. S., Toone, B. K., Carney, M. W., Flynn, T. G., Bottiglieri, T., Laundy, M., Chanarin, I., & Reynolds, E. H. (1990). Enhancement of recovery from psychiatric illness by methylfolate. *Lancet, 336*(8712): 392–395.

Goff, D. C., Henderson, D. C., & Amico, E. (1992). Cigarette smoking in schizophrenia: relationship to psychopathology and medication side-effects. *The American Journal of Psychiatry, 149*: 1189–1194.

Goff, D. C., Bottiglieri, T., Arning, E., Shih, V., Freudenreich, O., Evins, E., Henderson, D. C., Baer, L., & Coyle, J. (2004). Folate, homocysteine, and negative symptoms in schizophrenia. *The American Journal of Psychiatry, 161*: 1705–1708.

Gold, C., Heldal, T. O., Dahle, T., & Wigram, T. (2005). Music therapy for schizophrenia or schizophrenia-like illnesses. *Cochrane Database Systematic Review, 2*. Article No. CD004025.pub2. DOI: 10.1002/14651858. CD004025.

Gottesman, I. I. (1991). *Schizophrenia Genesis: The Origins of Madness.* New York: W. H. Freeman.

Gottesman, I. I., McGuffin, P., & Farmer, A. E. (1987). Clinical genetics as clues to the "real" genetics of schizophrenia. *Schizophrenia Bulletin, 13*: 23–47.

Gottschall, E. (1994). *Breaking the Vicious Cycle: Intestinal Health Through Diet.* Ontario: Kirkton Press.

Graham, H. L., Maslin, J., Copello, A., Birchwood, M., Mueser, K., McGovern, D., & Georgio, G. (2001). Drug and alcohol problems amongst individuals with severe mental health problems in an inner city area of the UK. *Social Psychiatry and Psychiatric Epidemiology*, 36(9): 448–455.

Granholm, E., McQuaid, J. R., McClure, F., Pedrelli, P., & Jeste, D. V. (2002). A randomized controlled pilot study of cognitive-behaviour social skills training for older patients with schizophrenia. *Schizophrenia Research*, 53: 167–169.

Greden, J. F., & Tandon, R. (1995). Long-term treatment for lifetime disorders? *Archives of General Psychiatry*, 52: 197–200.

Green, A. I., Faraone, S. V., Brown, W. A., Guttierz, J., & Tsuang, M. T. (1992). Neuroleptic dose reduction studies: clinical and neuro-endocrine effects. Presented at the 31st Annual Meeting of the American College of Neuropsychopharmacology, Dec 14–18, San Juan, Puerto Rico.

Green, B., Young, R., & Kavanagh, D. (2005). Cannabis use and misuse prevalence among people with psychosis. *The British Journal of Psychiatry*, 187(4): 306–313.

Greeno, C. G., & Wing, R. R. (1994). Stress-induced eating. *Psychological Bulletin*, 115(3): 444–464.

Gupta, S., Masand, P. S., Virk, S., Schwartz, T., Hameed, A., Frank, B. L., & Lockwood, K. (2004). Weight decline in patients switching from Olanzapine to Quetiapine. *Schizophrenia Research*, 70: 57–62.

Hahn, R. A. (1997). The nocebo phenomenon: concept, evidence, and implications for public health. *Preventive Medicine*, 26(5 (Pt 1)): 607–611.

Hajak, G. (1999). A comparative assessment of the risks and benefits of Zopiclone: a review of 15 years. *Drug Safety*, 21(6): 457–469.

Halstead, S. M., Barnes, T. R. E., & Speller, J. C. (1994). Akathisia: prevalance and associated dysphoria in an in-patient population with chronic schizophrenia. *The British Journal of Psychiatry*, 164: 177–183.

Hansen, C. J., Stevens, L. C., & Coast, J. R. (2001). Exercise duration and mood state: how much is enough to feel better? *Health Psychology*, 20: 267–275.

Harding, C. M., & Zahniser, J. H. (1994). Empirical correction of seven myths about schizophrenia with implications for treatment. *Acta Psychiatrica Scandinavica Supplement*, 90 (384 Suppl.): 140–146.

Harding, C., Zubin, J., & Strauss, J. (1987). Chronicity in schizophrenia: fact, partial fact or artifact? *Hospital and Community Psychiatry*, 38: 477–486.

Harris, A. E. (1988). Physical disease and schizophrenia. *Schizophrenia Bulletin*, *14*: 85–96.

Harrison, G., Hopper, K., Craig, T., Laska, E., Siegel, C., Wanderlling, J., Dube, K., Ganev, K., Giel, R., An Der Heiden, W., Holmberg, S., Janca, A., Lee, P. W. H., Leon, C. A., Malhotra, S., Marsella, A., Nakane, Y., Sartorius, N., Chen, Y., Skoda, C., Thara, R., Tsirkin, S. J., Varma, V. K., Walsh, D., & Wiersma, D. (2001). Recovery from psychotic illness: a 15 and 25-year international follow-up study. *The British Journal of Psychiatry*, *178*: 506–517.

Harrison, G., Owens, D., Holton, A., Neilson, D., & Boot, D. (1988). A prospective study of severe mental disorder in Afro-Caribbean patients. *Psychological Medicine*, *18*: 643–657.

Hart, L. (1997). *Phone At Nine Just to Say You're Alive*. London: Pan.

Hassett, A. (1998). A patient who changed my practice: the lady with a plumber in her roof. *Journal of Psychiatry in Clinical Practice*, *24*(4): 309–311.

Hattan, J., King, L., & Griffiths, P. (2002). The impact of foot massage and guided relaxation following cardiac surgery: a randomized controlled trial. *Journal of Advanced Nursing*, *37*(2): 199–207.

Hatzidimitriadou, E. (2002). Political ideology, helping mechanisms and empowerment of mental health self-help/mutual aid groups. *Journal of Community and Applied Social Psychology*, *12*(4): 271–285.

Health and Safety Executive (1988). *An Assessment of Employee Assistance and Workplace Counselling Programmes in British Organisations*. Health and Safety Executive.

Health and Safety Executive (1999). *Discussion Document: Managing Stress at Work*. Health and Safety Executive.

Healthcare Commission (2006). *Community Mental Health Service Users Survey*. London: Healthcare Commission.

Healy, D. (1990). Schizophrenia: basic, reactive, release and defect processes. *Human Psychopharmacology: Clinical and Experimental*, *5*(2): 105–121.

Healy, D. (1991). D1 and D2 and D3. *The British Journal of Psychiatry*, *159*: 319–324.

Healy, D. (2005). *Psychiatric Drugs Explained* (4th edn). London: Elsevier Churchill Livingstone.

Heinrichs, D. W., & Carpenter, W. T. (1981). The efficacy of psychotherapy: a perspective and review emphasizing controlled outcome studies, In: S. Arieti & H. K. Brodie (Eds.), *The American Handbook of Psychiatry*. New York: Basic Books.

Heinssen, R. K., Liberman, R. P., & Kopelowicz, A. (2000). Psychosocial skills training for schizophrenia: lessons from the laboratory. *Schizophrenia Bulletin, 26*(1): 21–46.

Hemmings, G. (2004). Schizophrenia. [Letter to the Editor]. *The Lancet, 364*(9442): 1312–1313.

Henry, G. (2005). Rid These Voices. In: *Celebrating Black Heritage: A Medley of Inspiration* (p. 7). Bradford: Sharing Voices (Bradford).

Herran, A., Garcia-Unzueta, M. T., Amado, J. A., Lopez-Cordovilla, J. J., Diez-Manrique, J. F., & Vazquez-Barquero, J. L. (1999). Folate levels in psychiatric outpatients. *Psychiatry Clinical Neuroscience, 53*: 531–533.

Heston, L. L. (1966). Psychiatric disorders in foster home reared children of schizophrenic mothers. *British Journal of Psychiatry, 112*: 819–825.

Hewitt, D. (1992). Massage with lavender oil lowered tension. *Nursing Times, 88*(25): 8.

Hibbeln, J. R. (1998). Fish consumption and major depression. [Letter to the Editor]. *The Lancet, 351*: 1213.

Hilliard, D. (1995). Massage for the seriously mentally ill. *Journal of Psychosocial Nursing in Mental Health, 33*(7): 29–30.

Hodgson, H. R., & Miller, P. (1982). *Selfwatching; Addictions, Habits, Compulsions: What To Do About Them.* London: Century.

Hogarty, G. E., Kornblith, S. J., Greenwald, D., DiBarry, A. L., Cooley, S., Ulrich, R. F., Carter, M., & Flesher, S. (1997a). Three-year trials of personal therapy among schizophrenic patients living with or independent of family: I. Description of study and effects on relapse rates. *The American Journal of Psychiatry, 154*(11): 1504–1513.

Hogarty, G. E., Greenwald, D., Ulrich, R. F., Kornblith, S. J., DiBarry, A. L., Cooley, S., Carter, M., & Flesher, S. (1997b). Three-year trials of personal therapy among schizophrenic patients living with or independent of family: II. Effects on adjustment of patients. *The American Journal of Psychiatry, 154*(11): 1514–1524.

Holmes, C., Hopkins, V., Hensford, C., MacLaughlin, V., Wilkinson, D., & Rosenvinge, H. (2002). Lavender oil as a treatment for agitated behaviour in severe dementia: a placebo controlled study. *International Journal of Geriatric Psychiatry, 17*(4): 305–308.

Holmes, G. & Hudson, M. (2003). Coming off medication. *OpenMind, 123*: 14–15.

Holmes, P. (1986). Fringe benefits. *Nursing Times, 82*: 20–22.

Holohan, A. (2004). Trials and tribulations. *The Schizophrenia Association of Great Britain Newsletter, 38*: 23.

Hooper, L., Thompson, R. L., Harrison, R. A., Summerbell, C. D., Ness, A. R., Moore, H. J., Worthington, H. V., Durrington, P. N., Higgins, J. P. T., Capps, N. E., Riemersma, R. A., Ebrahim, S. B. J., & Davey Smith, G. (2006). Risks and benefits of Omega 3 fats for mortality, cardiovascular disease, and cancer: systematic review. *The British Medical Journal, 332*: 752–760.

Horne, J. (1998). How much sleep do we need? *The Daily Telegraph,* 19 May.

Horrobin, D. (2001) *The Madness of Adam and Eve: How Schizophrenia Shaped Humanity.* London: Bantam.

Hughes, J. R., Hatsukami, D. K., Mitchell, J. E., & Dahlgren, L. A. (1986). Prevalence of smoking among psychiatric outpatients. *The American Journal of Psychiatry, 143*: 993–997.

Hummer, M., Malik, P., Gasser, R. W., Hofer, A., Kemmler, G., Naveda, R. C. M., Rettenbacher, M. A., & Fleischhacker, W. W. (2005). Osteoporosis in patients with schizophrenia. *The American Journal of Psychiatry, 162*(1): 162–167.

Hutchinson, G., Takei, N., Fahy, T. A., Bhugra, D., Gilvarry, C., Moran, P., Mallett, R., Sham, P., Leff, J., & Murray, R. M. (1996). Morbid risk of schizophrenia in first-degree relatives of White and African-Caribbean patients with psychosis. *The British Journal of Psychiatry, 169*: 776–780.

Illman, J. (2004). *Use Your Brain to Beat Depression: The Complete Guide to Understanding and Tackling Depressive Illness.* London: Cassell.

Jablensky, A., Sartorius, N., Ernberg, G., Ansker, M., Korten, A., Cooper, J. E., Day, R., & Bertelsen, A. (1992). Schizophrenia: manifestations, incidence and course in different cultures; a World Health Organisation ten country study. *Psychological Medicine Supplement, 20*: 1–97.

Janssen I., Krabbendam, L., Bak, M., Hanssen, M., Vollebergh, W., de Graaf, R., & van Os, J. (2004). Childhood abuse as a risk factor for psychotic experiences. *Acta Psychiatrica Scandinavica, 109*(1): 38–45.

Jarmcy, C., & Mojay, G. (1999). *Shiatsu: The Complete Guide.* London: HarperCollins.

Jeste, D. V., Potkin, S. G., Sinha, S., Feder, S., & Wyatt, R. J. (1979). Tardive dyskinesia: reversible and persistent. *Archives of General Psychiatry, 36*: 585–590.

Joannides, P. (2001). *Guide to Getting It On!* London: Vermillion.

John (2003). Tactile hallucinations: imagine a person you cannot see attacking you. *Voices,* Spring: 7.

Johns, L. C., & van Os, J. (2001). The continuity of psychotic experiences in the general population. *Clinical Psychology Review, 21*(8): 1125–1141.

Johnstone, E. C., Russell, K. D., Harrison, L. K., & Lawrie, S. M. (2003). The Edinburgh High Risk Study: Current status and future prospects. *World Psychiatry, 2*: 45–49.

Johnstone, L. (1999). Adverse psychological effect of ECT. *Journal of Mental Health, 8*(1): 69–85.

Johnstone, L. (2003). A shocking treatment? *The Psychologist, 16*(5): 236–239.

Jonas, W. B., & Crawford, C. C. (2003). Science and spiritual healing: a critical review of spiritual healing, "energy" medicine and intentionality. *Alternative Therapies, 9*(2): 56–61.

Jones, P. B., Rantakallio, P., Hartikainen, A., Isohanni, M., & Sipila, P. (1998). Schizophrenia as a long-term outcome of pregnancy, delivery, and perinatal complications: a 28-year follow-up of the 1966 north Finland general population birth cohort. *American Journal of Psychiatry, 155*: 355–364.

Joy, C. B., Adams, C. E., & Rice, K. (2004). Crisis intervention for people with severe mental illnesses. *The Cochrane Database of Systematic Reviews, 4*. Article No. CD001087.DOI:10.1002/14651858.CD001087. pub2.

Joy, C. B., Mumby-Croft, R., & Joy, L. A. (2003). Polyunsaturated fatty acid supplementation for schizophrenia. *The Cochrane Database of Systematic Reviews, 2*. Article No. CD001257.D01: 10.1002/14651858. CD001257.

Kales, A., Soldatos, C. R., & Kales, J. D. (1987). Sleep disorders: insomnia, sleepwalking, night terrors, nightmares, and enuresis. *The Annals of Internal Medicine, 106* (4): 582–592.

Kane, J. M., Woerner, M., Weinhold, P., Wegner, J., Kinon, B., & Bornstein, M. (1984). Incidence of tardive dyskinesia: five-year data from a prospective study. *Psychopharmacology Bulletin, 20*: 387–389.

Kanwal, G. S. (1997). Hope, respect and flexibility in the psychotherapy. *Contemporary Psychoanalysis, 33*: 133–150.

Kavanagh, D. (1992). Recent developments in expressed emotion and schizophrenia. *The British Journal of Psychiatry, 160*: 601–620.

Ke, S. X (2006). Personal communication.

Keck, P. E. Jr., and McElroy, S. R. (2003).Aripiprazole: a partial dopamine D2 receptor agonist antipsychotic. *Expert Opi Inv Drug, 12*: 665–662.

Kelly, C., & McCreadie, R. (1998). Psychiatric patients who smoke have more admissions to hospital. Presentation to the Annual Meeting of The Royal College of Psychiatrists, 22nd–25th June. Belfast: Northern Ireland.

Kelly, C., & McCreadie, R. (2000). Cigarette smoking and schizophrenia. *Advances in Psychiatric Treatment, 6*: 327–331.

Kendell, R. E., & Kemp, I. W. (1989). Maternal influenza in the etiology of schizophrenia. *Archives of General Psychiatry, 46*: 878–882.

Kessler, R., Chiu, W. T., Demler, O., Merikangas, K. R., & Walters, E. E. (2005). Prevalence, severity, and comorbidity of 12-month DSM-1V disorders in the national comorbidity survey replication. *Archives of General Psychiatry, 62*: 590–592.

Kety, S. S., Rosenthal, D., Wender, P. H., & Schulsinger, F. (1968). The types and prevalence of mental illness in the biological and adoptive families of adopted people with schizophrenia. In: D. Rosenthal & S. S. Kety (Eds.), *The Transmission of Schizophrenia*. Elmsford, NY: Pergamon.

Kety, S. S., Rosenthal, D., Wender, P. H., Schulsinger, F., & Jacobson, B. (1975). Mental Illness in the biological and adoptive families of adopted individuals who have become schizophrenic: A preliminary report based on psychiatric interviews. In: R. R. Fieve, D. Rosenthal, & H. Brill (Eds.), *Genetic Research in Psychiatry*. Baltimore, MD: Johns Hopkins University Press.

King, M., Coker, E., Leavey, G., Hoare, A., & Johnson-Sabine, E. (1994). Incidence of psychotic illness in London: comparison of ethnic groups. *The British Medical Journal, 309*: 1115–1119.

Kleijnen, J., Knipschild, P., & ter Riet, G. (1991). Clinical Trials of Homeopathy. *The British Medical Journal, 302*: 315–323.

Knegtering, R., Castelein, S., Bous, H., van der Linde, J., Bruggeman, R., Kluiter, H., & van den Bosch, R. J. (2004). A randomized open-label study of the impact of Quetiapine versus Risperidone on sexual functioning. *Journal of Clinical Psychopharmacology, 24*: 56–61.

Kuipers, E., & Bebbington, P. (2005). *Living with Mental Illness: A Book for Relatives and Friends* (3rd edn.). London: Souvenir.

Kuipers, E., Garety, P., Fowler, D., Dunn, G., Bebbington, P., Freeman, D., & Hadley, C. (1997). London–East Anglia randomized controlled trial of cognitive-behavioural therapy for psychosis I. Effects of the treatment phase. *The British Journal of Psychiatry, 171*: 319–327.

Kuipers, E., Fowler, D., Garety, P., Chisholm, D., Freeman, D., Dunn, G., Bebbington, P., & Hadley, C. (1998). London–East Anglia randomized controlled trial of cognitive-behavioural therapy for psychosis III. Follow-up and economic evaluation at 18 months. *The British Journal of Psychiatry, 173*: 61–68.

Kuipers, L. (1993). Family burden in schizophrenia: implications for services. *Social Psychiatry and Psychiatric Epidemiology, 28*: 207–210.

Kumar, S., Thara, R., & Rajkumar, S. (1989). Coping with symptoms of relapse in schizophrenia. *European Archives of Psychiatric Neurological Science, 239*: 213–215.

Labatte, L. A., Grimes, J. B., Hines, A. H., & Oleshansky, M. A. (1997). Sexual dysfunction induced by SSRIs. American Psychiatric Association Meeting, 150: Abstract 36.

Laing, R. D. (1965). *The Divided Self. An Existential Study in Sanity and Madness*. Harmondsworth: Penguin.

Laing, R. D., & Esterson, A. (1968). *Sanity, Madness and the Family*. Harmondsworth: Penguin.

Laviolette, S. R., & van der Kooy, D. (2003). Blockade of mesolimbic dopamine transmission dramatically increases sensitivity to the rewarding effects of nicotine in the ventral tegmental area. *Molecular Psychiatry, 8*(1): 50–59.

Lazarides, L. (2002). *Treat Yourself with Nutritional Therapy*. Twickenham: Merton Books.

Leatherwood, P. D., Chauffard, F., Heck, E., & Munoz-Box, R. (1982). Aqueous extract of valerian root (*valeriana officinalis* L.) improves sleep quality in man. *Pharmacology Biochemistry & Behaviour, 17*: 65–71.

Leete, E. (1989). How I perceive and manage my illness. *Schizophrenia Bulletin, 15*(2): 197–200.

Leff, J., Kuipers, L., Berkowitz, R., Eberlein-Vries, R., & Sturgeon, D. (1982). A controlled trial of social intervention in the families of schizophrenic patients. *The British Journal of Psychiatry, 141*: 121–134.

Leff, J., Sartorius, N., Jablensky, A., Korten, A., & Ernberg, G. (1992). The International Pilot Study of Schizophrenia: Five-year follow-up findings. *Psychological Medicine, 22*: 131–145.

Lehtinen, K. (2001). Finnish needs adapted project: five-year outcomes. Paper presented at the World Psychiatric Association International Congress, Madrid, Spain.

Lehtinen, V., Aaltonen, J., Koffert, T., Rakkolainen, V., & Syvalahti, E. (2000). Two-year outcome in first-episode psychosis treated according to an integrated model. Is immediate neuroleptisation always needed? *European Psychiatry, 15*: 312–320.

Lejoyeux, M., Ades, J., & Mourad, I. (1996). Antidepressant withdrawal syndrome: recognition, prevention and management. *CNS Drugs, 5*: 278–292.

Lepore, S. J., & Smyth, J. M. (Eds.) (2002). *The Writing Cure: How Expressive Writing Promotes Health and Emotional Wellbeing*. Washington, DC: American Psychological Association.

Leucht, S., Wahlbeck, K., Hamann, J., & Kissling, W. (2003). New generation antipsychotics versus low-potency conventional antipsychotics: a systematic review and meta-analysis. *Lancet, 361*(9369): 1581–1589.

Lewis, S. W. (1989). Congential risk factors for schizophrenia. *Psychological Medicine, 19*: 5–13.

Lieberman, J. A., Kane, J. M., & Alvir, J. (1987). Provocative tests with psychostimulant drugs in schizophrenia. *Psychopharmacology, 91*: 415–433.

Lilly, S. (2002). *Illustrated Elements of Crystal Healing: A Practical Guide to Using Crystal for Health and Well-being*. London: Haper/Element.

Lima, A. R., Weiser, K. V. S., Bacaltchuk, J., & Barnes, T. R. E. (2004). Anticholinergics for neuroleptic-induced acute akathisia. *The Cochrane Database of Systematic Reviews, 4*. Article no. CD003727. DOI:10.1002/14651858.CD003727.

Linde, K., & Melchart, D. (1998). Randomized controlled trials of individualised homeopathy: a state-of-the-art review. *Journal of Alternative Complementary Medicine, 4*(4): 371–388.

Linde, K., Ramirez, G., Mulrow, C. D., Pauls, A., Weidenhammer, W., & Melchart, D. (1996). St John's Wort for depression—an overview and meta-analysis of randomized clinical trials. *The British Medical Journal, 313*: 253–258.

Link, B. G., Mirotznik, J., & Cullen, F. T. (1991). The effectiveness of stigma coping orientation: can negative consequences of mental illness labelling be avoided? *Journal of Health and Social Behavior, 32*: 302–320.

Link, B. G., Struening, E. L., Rahav, M., Phelan, J., & Nuttbrock, L. (1997). On stigma and its consequences: evidence from a longitudinal study of men with dual diagnoses of mental illness and substance abuse. *Journal of Health and Social Behavior, 38*: 177–190.

Linszen, D. H., Dingemans, P. M., & Lenior, M. E. (1994). Cannabis abuse and the course of recent-onset schizophrenic disorders. *Archives of General Psychiatry, 51*: 273–279.

Longhofer, J., & Floersch, J. (1993). African drumming and psychiatric rehabilitation. *Psychosocial Rehabilitation Journal, 16*(4):3–10.

Loughborough Sleep Research Centre (2006). Exercise, heat load and effects on sleep. Non-clinical basic research, www.lboro.ac.uk/departments/hu/groups/sleep/nonclin.htm

Macdonald, S., Halliday, T., MacEwan, T., Sharkey, V., Farrington, S., Wall, S., & McCreadie, R. G. (2003). Nithsdale Schizophrenia Surveys 24: sexual dysfunction. Case control study. *The British Journal of Psychiatry, 182*: 50–56.

Maher, B. A. (1988). Anomalous experience and delusional thinking: The logic of explanations. In: T. F. Oltmanns & B. A. Maher (Eds.), *Delusional Beliefs* (pp 15–33). New York: Wiley.

Malla, N. R. M. (1993). Stressful life events and schizophrenia: a review of the research. *The British Journal of Psychiatry, 162*: 161–166.

Mallett, R., Leff, J., Bhugra, D., Pang, D., & Zhao, J. H. (2002). Social environment, ethnicity and schizophrenia. A case-control study. *Social Psychiatry and Social Epidemiology, 37*(7): 329–335.

Malmberg, L., & Fenton, M. (2001). Individual psychodynamic psychotherapy and psychoanalysis for schizophrenia and severe mental illness. *The Cochrane Database of Systematic Reviews, 3*. Article No. CD001360.DOI:10.1002/14651858.CD001360.

Malzacher, M., Merz, J., & Ebnother, D. (1981). Marked life events prior to an acute schizophrenic episode: comparison of a sample of first admissions with a normal sample. Translated by the authors. *Archiv für Psychiatrie und Nervenkrankheiten, 230*: 227–242.

Marder, S. R., van Putten, T., & Mintz, J. (1987). Low and conventional dose maintenance therapy with fluphenazine decanoate: two-year outcome. *Archives of General Psychiatry, 44*: 518–521.

Martin, D. J., Garske, J. P., & Davis, M. K. (2000). Relation of the therapeutic alliance with outcome and other variables: a meta-analytic review. *Journal of Consulting and Clinical Psychology, 68*(3): 438–450.

Martin, L. R., Friedman, H. S., Tucker, J. S., Tomlinson-Keasey, C., Criqui, M. H., & Schwartz, J. E. (2002). A life course perspective on childhood cheerfulnesss and its relation to mortality risk. *Personality and Social Psychology Bulletin, 28*(9): 1155–1165.

Matthysse, S. (1973). Antipsychotic drug actions: a clue to the neuropathology of schizophrenia? *Federation Proceedings, 32*(2): 200–205.

Maxwell-Hudson, C. (1999). *Massage: The Ultimate Illustrated Guide.* London: Dorling Kindersley.

Maxwell-Hudson, C. (2006). Personal communication.

May, P. R., Van Putten, T., Yale, C., Potepan, P., Jenden, D. J., Fairchild, M. D., Goldstein, M. J., & Dixon, W. J. (1976). Predicting individual responses to drug treatment in schizophrenia: a test dose model. *The Journal of Nervous and Mental Disease, 162*(3): 177–183.

McCandless-Glimcher, I., McKnight, S., Hamera, E., Smith, B. L., Peterson, K., & Plumlee, A. A. (1986). Use of symptoms by schizophrenics to monitor and regulate their illness. *Hospital and Community Psychiatry*, 37: 929–933.

McCreadie, R. G. (2002). Use of drugs, alcohol and tobacco by people with schizophrenia: case-control study. *The British Journal of Psychiatry*, 181: 321–325.

McCreadie, R. G., & Kelly, C. (2000). Patients with schizophrenia who smoke: private disaster, public resource. *The British Journal of Psychiatry*, 176: 109.

McGlashan, T. H. (1988). A selective review of North American long-term follow-up studies of schizophrenia. *Schizophrenia Bulletin*, 14: 515–542.

McGrath, J. J. (2005). Myths and plain truths about schizophrenia epidemiology—the Nape Lecture, 2004. *Acta Psychiatrica Scandinavica*, 111(1): 4–11.

McGrath, J. J., Saha, S., Welham, J., El Saadi, O., MacCauley, C., & Chant, D. (2004). A systematic review of the incidence of schizophrenia: the distribution of rates and the influence of sex, urbanicity, migrant status and methodology. *BMC Medicine*, 2: 2–13.

McGuire, P., Silbersweig, D., Wright, I., David, A., Murray, R. M., Frackowiak, R., & Frith, C. (1995). Abnormal monitoring of inner speech: a physiological basis for auditory hallucinations. *Lancet*, 346: 596–600.

McQuade, R. D., Stock, E., Marcus, R., Fody, D., Gharbia, N. A., Vanveggel, S. Archibald, D., & Carson, W. H. (2004). A comparison of weight change during treatment with Olanzapine or Aripiprazole: Results from a randomized, double-blind study. *Journal of Clinical Psychiatry*, 65(Suppl.) 18: 47–56.

McQuaid, J. R., Granholm, E., McClure, F. S., Roepke, S., Pedrelli, P., Patterson, T. L., & Jeste. D. V. (2000). Cognitive–behavioural and social skills training intervention for older patients with schizophrenia. *Journal of Psychotherapy Practice and Research*, 9: 149–156.

Medicines and Healthcare Products Regulatory Agency (MHRA) (2006). Statement on SSRs and suicidal behaviour. Personal communication.

Mellor, J. E., Laugharne, J. D., & Peet, M. (1995). Schizophrenic symptoms and dietary intake of n3 fatty acids. *Schizophrenia Research*, 18: 85–86.

Meltzer. H. Y., Alphs, L., Green, A. I., Altamura, A. C., Anand, R., Bertoldi, A., Bourgeois, M., Chouinard, G., Islam, Z., Kane, J.,

Krishnan, R., Lindenmayer, J. P., & Potkin, S. (International Suicide Prevention Trial Study Group) (2003). Clozapine treatment for suicidality in schizophrenia. *Archives of General Psychiatry, 60*: 82–91.

Merikangas, K. R., Mehta, R. L., Molnar, B. E., Walters, E. E., Swendsen, J. D., Aguilar-Gaziola, S., Bijl, R., Borges, G., Caraveo-Anduaga, J. J., DeWit, D. J., Kolody, B., Vega, W. A., Wittchen, H. U., & Kessler, R. C. (1998). Comorbidity of substance use disorders: results of the international consortium in psychiatric epidemiology. *Addictive Behaviors, 6*: 893–907.

Menezes, P. R., Johnson, S., Thornicroft, G., Marshall, J., Prosser, D., Bebbington, P., & Kuipers, E. (1996). Drug and alcohol problems among individuals with severe mental illness in South London. *The British Journal of Psychiatry, 168*: 612–619.

Meyer, J. M. (2001). Effects of atypical antipsychotics on weight and serum lipid levels. *Journal of Clinical Psychiatry, 62*(Suppl.) 27: 27–34.

Miller, P., Lawrie, S. M., Hodges, A., Clafferty, R., Cosway, R., & Johnstone, E. C. (2001). Genetic liability, illicit drug use, life stress and psychotic symptoms: preliminary findings from the Edinburgh study of people at high risk for schizophrenia. *Social Psychiatry and Psychiatric Epidemiology, 36*(7): 338–342.

Miller, R. N. (1982). Study on the effectiveness of remote mental healing. *Medical Hypotheses, 8*: 481–490.

Mind (2000). *Counting the Cost.* London: Mind.

Mind (2001a). *Exercise Your Mind.* London: Mind.

Mind (2001b). *Roads to Recovery.* London: Mind.

Mind (2002). *My Choice.* London: Mind.

Mind (2005a). *Coping with Coming Off—Mind's Research into the Experiences of People Trying to Come off Psychiatric Drugs.* London: Mind.

Mind (2005b). *Making Sense of Coming Off Psychiatric Drugs.* London: Mind.

Mind (2005c). *Guide to Managing Stress.* London: Mind.

Modell, S., Jody, D., Kujawa, M., Carson, W., Stringfellow, J., Iwamoto, T., Marcus, R., & Stock, E. (2004). Efficacy of Aripiprazole and Perphenazine in severe schizophrenia resistant to treatment with atypical antipsychotics. Presentation at the 17th Congress of the European College of Neuropsychopharmacology. Stockholm: 9–13th October.

Mojtabai, R., Nicholson, R., & Carpenter, B. (1998). Role of psychosocial treatments in management of schizophrenia: a meta-analytic review of controlled outcome studies. *Schizophrenia Bulletin, 24*(4): 569–587.

Moller, H. J. (1999). Effectiveness and safety of benzodiazepines (benzo-diazepine dependence and withdrawal: myths and management.) *Journal of Clinical Psychopharmacology, 19*(Suppl. 2): 2s–11s.

Moncrieff, J. (2006a). Does antipsychotic withdrawal provoke psychosis? Review of the literature on rapid onset psychosis (supersensitivity psychosis) and withdrawal-related relapse. *Acta Psychiatrica Scandanavica, 114*(1): 3–13.

Moncrieff, J. (2006b). Why is it so difficult to stop psychiatric drug treatment? It may be nothing to do with the original problem. *In press.*

Monahan, J. (1996). Mental illness and violent crime. In: *Violent Behavior: One of the Consequences of Failing to Treat Severe Mental Illnesses* (p. 2). Treatment Advocacy Center Briefing Paper (2003). Arlington,. VA: J. Monahan.

Montejo-Gonzalez, A. L., Llorca, G., Izquierdo, J. A., Ledesma, A., Bousono, M., Calcedo, A., Carrasco, J. L., Ciudad, J., Daniel, E., De la Gandara, J., Derecho, J., Franco, M., Gomez, M. J., Macias, J. A., Martin, T., Perez, V., Sanchez, J. M., Sanchez, S., & Vicens, E. (1997). SSRI induced sexual dysfunction: fluoxetine, paroxetine, sertraline and fluvoxamine in a prospective, multicenter and descriptive clinical study of 344 patients. *Journal of Sex and Marital Therapy, 23*(3): 176–194.

Mosher, L. R. (1999). Soteria and other alternatives to acute psychiatric hospitalization: a personal and professional review. *The Journal of Nervous and Mental Disease, 187*: 142–149.

Mueser, K. T., & Berenbaum, H. (1990). Psychodynamic treatment of schizophrenia: is there a future? *Psychological Medicine, 20*: 253–262.

Muller, P., & Seeman, P. (1978). Dopaninergic supersensitivity after neuroleptics: time course and specificity. *Psychopharmacology, 60*: 1–11.

Muller, W. E., Rolli, M., Schafer, C., & Hafner, U. (1997). Effects of hypericum extract (L1 160) in biochemical models of antidepressant activity. *Pharmacopsychiatry, 30*(Suppl. 2): 102–107.

Munro, J., O'Sullivan, D., Andrews, C., Arana, A., Mortimer, A., & Kerwin, R. (1999). Active monitoring of 12,760 Clozapine recipients in the UK and Ireland. Beyond pharmacovigilance. *British Journal of Psychiatry, 175*: 576–580.

Nathans-Barel, I., Feldman, P., Berger, B., Modai, I., & Silver, H. (2005). Animal-assisted therapy ameliorates anhedonia in schizophrenia patients: a controlled pilot study. *Psychotherapy and Psychosomatics, 74*: 31–35.

National Centre for Volunteering (2003). *Volunteering for Mental Health. Research Bulletin.* National Centre for Volunteering.

NICE (National Institute for Health and Clinical Excellence) (2002a). *Schizophrenia: Core interventions in the treatment and management of schizophrenia in primary and secondary care.* London: NICE.

NICE (National Institute for Health and Clinical Excellence) (2002b). Health Technology Appraisal No 43. *The Clinical Effectiveness and Cost Effectiveness of Newer Atypical Antipsychotic Drugs for Schizophrenia.* London: NICE.

NICE (National Institute for Health and Clinical Excellence) (2003). *Guidance on the use of Electroconvulsive Therapy.* London: NICE.

NICE (National Institute for Health and Clinical Excellence) (2004). *Depression: Management of Depression in Primary and Secondary Care.* London: NICE.

National Institute for Mental Health in England (NIMHE)/Care Services Improvement Partnership (CSIP) (2006). *Treat Home-based Care and Support as the Norm for the Delivery of Mental Health Services. 10 High Impact Changes for Mental Health Services.* London: NIMHE.

Norman (1994). Letter to the Editor. *Voices, 14*: 3.

Norman, L., Cowan, T., & Conran, T. (1989). *The Reflexology Handbook: A Complete Guide.* London: Piatkus.

Nutt, D. J., & Wilson, S. (1999). Evaluation of severe insomnia in the general population—implications for the management of insomnia: the UK perspective. *Journal of Psychopharmacology, 13*(Suppl. 1): 33–34.

O'Reilly, P. O., & Handforth, J. R. (1955). Occupational therapy with "refractory" patients. *The American Journal of Psychiatry, 111*: 763–766.

Oh, V. M. S. (1994). The placebo effect: can we use it better? *British Medical Journal, 309*: 69–70.

Oken, B. S., Storzbach, D. M., & Kaye, J. A. (1998). The efficacy of ginkgo biloba on cognitive function in Alzheimer Disease. *Archives of Neurology, 55*: 1409–1415.

Ohlsen, R. I., Treasure, J., & Pilowsky, L. S. (2004). A dedicated nurse-led service for antipsychotic-induced weight gain. *Psychiatric Bulletin, 28*: 164–166.

Parkinson, S., & Nelson, G. (2003). Consumer/survivor stories of empowerment and recovery in the context of supported housing (2003). *The International Journal of Psychosocial Rehabilitation, 7*: 103–118.

Passant, H. (1990). A holistic approach in the ward. *Nursing Times*, *86*(4): 26–28.

Paton, C., Banham, S., & Whitmore, J. (2000). Benzodiazepines in schizophrenia. Is there a trend towards long-term prescribing? *Psychiatric Bulletin*, *24*: 113–115.

Peet, M., & Horrobin, D. F. (2002a). A dose-ranging exploratory study of the effects of ethyl-eicosapentaenoate in patients with persistent schizophrenic symptoms. *Journal of Psychiatry Research*, *36*(1): 7–18.

Peet, M., & Horrobin, D. F. (2002b). A dose-ranging exploratory study of the effects of ethyl-eicosapentaenoate in patients with ongoing depression despite apparently adequate treatment with standard drugs. *Archives of General Psychiatry*, *59*: 913–919.

Peet, M., Laugharne, J. D., Mellor, J., & Ramchand, C. N. (1996). Essential fatty acid deficiency in erythrocyte membranes from chronic schizophrenic patients and the clinical effects of dietary supplementation. *Prostaglandins Leukot Essential Fatty Acids*, *55*: 71 75.

Peet, M., Laugharne, J. D. E., & Mellor, J. (1997). Double-blind trial of n-3 fatty acid supplementation in the treatment of schizophrenia. Presented at the International Congress on Schizophrenia Research, April 1997, Colorado Springs, Colorado, USA.

Pekkala, E., & Merinder, L. (2002). Psychoeducation for schizophrenia. *The Cochrane Database of Systematic Reviews*, *2*. Article No. CD002831.DOI: 10.1002/14651858.CD002831.

Pendlebury, J., & Ost, D. (2002). Cromwell House weight management programme for patients with severe enduring mental illness: preliminary results. Poster Presented at ECNP Annual Congress, Barcelona, Spain 5–9 October.

Pfeiffer, C., & Holford, P. (1996). *Mental Illness The Nutrition Connection: How to Beat Depression, Anxiety and Schizophrenia*, and *How to Enhance your Mental and Emotional Well being*. London: Ion Press.

Piazza, L. A., Markowitz, J. C., Kocsis, J. H., Leon, A. C., Portera, L., Miller, N. L., & Adler, D. (1997). Sexual functioning in chronically depressed patients treated with SSRI antidepressants: a pilot study. *The American Journal of Psychiatry*, *154*(12): 1757–1759.

Pigott, T. A., Carson, W. H., Saha, A. R., Torbeyns, A. F., Stock, E. G., & Ingenito, G. G. (2003). Aripiprazole for the Prevention of Relapse in Stabilised Patients with Chronic Schizophrenia: A placebo-controlled 26-week study. *Journal of Clinical Psychiatry*, *64* (9): 1048–1056.

Pilling, S., Bebbington, P. E., Kuipers, E., Garety, P., Geddes, J., Martindale, B., Orbach, G., & Morgan, C. (2002). Psychological treatments in schizophrenia II: Meta-analyses of randomized controlled trials of social skills, training and cognitive remediation. *Psychological Medicine*, 32: 783–791.

Pitt, L., & Kilbride, M. (2006). Researching recovery from psychosis. *Mental Health Practice*, 9(7): 20–23.

Potkin, S. G., Saha, A. R., Kujawa, M. J., Carson, W. H., Ali, M., Stock, E., Stringfellow, J., Ingenito, G., & Marder, S. R. (2003). Aripiprazole, an antipsychotic with a novel mechanism of action, and Risperidone vs placebo in patients with schizophrenia and schizoaffective disorder. *Archives of General Psychiatry*, 60(7): 681–690.

Pretty, J., Griffin, M., Sellens, M., & Pretty, C. (2003). Green exercise: complementary roles of nature, exercise and diet in physical and emotional well-being and implications for public health policy. Centre for Environment and Society Occasional Paper. University of Essex.

Prien, R. F., Cole., J. O., & Belkin, N. F. (1968). Relapse in chronic schizophrenics following abrupt withdrawal of tranquillizing medication. *British Journal of Psychiatry*, 115(523): 679–686.

Pristach, C. A., & Smith, C. M. (1990). Medication compliance and substance abuse among schizophrenic patients. *Hospital and Community Psychiatry*, 41: 1345–1348.

Prout, C. T., & White, M. A. (1951). A controlled study of personality relationships in mothers of schizophrenic male patients. *American Journal of Psychiatry*, 107: 251–256.

Puri, B. K., & Richardson, A. J. (1998). Sustained remission of positive and negative symptoms of schizophrenia following treatment with EPA. *Archives of General Psychiatry*, 55: 188–189.

Puri, B. K. Brown, R. A., McKee, H. J., & Treasadan, I. H. (2005). *Mental Health Law: A Practical Guide*. London: Hodder Arnold.

Puri, B. K., Richardson, A. J., Horrobin, D. F., Easton, T., Saeed, N., Oatridge, A., Hajnal, J. V., & Bydder, G. M. (2000). Eicosapentaenoic acid treatment in schizophrenia associated with symptom remission, normalisation of blood fatty acids, reduced neuronal membrane phospholipid turnover and structural brain changes. *International Journal of Clinical Practice*, 54: 57–63.

Quilliam, S. (2003). *Positive Thinking*. London: Dorling Kindersley.

Ralph, R. O. (2000). Recovery. *Psychiatric Rehabilitation Skills*, 4(3): 480–517.

Ramaratnam, S., & Sridharan, K. (2002). Yoga for epilepsy. *The Cochrane Database of Systematic Reviews, 1.* Article No. CD001524.DOI:10. 1002/14651858.CD001524.

Ran, M., Xiang, M., Huang, M., & Shan, Y. (2001). Natural course of schizophrenia: 2-year follow-up study in a rural Chinese community. *British Journal of Psychiatry, 178*: 54–158.

Rankin, J. (2005). *A Good Choice for Mental Health, Mental Health in the Mainstream Working Paper Three.* London: Institute for Public Policy Research.

Rathbone, J., & Xia, J. (2005). Acupuncture for schizophrenia. *The Cochrane Database of Systematic Reviews, 4.* Article No. CD005475. DOI:10.1002/14651858.CD005475.

Rathbone, J., Zhang, L., Zhang, M., Xia, J., Xiehe, L., & Yanchun, Y. (2005). Chinese herbal medicine for schizophrenia. *The Cochrane Database of Systematic Reviews, 4.* Article No. CD003444. DOI: 10. 10002/14651858.CD003444.

Rector, N. A., & Beck, A. T. (2001). Cognitive behavioural therapy for schizophrenia: an empirical review. *The Journal of Nervous and Mental Disease, 189* (5): 278–287.

Regier, D. A., Farmer, M. E., Rae, D. S., Locke, B. Z., Keith, S. J., Judd, L. L., & Goodwin, F. K. (1990). Comorbidity of mental disorders with alcohol and other drug abuse: results from the epidemiologic catchment area (ECA) study. *Journal of the American Medical Association, 264*(19): 2511–2518.

Reichelt, K. L., & Landmark, J. (1995). Specific IgA antibody increases in schizophrenia. *Biological Psychiatry, 37*: 410–413.

Reichenberg-Ullman, J., & Ullman, R. (1990). Healing through homeopathy: a case of schizophrenia. *Townsend Letter for Doctors & Patients, June*: 364–365.

Repper, J., & Perkins, R. (2003). *Social Inclusion and Recovery: A Model for Mental Health Practice.* London: Bailliere Tindall.

Rethink (2005). *Future Perfect: Mental Health Service Users Set Out a Vision for the 21st Century.* (Pdf file for download).

Reynolds, E. H., Carney, M. W., & Toone, B. K. (1984). Methylation and mood. *The Lancet, 2*(8396): 196–198.

Reynolds, W., Lauder, W., Sharkey, S., Maciver, S., Veitch, T., & Cameron, D. (2004). The effects of a transitional discharge model for psychiatric patients. *Journal of Psychiatric and Mental Health Nursing, 11*: 82–88.

Richardson, A. J., Easton, T., & Puri, B. K. (2000). Red cell and fatty acid plasma changes accompanying symptom remission in a patient with schizophrenia treated with eicosapentaenoic acid. *European Neuropsychopharmacology*, 10(3): 189–193.

Ried, L. D., Renner, B. T., Bengtson, M. A., Wilcox, B. M., & Acholonu, W. W. Jnr (2003). Weight change after an atypical antipsychotic switch. *Annals of Pharmacotherapy*, 37(10): 1381–1386.

Rihs, M., Muller, C., & Bauman, P. (1996). Caffeine consumption in hospitalised psychiatric patients. *European Archives of Psychiatry and Clinical Neuroscience*, 246(2): 83–92.

Roberts, L., Ahmed, I., & Hall, S. (2000). Intercessory prayer for the alleviation of ill health. *The Cochrane Database of Systematic Reviews*, 2. Article No. CD000368.DOI:10.1002/14651858.CD000368.

Romme, M. (2004). Personal communication.

Rosenbaum, J. F., Fava, M., Hoog, S. F., Ashcroft, R. C., & Krebs, W. B., (1998). Selective serotonin reuptake inhibitor discontinuation syndrome: a randomized clinical trial. *Biological Psychiatry*, 44: 77–87.

Ruddy, R., & Milnes, D. (2005). Art therapy for schizophrenia or schizophrenia-like illnesses. *The Cochrane Systematic Reviews*, 1. Article No. CD003728. DOI: 10.1002/14651858.CD003728.

Rund, B. R. (1994). The relationship between psychosocial and cognitive functioning in schizophrenic patients and expressed emotion and communication deviance in their parents. *Acta Psychiatrica Scandinavica*, 90: 133–140.

Sanderson, H. & Ruddle, J. (1992). Aromatherapy and occupational therapy. *British Journal of Occupational Therapy*, 55(8): 310–314.

Sawynok, J. (1995). Pharmacological rationale for the clinical use of caffeine. *Drugs*, 49: 37–50.

Segraves. R. T. (1989). Effects of psychotropic drugs on human erection and ejaculation. *Archives of General Psychiatry*, 46(3): 275–284.

Sempik, J., Aldridge, J., & Becker S. (2005). *Growing Together—A Practice Guide to Social Inclusion Through Gardening and Horticulture*. Bristol: The Policy Press.

Shapiro, C. M. (1993). *ABC of Sleep Disorders*. London: BMJ Publishing Group.

Shapiro, M. B., & Ravenette, A. T. (1959). A preliminary experiment on paranoid delusions. *Journal of Mental Science*, 105: 295–312.

Sharma, H. (1996). Maharishi Ayurveda: research review, part two: Maharishi Ayurveda herbal food supplements and additional strategies. *Complementary Medicine International*, March/April: 17–28.

Shepherd, G., Murray, A., & Muijen, M. (1995). Perspectives on schizophrenia: a survey of user, family care and professional views regarding effective care. *Journal of Mental Health*, 4: 403–422.

Sheps, D. S., McMahon, R. P., Becker, L., Carney, R. M., Freedland, K. E., Cohen, J. D., Sheffield, D., Goldberg, A. D., Ketterer, M. W., Pepine, C. J., Raczynski, J. M., Light, K., Krantz, D. S., Stone, P. H., Knatterud, G. L., & Kaufmann, P. G. (2002). Mental stress-induced ischemia and all-cause mortality in patients with coronary artery disease: results from the psychophysiological investigations of myocardial ischemia study. *Circulation, 105*: 1780–1784.

Shreeve, C. M. (2003). *Effortless Exercise*. London: Sheldon Press.

Simpson, J. (1997). Who's normal? I am! *Voices, 18*: 8.

Sims, S. (1986). Slow stroke back massage for cancer patients. *Nursing Times, 82*: 47–50.

Singh, M. M., & Kay, S. R. (1976). Wheat gluten as a pathogenic factor in schizophrenia. *Science, 191*(4225): 401–402.

Smith, R. C. (1994). Lower dose therapy with traditional neuroleptics in chronically hospitalised schizophrenic patients. *Archives General Psychiatry, 51*: 427–429.

Smith, S. (2003). Effects of antipsychotics on sexual and endocrine function in women: implications for clinical practice. *Journal of Clinical Psychopharmacology, 23*(Suppl. 1): 27–32.

Smith, S., O'Keane, V., & Murray, R. (2002). Sexual dysfunction in patients taking conventional antipsychotic medication. *The British Journal of Psychiatry, 181*: 49–55.

Snyder, S. H., Banerjee, S. P., Yamamura, H. I., & Greenberg, D. (1974). Drugs, neurotransmitters and schizophrenia. *Science, 184*: 1243–1253.

Soares, K. V. S., & McGrath, J. J. (2000). Anticholinergic medication for neuroleptic-induced tardive dyskinesia. *The Cochrane Database of Systematic Reviews, 2*. Article no. CD000204.DOI:10.1002/14651858. CD000204.

Soares, K. V. S., & McGrath, J. J. (2001). Vitamin E for neuroleptic-induced tardive dyskinesia. *The Cochrane Database of Systematic Reviews, 4*. Article no. CD000209.DOI:10.1002/ 14651858.CD000209.

Sommer, S. (2002). *The Little Book of Bach Flower Remedies*. London: Vermillion.

Stallibrass, C. (1997). An evaluation of the Alexander Technique for the management of disability in Parkinson's Disease—a preliminary study. *Clinical Rehabilitation, 11*(1): 8–12.

Stallibrass, C., Sissons, P., & Chalmers, C. (2002). Randomized controlled trial of the Alexander Technique for idiopathic Parkinson's Disease. *Clinical Rehabilitation, 16*: 705–718.

Stanton, B., & David, A. S. (2000). First-person accounts of delusions. *Psychiatric Bulletin, 24*: 333–336.

Stevenson, C. (1992). Holistic power. *Nursing Times, 88*(38): 68–70.

Stiles, W. B., Barkham, M., Twigg, E., Mellor-Clark, J., & Cooper, M. (2006). Effectiveness of cognitive-behavioural, person-centred and psychodynamic therapies as practised in UK National Health Service settings. *Psychological Medicine, 36*: 555–566.

Storms, L. H., Clopton, J. M., & Wright, C. (1982). Effects of gluten on schizophrenics. *Archives of General Psychiatry, 39*(3): 323–327.

Su, K.-P., Shen, W., Huang, S.-Y. (2001). Omega-3 fatty acids as a psychotherapeutic agent for a pregnant schizophrenic patient. *European Neuropsychopharmacology, 11*(4): 295–299.

Sullivan, W. P. (1994). A long and winding road: The process of recovery from severe mental illness. *Innovations and Research, 3*: 19–27.

Tan, S. A., Tan, L. G., Berk, L. S., Lukman, S. T., & Lukman, L. F. (1997). Mirthful laugher an effective adjunct in cardiac rehabilitation. *Canadian Journal of Cardiology, 13*(Suppl. B): 190.

Tang, W., Yao, X., & Zheng, Z. (1994). Rehabilitative effect of music therapy for residual schizophrenia: a one-month radomised controlled trial in Shanghai. *British Journal of Psychiatry Supplement, 24*: 38–44.

Tanskanen, A., Hibbeln, J. R., Tuomilehto, J., Uutela, A., Haukkala, A., Viinamaki, H., Lehtonen, J., & Vartiainen, E. (2001). Fish consumption and depressive symptoms in the general population in Finland. *Psychiatric Services, 52*: 529–531.

Tarrier, N. (1987). An investigation of residual psychotic symptoms in discharged schizophrenic patients. *The British Journal of Clinical Psychology, 26*: 141–143.

Tarrier, N. (1991). Some aspects of family interventions in schizophrenia: 1. Adherence to intervention programmes. *The British Journal of Psychiatry, 159*: 475–480.

Tarrier, N., Barrowclough, C., Porceddu, K., & Fitzpatrick, E. (1994). The Salford family intervention project: relapse rates of schizophrenia at five and eight years. *The British Journal of Psychiatry, 165*: 829–832.

Tarrier N., Kinney, C., McCarthy, E., Humphreys, L. Wittkowski, A., & Morris, J. (2000). Two-year follow-up of cognitive–behavioural therapy and supportive counselling in the treatment of persistent symptoms in chronic schizophrenia. *Journal of Consulting and Clinical Psychology, 68*(5): 917–922.

Tarrier, N., Kinney, C., McCarthy, E., Wittkowski, A., Yusupoff, L., Gledhill, A., Morris, J., & Humphreys, L. (2001). Are some types of psychotic symptoms more responsive to cognitive–behaviour therapy? *Behavioural and Cognitive Psychotherapy, 29*: 45–55.

Tarrier, N., Lewis, S., Haddock, G., Bentall, R., Drake, R., Kinderman, P., Kingdon, D., Siddle, R., Everitt, J., Leadley, K., Benn, A., Grazebrook, K., Haley, C., Akhtar, S., Davies, L., Palmer, S., & Dunn, G. (2004). Cognitive–behavioural therapy in first-episode and early schizophrenia. *The British Journal of Psychiatry, 184*: 231–239.

Tarrier, N., Yusupoff, L. McCarthy, E., Kinney, C., & Wittkowski, A. (1998). Some reasons why patients suffering from chronic schizophrenia fail to continue in psychological treatment. *Behavioural and Cognitive Psychotherapy, 26*: 177–181.

Tarrier, N., Wittkowski, A., Kinney, C., McCarthy, E., Morris, J., & Humphreys, L. (1999). Durability of the effects of cognitive–behavioural therapy in the treatment of chronic schizophrenia: 12-month follow-up. *The British Journal of Psychiatry, 174*: 500–504.

Tattan, T., & Tarrier, N. (2000). The expressed emotion of case managers of the seriously mentally ill: the influence of expressed emotion on clinical outcomes. *Psychological Medicine, 30*: 195–204.

Taylor, D. (2006). Personal communication.

Taylor, D., Paton, C., & Kerwin, R. (2005). *The Maudsley 2005–2006 Prescribing Guidelines* (8th edn). London: Taylor and Francis.

Taylor, P. (1985). Motives for offending amongst violent and psychotic men. *The British Journal of Psychiatry, 147*: 491–498.

Thakore, J. H. (2005). Metabolic syndrome and schizophrenia. *The British Journal of Psychiatry, 186*: 455–456.

Tharyan, P., & Adams, C. E. (2002). Electroconvulsive therapy for schizophrenia. *Cochrane Database of Systematic Reviews, 2*. CD000076.

The Mental Health Foundation (1997). *Knowing Our Own Minds: A Survey of how People in Emotional Distress Take Control of Their Own Lives*. London: The Mental Health Foundation.

The Mental Heath Foundation (1998). *Healing Minds*. London: The Mental Health Foundation.

The Mental Heath Foundation (1999). *Complementary Therapies in Mental Health, Mental Health Briefing (23)*. London: The Mental Health Foundation.

The Mental Health Foundation (2000a). *Pull Yourself Together! A Survey of the Stigma and Discrimination Faced by People Who Experience Mental Distress*. London: The Mental Health Foundation.

The Mental Health Foundation (2000b). *Strategies for Living. A Survey of the Effect of Employment on People Who Experience Mental Distress.* London: The Mental Health Foundation.

The Mental Health Foundation (2002). *Out at Work: A Survey of the Experiences of People with Mental Health Problems Within the Workplace.* London: The Mental Health Foundation.

The Mental Health Foundation (2003). *Strategies for Living: The Research Report.* London: The Mental Health Foundation.

The Mental Health Foundation (2005). *Up and Running: The Research Report.* London: The Mental Health Foundation.

The Mental Health Foundation & Rethink (2004). *Self-help Groups for Individuals who Experience Mental Distress: Proceedings of a Self-help Group Members' Symposium and a Review of Selected Literature.* London: The Mental Health Foundation.

The Royal College of Psychiatrists (1995). *The ECT Handbook.* London: Royal College of Psychiatrists.

The Royal College of Psychiatrists (2006). *High-dose Antipsychotic Medication: New Consensus Statement.* London: Royal College of Psychiatrists.

Thomas, H. (1993). Psychiatric symptoms in cannabis users. *The British Journal of Psychiatry, 163*: 141–149.

Thomas, P., & May, R. (2003). *Advice on Medication.* Manchester: Hearing Voices Network.

Thornicroft, G. (1990). Cannabis and psychosis. Is there epidemiological evidence for an association? *The British Journal of Psychiatry, 157*: 25–33.

Thornton, J. A. & Wahl, O. F. (1996). Impact of a newspaper article on attitudes toward mental illness. *Journal of Community Psychology, 24*(1): 17–25.

Tien, A. Y., & Anthony, J. C. (1990). Epidemiological analysis of alcohol and drug use as risk factors for psychotic experiences. *The Journal of Nervous and Mental Disease, 178*: 473–480.

Tooth, B., Kalyanasundaram, V., Glover, H., & Momedzadah, S. (2003). Factors consumers identify as important to recovery from schizophrenia. *Australasian Psychiatry, 11*(Suppl.): S70–S77.

Torrey, E. F. (2006). *Surviving Schizophrenia: A Manual for Families, Consumers and Providers* (5th edn). New York: HarperCollins.

Torrey, E. F., & Rawlings, R. R. (1996). Fluctuations in schizophrenic birth by year. *The British Journal of Psychiatry, 169*: 772–775.

Torii, S., Fukada, H., Kanemoto, H., Miyanchi, R., Hamauzu, V., & Kawasaki, M. (1988). Contingent negative variation (CNV) and the psychological effects of odour. In: S. Van Toller & G. H. Dodd (Eds.), *Perfumery—the Psychology and Biology of Fragrance* (pp. 107–120). London: Chapman and Hall.

Trevelyan, J. (1996). A true complement? *Nursing Times, 92*(5): 42–43.

Tsay, S. L., Cho, Y., & Chen, M. L. (2004). Acupressure and transcutaneous electrical acupoint stimulation in improving fatigue, sleep quality and depression in hemodialysis patients. *American Journal of Chinese Medicine, 32*(3): 407–416.

Tsuang, M., & Faraone, S. (1997). *Schizophrenia: The Facts*. Oxford: Oxford University Press.

Turton, N. (1989). Therapeutic touch: its place in nursing care. In: A. P. Pritchard (Ed.), *Cancer Nursing—A Revolution in Care. Proceedings from the Fifth International Conference in Cancer Nursing*. London: Macmillan.

Unnithan, S. B., & Cutting, J. C. (1992). The cocaine experience: refuting the concept of a model psychosis? *Psychopathology, 25*(2): 71–78.

van Os, J., Castle, D. J., Takei, N., Der, G., & Murray, R. M. (1996). Psychotic illness in ethnic minorities: clarification from the 1991 Census. *Psychological Medicine, 26*: 203–208.

van Os, J., Verdoux, H., Maurice-Tison, S., Gay, B., Liraud, F., Salamon, R., & Bourgeois, M. (1999). Self-reported psychosis-like symptoms and the continuum of psychosis. *Social Psychiatry and Psychiatric Epidemiology, 34*(9): 459–463.

Van Putten, T. (1974). Why do schizophrenic patients refuse to take their drugs? *Archives of General Psychiatry, 31*: 67–72.

Van Putten, T., May, R. R. A., Marder, S. R., & Wittman, L. A. (1981). Subjective response to antipsychotic drugs. *Archives of General Psychiatry, 38*: 187–190.

Vaughn, C. & Leff, J. (1976). The influence of family and social factors on the course of psychiatric illness. *The British Journal of Psychiatry, 129*: 125–137.

Vedanthan, P. K., Kesavalu, L. N., Murthy, K. C., Duvall, K., Hall, M. J., Baker, S., & Nagarathna, S. R. (1998). Clinical study of yoga techniques in university students with asthma: a controlled study. *Allergy Asthma Proceedings, 19*(1): 3–9.

Veltman, A., Cameron, J. I., & Stewart, D. (2002). The experience of providing care to relatives with chronic mental illness. *The Journal of Nervous and Mental Disease, 190*(2): 108–114.

Viguera, A. C., Baldessarini, R. J., Hegarty, J. D., van Kammen, D., & Tohen, M. (1997). Clinical risk following abrupt and gradual withdrawal of maintenance neuroleptic treatment. *Archives of General Psychiatry, 54*: 49–55.

Volz, H. P. (1997). Controlled clinical trials of hypericum extracts in depressed patients: an overview. *Psychopharmacology, 30*(Suppl. 2): 72–76.

Waddington, J. L., Youssef, H. A., & Kinsella, A. (1995). Sequential cross sectional and 10 year prospective study of severe negative symptoms in relation to duration of initially untreated psychosis in chronic schizophrenia. *Psychological Medicine, 25*: 849–857.

Waines, A. (2004). *The Self-Esteem Journal.* London: Sheldon Press.

Walach, H., Reuter, K., Wiesendanger, H., & Werthmuller, L. (2000). Distant healing improves quality of life in chronically ill patients: results of a waiting list controlled randomized study. *Forsch Komple, 7*(l): 54–55.

Walker, A. M., Lanza, L. L., Arellano, F., & Rothman, K. J., (1997). Mortality in current and former users of clozapine. *Epidemiology, 8*: 671–677.

Wallcraft, J. (1998). *Healing Minds.* London: The Mental Health Foundation.

Walsh, E., Buchanan, A., & Fahy, T. (2002). Violence and schizophrenia: examining the evidence. *The British Journal of Psychiatry, 180*: 490–495.

Walters, C. (1998). *Aromatherapy: An Illustrated Guide.* Shaftesbury: Element.

Wardell, D. W., & Engebretson, J. (2001). Biological correlates of Reiki touch healing. *Journal of Advanced Nursing, 33*: 439–445.

Warner, R. (1994). *Recovery from Schizophrenia: Psychiatry and Political Economy* (2nd edn). London: Routledge.

Weisenberg, M., Raz, T., & Hener, T. (1998). The influence of film mood on pain perception. *Pain, 76*: 365–375.

Weisenberg, M., Tepper, I., & Schwarzwald, J. (1995). Humour as a cognitive technique for increasing pain tolerance. *Pain, 63*(2): 207–212.

Wessely, S., Castle, D., Der, G., & Murray, R. (1991). Schizophrenia and Afro-Caribbeans: a case-control study. *The British Journal of Psychiatry, 159*: 795–801.

Whicher, E., Morrison, M., & Douglas-Hall, P. (2002). "As required" medication regimens for seriously mentally ill people in hospital. *The Cochrane Database of Systematic Reviews, 1.* Article no. CD003441.DOI:10.1002/14651858.CD003441.

Whitaker, R. (2002). *Mad in America: Bad Science, Bad Medicine and the Enduring Mistreatment of the Mentally Ill.* New York: Perseus.

Whitaker, R. (2004). The case against antipsychotic drugs: a 50-year record of doing more harm than good. *Medical Hypotheses, 62*: 5–13.

Williams, J. (2006). The uses of humour and other coping strategies. *Voices*, Summer: 3.

Willner, P. (1997). The dopamine hypothesis of schizophrenia: current status, future prospects. *International Clinical Psychopharmacology, 12*(6): 297–308.

Winefield, H. (1996). Barrier to an alliance between family and professional caregivers in chronic schizophrenia. *Journal of Mental Health, 5*: 223–232.

Wolkowitz, O. M., & Pickar, D. (1991). Benzodiazepines in the treatment of schizophrenia: A review and reappraisal. *The American Journal of Psychiatry, 148*: 714–726.

Wolkowitz, O. M., Turetsky, N., Reus, V. I., & Hargreaves, W. (1992). Benzodiazepine augmentation of neuroleptics in treatment-resistant schizophrenia. *Psychopharmacology Bulletin, 28*: 291–295.

Wong, A. H., Smith, M., & Boon, H. S. (1998). Herbal remedies in psychiatric practice. *Archives of General Psychiatry, 55*: 1033–1044.

Wood, N. (1994). Letter to the Editor. *Voices*, 3.

Woolery, A., Myers, H., Sternlieb, B., & Zeltzer, L. (2004). A Yoga intervention for young adults with elevated symptoms of depression. *Alternative Therapies in Health and Medicine, 10*(2): 60–63.

World Health Organization (WHO) (2004). *Global Status Report on Alcohol*. Geneva: WHO.

Wyatt, R. J. (1991). Neuroleptics and the natural course of schizophrenia. *Schizophrenia Bulletin, 17*: 325–351.

Xuan Ke, S. (2006). Personal communication.

Yip, Y. B., & Tse, S. H. (2004). The effectiveness of relaxation acupoint stimulation and acupressure with aromatic lavender essential oil for non-specific low back pain in Hong Kong: a randomized controlled trial. *Complementary Therapies in Medicine, 12*(1): 28–37.

Zhang, X. Y., Zhou, D. F., Su, J. M., & Zhang, PY. (2001). The effect of extract of ginkgo biloba added to haloperidol on superoxide dismutase in inpatients with chronic schizophrenia. *Journal of Clinical Psychopharmacology, 21*(1): 85–88.

Zhang X. Y., Zhou, D. F., Zhang, P. Y., Wu, G. Y., Su, J. M., & Cao, L. Y. (2001). A double-blind, placebo-controlled trial of extract of ginkgo biloba added to haloperidol in treatment-resistant patients with schizophrenia. *Journal of Clinical Psychiatry, 62*(11): 878–883.

Zhang, X. Y., Zhou, D. F., Cao, L. Y., Xu, C. Q., Chen, D. C., & Wu, G. Y. (2004). The effect of vitamin E treatment on tardive dyskinesia and blood superoxide dismutase: a double-blind placebo controlled trial. *Journal of Clinical Psychopharmacology, 24*(1): 83–86.

Zhou, D., Zhang, X., Su, J., Nan, Z., Cui, Y., Liu, J., Guan, Z., Zhang, P., & Shen, Y. (1999). The effects of classic antipsychotic haloperidol plus the extract of ginkgo biloba on superoxide dismutase in patients with chronic refractory schizophrenia. *Chinese Medical Journal (England), 112*(12): 1093–1096.

INDEX